A YEAR
of
DEVOTION

WRITTEN BY
ANDREW WOMMACK
BOB NICHOLS
BOB YANDIAN

ANDREW WOMMACK MINISTRIES

Unless otherwise indicated, all Scripture quotations are taken from the King James Version of the Bible.

A Year of Devotion
ISBN:1-59548-069-2
Copyright ©2006 by Andrew Wommack Ministries, Inc.
850 Elkton Dr.
Colorado Sptings, CO 80907

TABLE OF CONTENTS

TABLE OF CONTENTS

TABLE OF CONTENTS

TABLE OF CONTENTS

TABLE OF CONTENTS

TABLE OF CONTENTS

TABLE OF CONTENTS

TABLE OF CONTENTS

TABLE OF CONTENTS

TABLE OF CONTENTS

TABLE OF CONTENTS

TABLE OF CONTENTS

The author's initials follow each daily reading:
(AW) = Andrew Wommack
(BN) = Bob Nichols
(BY) = Bob Yandian

JANUARY 1
PROSPERITY PLEASES GOD
3 JOHN 2

"Beloved, I wish above all things that thou mayest prosper and be in health, even as thy soul prospereth" *(3 John 2).*

The Apostle John, inspired by the Holy Spirit, wished above everything else that we prosper as our souls prosper. That's God's will for us! This shouldn't be surprising. It just stands to reason that anyone who loved us enough to sacrifice His Son to purchase our freedom would do anything for our welfare (Rom. 8:32). Yet today, many people think that our heavenly Father, who gave His only begotten Son for us, either delights in or is apathetic toward our poverty and sickness.

The word *prosper* means "to be successful; thrive." *Euodoo* is the Greek word used twice in this verse for "prosper" and "prospereth." It means "to help on the road, i.e. succeed in reaching; fig. to succeed in business affairs." Prosperity isn't limited to, but certainly includes, financial abundance. As King David put it, the Lord has ***"pleasure in the prosperity of his servant"*** (Ps. 35:27).

One of the purposes of this daily devotional is to open your heart to the love and provision of the Lord for prosperity in every area of your life—spiritual, emotional, mental, and physical. Not believing this truth has caused many people to see God as only relevant to their eternal needs. However, the Word plainly teaches that our great salvation includes so much more! As we believe, experience, and preach a full Gospel, we'll see God's reality and power manifest in the here and now.

Jesus gave Himself to deliver us from this present evil world (Gal. 1:4). We shouldn't reject what He died to accomplish for any reason. God is glorified when we let Him prosper us (Ps. 35:27). Let's bring pleasure to the Lord this year by walking in a whole new level of prosperity! (AW)

JANUARY 2
THE BIG THREE
1 CORINTHIANS 13:1-13

"And now abideth faith, hope, charity, these three; but the greatest of these is charity" *(1 Cor. 13:13).*

Faith, hope, and charity (God's kind of love) are godly attributes. Satan possesses none of them and hates those who do. God is a God of faith, hope, and love. These are His characteristics. Those who genuinely possess them are "God-possessed," for they only come from and through the Lord.

People in today's society often lack these qualities, but they have existed since God breathed His life into man, and they'll be here as long as He continues to live in believers' hearts. They abide regardless of political systems. People, under the direction of the devil, have tried to eradicate them, but their efforts have fallen short and always will. Love never fails (1 Cor. 13:8). Faith overcomes the world (1 John 5:4). We are saved by hope (Rom. 8:24).

These are the qualities that give life meaning and enjoyment. They distinguish human beings from the rest of creation. Remove them, and people act like animals. Faith, hope, and love can melt even the vilest heart and reshape it in the image of God. But to live without them is to live with a low quality of life.

Satan seeks to strip men and women of faith, hope, and love, while the Lord never wills us to be without them. Warfare constantly rages between the kingdom of God and the kingdom of darkness over these virtues. Let the Lord fill you today with His faith, hope, and love. Then turn around and release them to those who are faithless, hopeless, and starving for true "agape" love. (AW)

JANUARY 3
THE SIGN OF A CHRISTIAN
JOHN 13:31-35

"By this shall all men know that ye are my disciples, if ye have love one to another" (John 13:35).

This is an amazing statement by Jesus! The distinguishing characteristic of a Christian, according to the Head of all Christendom, is our love for one another. This doesn't appear to be common knowledge in the church today. Possessing true love for other believers isn't a top priority for most Christians. Yet Jesus said that this is the number one thing that will show unbelievers that He's real and alive in us today.

The body of Christ has invested vast amounts of money and effort to reach the lost. We've built fancy churches, padded the seats, and air-conditioned the auditoriums to attract more people. We've traveled around the world and held mass crusades. Yet love for each other, which Jesus said would represent Him the best, is lacking or non-existent. We have bumper stickers on our cars, but no love in our hearts.

The first-century church didn't have tapes, books, or videos. Neither did they put bumper stickers on every camel that crossed the desert. They met in homes without the benefit of radio or television, but they made an infinitely greater impact on their world with the Gospel. How could this be? They had God's kind of love for Him and for each other!

Jude spoke of the early church meetings as being *"feasts of charity"* (Jude 1:12). Love abounded and so did the Gospel—and there's a direct relationship between the two. Choose to be a living advertisement for the Gospel today. As you allow His love to shine through, unbelievers will know that Jesus is alive. (AW)

JANUARY 4
FAITHFUL IN SOWING, AGGRESSIVE IN RECEIVING
MATTHEW 25:14-30

"For the kingdom of heaven is as a man travelling into a far country, who called his own servants, and delivered unto them his goods" (Matt. 25:14).

God is the true owner of the goods, and we are His stewards. From this portion of Scripture, we see that "talents" are literally money, not abilities. My working definition of a steward is: Faithful in giving, aggressive in receiving. Our stewardship, giving, and sowing isn't limited to money. It could be anything. But notice here that the master didn't bless them because of what they gave. He blessed them because of what they received. Some stewardship problems aren't so much in the sowing as they are in the receiving. We can't be like farmers who scatter seed and say, "See you later. I'll be back in six months." If we do that, there won't be anything there for us to harvest! Some say they've been tithing and giving for six months, eight months, a year, but it doesn't seem to be "working." God's way always works! Are they aggressive in their receiving? We don't just sow into the Spirit, we also reap from the Spirit. We don't just want to sow financially into the kingdom, we must also reap a harvest!

Those who are aggressive in their receiving keep some kind of a log that says, "God, here is the seed sown. I believe You for the harvest!" Aggressive receivers have scriptural promises that they pray and confess over their seed sown. Water the seed you've sown in faith with the Word. Take Luke 6:38 and pray like this: "I give, so it shall be given unto me; good measure, pressed down, and shaken together, and running over, shall men give into my bosom!" Then confess Proverbs 11:24: "I scatter, and yet I increase!" Speak God's Word in faith over your seed!

This principle will enable the church to maintain and spread revival, because the focus won't have to be on finances. We must become more radical in our receiving because there are projects that need to be funded. That's what being a steward is about. God always has more in store so that we can bring more people into His kingdom. It's about more than just sowing seed. It's about increase! Yes, it's about sowing seed. But it's also about reaping the harvest off that seed. Some seed from each harvest should be planted to produce future harvests. Be faithful in your sowing, but remember also to be aggressive in your receiving! (BN)

JANUARY 5
FAITH WORKS BY LOVE
GALATIANS 5:1-6

"For in Jesus Christ neither circumcision availeth any thing, nor uncircumcision; but faith which worketh by love" *(Gal. 5:6).*

When Jamie and I started out in the ministry, we were so poor we couldn't even pay attention! I was believing God for prosperity with all I knew, but we constantly struggled. At one time, all we had to eat was a bag of Fritos and some cokes that a friend had given us. We rationed them out for days!

Then Jamie took the car and our last seventy-five cents and went to the Laundromat. While she was gone, I did some serious praying. It seemed like the Lord wasn't meeting our needs. I said, "God, I'd give my right arm to feed Jamie!" He immediately responded, "I gave My Son to feed you." Then He reminded me of Luke 12:32, which says, ***"Fear not, little flock; for it is your Father's good pleasure to give you the kingdom."***

That broke my heart. I realized that I had let circumstances deceive me about God's love for us. I tried to operate in faith without love. I repented and received God's love. When Jamie returned, I told her we would eat meat that day.

After church that night, a friend invited us to his house. He gave us over ten pounds of fish, potatoes, and other food. Just before midnight, we sat down to a feast. The amazing thing was that he had tried to bring us the food earlier that day, but when he came by our apartment, our car was gone, so he supposed no one was home. The only time our car was gone was when Jamie was at the Laundromat washing clothes and God was showing me His love for us. At the precise moment I received His love, my faith worked and our need was met. Let God's love for you abound, and your faith will too! (AW)

JANUARY 6
FAITH & HOPE
HEBREWS 11:1-6

"Now faith is the substance of things hoped for, the evidence of things not seen" *(Heb. 11:1).*

There's a direct relationship between faith and hope. You can't have one without the other. Faith gives substance to things we hope for. Remove hope, and faith has no goal to achieve.

A hillbilly from the backwoods of North Carolina wandered into a church service once. As the people started praising the Lord that warm summer day, the temperature in the auditorium began to rise. Just then, an usher walked over to the wall and adjusted a little device. Within seconds, cool air blew out of the vent and touched this hillbilly. Utterly amazed, he thought this must be one of the greatest things he'd ever experienced!

Immediately, he asked the usher what the device on the wall was and how he could get one. The usher told him that it was a thermostat and all hardware stores sold them. The man could hardly wait to get out of the church service and go buy one. After purchasing a thermostat, he took it home and mounted it on the wall of his house. But no matter how much he turned the dial, cool air never came out.

He didn't realize that the thermostat doesn't produce the cool air we get from air-conditioning. It only turns the power unit on and off. That's a beautiful picture of the way faith and hope work together.

Although faith is the victory that overcomes the world, hope is what provides the motivation for faith. Remove hope, and our faith will never be activated. Hope is much more important in our lives than most of us understand. Let God build a strong hope in you today! (AW)

JANUARY 7
MEEK, NOT WEAK!
JAMES 1:21

"Receive with meekness the engrafted word, which is able to save your souls" (James 1:21).

Where have we come up with the idea that to be meek means to be weak? Maybe since the words rhyme, we assume they mean the same thing. Dog and hog rhyme, but they aren't the same. This misinterpretation has led us to picture a meek person as one without stamina, who won't look you in the eye when they speak, who dresses shabbily, eats lettuce and birdseed, and lets others walk all over them. Jesus was called meek (Matt. 11:29), but He certainly never failed to look a person in the eye when He spoke. He was also far from being weak or letting others push Him around. He even picked up the moneychangers and threw them out of the temple!

The predominant Greek word for meek is *praus*. The root of this word comes from a horse that can easily be controlled by the bit in his mouth, a horse that can be quickly trained. The word means "to be *teachable*."

A meek person knows there is more to be learned. A teachable person will never have a problem with pride or arrogance. An arrogant person thinks they have arrived and are not teachable. This is a sure sign of coming destruction. A truly meek person knows that the more they learn, the more there is to be learned. Knowledge is a two-edged sword. Learning reveals what you don't know.

James tells us we are to *"receive with __meekness__ the engrafted word"* (James 1:21, emphasis added). We must always maintain a teachable attitude when we learn the Word of God. While sitting under the teaching ministry of others, we should listen with a teachable attitude, not a critical one. There's much to be learned—even from those we disagree with.

Jesus told us *"the __meek__...shall inherit the earth"* (Matt. 5:5, emphasis added). Teachable people understand God's message of prosperity and will inherit land, possessions, and finances in the earth. It pays to be teachable! (BY)

JANUARY 8
RELUCTANT COMPLIANCE
LUKE 5:1-11

"Let down your nets...I will let down the net" (Luke 5:4-5).

Jesus had just used Peter's boat while preaching to the people. He wanted to bless him for this and also show him how He could meet all of his needs. Jesus told Peter to let down his nets for a catch. At that moment, all the fish in the lake started swimming for Peter's boat.

Peter had been fishing all night and had caught nothing. He certainly wasn't going to have any better luck now. Jesus may have been a wonderful preacher, but what did He know about fishing? Peter was the expert there. It's to his credit that he obeyed, but he didn't do it wholeheartedly. Jesus told him to cast his nets (plural) into the sea. Peter only threw in one net. He obeyed, but he wasn't expecting much.

The results were that all the fish that were intended to fill two or more nets jumped into Peter's one net. The net wasn't able to handle all the fish and it began to break. This was the biggest catch of Peter's life, yet it could've been even bigger! The fish were actually fighting to get into his net, but he wasn't prepared. No doubt, many fish that Jesus commanded to be caught were unable to comply because Peter wasn't prepared.

We often miss some of God's supply because of our own little faith. The widow in 2 Kings 4:6 could have had more oil, but she ran out of vessels to fill. Joash, the king of Israel, could have completely destroyed his enemies, but he wasn't aggressive enough (2 Kin. 13:18-19). Likewise, we often limit what God wants to do for us because of our unbelief (Ps. 78:41).

What has He told you to do? Do it with all your heart, and make plans for big results. Your faith determines the manifestation of God's supply! (AW)

JANUARY 9
HOPE
ROMANS 8:19-25

"For we are saved by hope: but hope that is seen is not hope:
for what a man seeth, why doth he yet hope for?" (Rom. 8:24).

Most people don't fully appreciate the power of hope. They say "I hope so," when really they've given up. Often in our love of faith, we have relegated hope to a despised position. But hope is the "thermostat" that turns our faith on (see Jan. 6).

Before faith can operate, we must have hope. Hope is the beginning of faith. Before a person can truly believe the good news of their salvation, they must hope that these things are true. The first step in believing for healing is to hope that you'll be healed. Sometimes the person who says "I hope I'll be healed" is ridiculed by those who respond, "You can't hope you're healed—you must believe!"

Until we move into true biblical faith, our healing won't manifest. But we need to realize that there are steps to faith. Some people are so far removed from believing with all their hearts what they pray for will come to pass that it looks impossible for them to reach their goals. It is impossible if we try to cover the distance in one giant leap, but inch-by-inch, it's a cinch. We can cover large distances if we take enough steps.

One of Jesus' parables of the kingdom states that there's *"first the blade, then the ear, after that the full corn in the ear"* (Mark 4:28). This shows that there are steps toward receiving a harvest. Before we can believe for a million dollars, we need to believe for one dollar. Before we can believe, we need to hope. Let hope be an important part of your life today! (AW)

JANUARY 10
FAITHFUL STEWARDS
1 CORINTHIANS 4:2

"Moreover it is required in stewards, that a man be found faithful" (1 Cor. 4:2).

As stewards, we are not owners, but we are entrusted with the oversight of everything we have. It all belongs to God (Ps. 24:1-2). This applies to every person in the world. Everyone has something, even if it seems like they don't. If there wasn't any other possession you had, you're at least clothed, in your right mind, and can read. You have something to steward over!

When people separate just one little area of life and say "Well, finances are everything we're stewards over," they leave room for the Enemy to get glory from their life. If someone is a faithful steward over their ministry anointing, but isn't faithful with finances, there are problems. Right now there are preachers in jail who have an anointing, but they weren't good stewards over finances. The law is the law whether you have a preacher's card or a union card. You can't just steward over one area of your life and expect to get a *"Well done, thou good and faithful servant"* (Matt. 25:21). We are a package—spirit, soul, and body. The financial and social realms are part of that package.

That's why it's important how you treat your car, your house, your cow, and your spouse—they all belong to God! He's just entrusted them to us. That's why we must take good care of the clothes we have. We wash them. If they need mending, we mend them. Why? Because they belong to the Lord! We are being faithful stewards over what God has entrusted to us. If you want to see if someone has the heart of a steward, watch them in a rental car. Some people rent a car, and suddenly, to them, speed bumps don't exist. God notices that. It's His car. It may have a rental company's name on the bumper, but Daddy God owns it. If you're living in an apartment and you want God to bless you with a house someday, don't tear up that apartment. Take good care of it. You're sowing seed when you are thankful for the beat up old car you may be driving. Wash it! If you only have one hubcap, shine it, and believe God for the rest. Vacuum the inside and keep it clean. In some folks' cars, you must brush aside five fast food bags just to get in. Then, once you're there, you wish you had a breather mask and a large can of Lysol. That's not being a good steward!

My assistant had a car with holes in the floorboards. When you were riding in it you could see the pavement zipping by. If it rained, you could get splashed right in the eye. He bought a floor mat and praised God for what he had. I saw him awhile after he had stopped working with me. He was driving a brand-new Honda. I remembered how he was with his old car and thought, *Now there goes someone who has ahold of something.* Be thankful. Be a good steward over what you've already been given. You might be surprised what the Lord will do for you! (BN)

JANUARY 11
COMMANDING GOD
ISAIAH 45:1-19

"Thus saith the LORD, the Holy One of Israel, and his Maker, Ask me of things to come concerning my sons, and concerning the work of my hands command ye me" *(Is. 45:11).*

This is an amazing scripture! What does it mean to command God? The answer lies in understanding that His kingdom is established on laws. There are laws that govern God's actions, and these laws are at our command.

When someone wants to turn the lights on in their home, they don't call the electric company and beg them to send a worker out to do it. The electric company generates the power and delivers it to the house, but it's the individual's responsibility to turn on the lights. In a sense, they must "command" the electricity to come on by flipping the switch on the wall. Does this mean they produced the power by their own might? No. The power doesn't come from them, but it is at their disposal.

Likewise, God has already met our every need through the atonement of Christ. Our salvation, healing, deliverance, and prosperity were already generated long before we ever needed them. His power has already been placed within the born-again spirit of every believer. But we must flip the switch! We do that through putting the laws of faith into action. Crying out to God in desperation is like the homeowner calling the electric company and pleading with them to turn on the lights. No amount of begging will get them to do what we're supposed to do. And no amount of begging will get God to do what He's told us to do!

Act on the Word in faith today, and see if the lights don't come on. You just might discover that God's power was in you all along! (AW)

JANUARY 12
FAITH PRODUCES VICTORY
1 JOHN 5:1-5

"For whatsoever is born of God overcometh the world: and this is the victory that overcometh the world, even our faith" *(1 John 5:4).*

I was listening to a preacher on television minister on this passage of Scripture. He was preaching absolute victory—and I was offended. You see, it was just three weeks before the due date of our first child and we were broke. We hadn't paid any of the doctor bills and we didn't have any money for the hospital. We'd even lost our rental house and had to move in with our parents. I tried to believe that the Lord would supply our needs, but it just didn't work. That's what I was telling myself as I listened to this man preach.

It was as though he heard my thoughts. He said, "Don't tell me it doesn't work. Faith always overcomes the world!" I thought, *Well, I've taught that myself, but this time it's too late.* He came right back with, "It's never too late. Believe God!" I thought, *I just can't. I'm ready to quit.* He said, "Don't give up. Don't quit. You can do it!"

I decided to get back in the fight and believe God. If I was going to fail, I would do it believing God with all my heart. Of course, when I operated in faith, I didn't fail. Our need was supernaturally supplied, and we overcame the world in that situation.

It's true for you too! Faith overcomes the world. If you aren't overcoming the world, you need a good dose of faith. Don't quit. Don't give up. Use the powerful weapon of faith that the Lord has put in your heart. Faith will quench ALL the fiery darts of the devil (Eph. 6:16). (AW)

JANUARY 13
A LITTLE SIN, A BIG STUMBLING BLOCK
HEBREWS 12:1, 3

"Let us lay aside every weight, and the sin which doth so easily beset...consider him...lest ye be wearied and faint in your minds" (Heb. 12:1,3).

One day I looked at this verse more closely. The sin, which does so easily beset, is singular. Furthermore, that sin is defined in verse 3 as "fainting in your mind." Therefore, the sin, which does so easily beset us as believers, is *discouragement*. Discouragement can be brought on by a number of circumstances in life.

1. Pressures of life: Every believer faces trouble. It's not only prophesied, but promised and guaranteed. *"Many are the afflictions of the righteous: but the Lord delivereth him out of them all"* (Ps 34:19). God has given us weapons to handle Satan's attacks, but one thing we must not do is give up.

2. Satanic attack: Our troubles may not come by way of circumstances, but can come directly from demons. Whether they be "serpents" or "scorpions," God has given us authority over all of Satan's power (Luke 10:19). But we must not give up.

3. Personal failure: Every one of us has failed as a Christian. We've promised the Lord our all and failed to come through on our promises. But again, we can't let ourselves become discouraged and give up. We must heed Hebrews 12:12-13 and *"lift up the hands which hang down, and the feeble knees; And make straight paths for your feet."*

4. Doing right with little results: This can be one of the greatest areas of discouragement in our spiritual walk. Paul warns us to *"not be weary in well doing: for in due season we shall reap, if we faint not"* (Gal. 6:9, emphasis added).

In all cases, discouragement comes when we take our eyes off the Lord and put them onto ourselves or our circumstances. Self-pity will bring on discouragement every time. Lay discouragement aside, set your eyes on God's Word again, and you'll be back on the road to success. Be encouraged—you'll pull through very soon! (BY)

JANUARY 14
THE MEASURE OF FAITH
ROMANS 12:1-12

"For I say, through the grace given unto me, to every man that is among you, not to think of himself more highly than he ought to think; but to think soberly, according as God hath dealt to every man the measure of faith" (Rom. 12:3).

If someone was serving different people soup out of a large pot with just one ladle, the ladle would be *the* measure, and everyone would receive the same amount of soup. Likewise, the Lord doesn't give us different amounts of faith. He's given every believer *"the measure of faith"* (emphasis added).

What about the places in Scripture where Jesus speaks of great faith (Matt. 8:10) and little faith (Matt. 8:26)? He's saying that we can use (manifest) great faith or little faith, but this doesn't affect the amount we've actually been given. That's the same—*the* measure of faith.

Paul said the faith he used was *"the faith of the Son of God"* (Gal. 2:20, emphasis added). Notice he didn't say "faith in the Son of God," but *"the faith of the Son of God."* (Translations other than the *King James Version* tend to obscure this truth by misinterpreting the Greek.) If we all have the same measure of faith and Paul's measure was the same as Jesus', then ours is too. There isn't a shortage of faith. There's just a shortage of people who use the faith God gave them!

There are many things we can do to release the God-given faith that's in us, but before we can do any of them, we must believe the faith is there. Instead of acknowledging your lack today, acknowledge the faith of Jesus that you have in your heart. This is the first step toward making your faith effective (Philem. 1:6). (AW)

JANUARY 15
THE LAW OF FAITH
ROMANS 3:19-31

"Where is boasting then? It is excluded. By what law? of works?
Nay: but by the law of faith" *(Rom. 3:27).*

Paul speaks here of *"the law of faith."* Faith is a law. Just as there are laws in the physical world, there are laws in the spiritual realm also. Failure to understand this is at the heart of many Christians' frustrations. They don't understand why God doesn't do something to end their pitiful situation or that there are laws they must learn to obey.

A person who walks off a ten-story building shouldn't be upset with God when they fall. Sure, it is the law of gravity, which God created, that will hurt or kill them, but it's nothing personal on God's part. The law of gravity is a constant that God will not cancel for our convenience. If the Lord were to stop gravity so the person walking off the ten story building wouldn't get hurt, there would be untold other deaths from car and train wrecks, etc. That's what makes gravity a law. It's constant and universal.

Likewise, there are laws of faith that God has to honor. He loves us and wants to answer our prayers, but God will not violate His laws of faith to do it. There is a law of sowing and reaping in the physical world. The farmer who doesn't sow shouldn't be upset with God when the crop he prayed for doesn't grow. He didn't cooperate with the laws that God established. In the same way, many Christians don't cooperate with God's laws for prosperity, healing, joy, etc., yet they can't understand why they aren't reaping positive results. We need to learn God's spiritual laws and conform our lives to them. Only then will we enjoy the benefits God wants us to have. (AW)

JANUARY 16
AGGRESSIVE RECEIVERS ARE RADICAL THANK-ERS
2 CORINTHIANS 9:11

"Being enriched in every thing to all bountifulness, which causeth
through us thanksgiving to God" *(2 Cor. 9:11).*

People who know how to prosper in the Lord are radical in their thanksgiving. Every time you thank God for what He's already done, it is sowing seed for the next need or miracle. It's like putting another baited hook in the water and getting ready to haul in "the big one." When you thank God, He can hardly stand it and just loves to move on your behalf. It's as if He says, "They're thankful for what I've already given them. Send them some more. They're faithful people—faithful to give me praise and thanksgiving. Let's bless their socks off!" You need to get radically thankful for what you've already been given! It's sad that some people believe God for some "big thing" and when He does it, they run off and enjoy it without ever stopping to say, "Thank You, Lord, for what You've done." Like the ten lepers in Luke 17, only one returned to thank Jesus—and he was made completely whole! I believe that all ten were cleansed—meaning the leprosy ceased—but the thankful one was completely restored by creative miracles. New fingers, new toes—whatever he lost was restored!

Aggressively thankful people are ready to jump in and thank God from their hearts when others get blessed. If your blessing ship hasn't come in yet, start getting radically thankful any time anybody around you gets blessed. Then watch God notice you. Why? It raises up a memorial to Him. The worst thing in the world you could do is gripe about the "old clunker" you're driving. That's the worst seed you can sow! Be thankful that things are as good as they are. Be thankful for what you do have. To receive aggressively, you must thank aggressively. Aggressive receivers are aggressive thank-ers! (BN)

JANUARY 17
A WILLING SACRIFICE
GENESIS 22:1-18

*"And they came to the place which God had told him of; and Abraham built
an altar there, and laid the wood in order, and bound Isaac his son,
and laid him on the altar upon the wood"* (Gen. 22:9).

This amazing account of Abraham offering his son Isaac to God as a sacrifice has inspired people through the ages. Yet Abraham wasn't the only one to express amazing faith and faithfulness. Isaac's actions were pretty awesome too!

Most scholars believe that Isaac was about seventeen years old at this time. This means that Abraham was 117. Isaac probably could have overpowered Abraham. Certainly, he could have outrun dear old dad. But Isaac allowed his father to bind him and place him on the altar knowing full well that Abraham intended to make him a sacrifice. There is no indication that Isaac was screaming for help or that he resisted in any way. Isaac had complete trust in God, his father, or both.

This is a perfect picture of how God sacrificed His Son Jesus for us. It was an astonishing act of love for us on God's part, but it was equally wonderful what Jesus did. The scriptures say, *"He was oppressed, and he was afflicted, yet he opened not his mouth: he is brought as a lamb to the slaughter, and as a sheep before her shearers is dumb, so he openeth not his mouth"* (Is. 53:7). Jesus could have called for legions of angels to deliver Him, but He didn't (Matt. 26:53). He yielded Himself to His Father just as Isaac did, even unto death.

Such love and sacrifice certainly had a purpose. If God gave His Son so freely for us, how could we ever doubt that He will supply our every need (Rom. 8:32). God loves us and delights in our prosperity (Ps. 35:27). He's proven that beyond any reasonable doubt. (AW)

JANUARY 18
WHAT ARE YOU THINKING?
GENESIS 22:1-18

"I and the lad will go yonder and worship, and come again to you" (Gen. 22:5).

It is hard for most of us to relate to the story of Abraham offering his son, Isaac, to God as a sacrifice. Much of the reason is because we incorrectly imagine how hard this must have been on Abraham.

One movie about this incident depicts Abraham hitting his fist against a stone wall and crying out, "No God! Anything but Isaac!" It portrays Abraham wrestling with God all night and finally grudgingly giving in to the Lord and complying with His demand. But that's not what the Bible states. There is no hint of any resistance on Abraham's part. In fact, verse 3 shows Abraham rising early the next morning and heading to the place of sacrifice.

The reason we'd be unable to sacrifice our own child is because we'd think about our son being dead and imagine our guilt from knowing that it happened by our own hand. Abraham didn't think that way. He told his servants, *"We will worship and then we will come back to you"* (Gen. 22:5, NIV).

In Hebrews 11:19, we find that Abraham was believing God to raise Isaac from the dead. You see, Abraham never saw Isaac dead and gone. He had a promise that God was going to give him a multitude of children through Isaac, and Isaac hadn't had any children yet. Therefore, he had to live. Abraham wasn't thinking on death; he was thinking about resurrection.

What are you thinking about? Are you looking at the sacrifice or the reward? What you think upon will determine your reaction. If you, like Abraham, think on the promise, you'll have faith like Abraham to sacrifice anything. The choice is yours, and your choice will determine whether you rejoice or resist. (AW)

JANUARY 19
GOD IS GREATER
GENESIS 22:1-18

"And he said, Take now thy son, thine only son Isaac, whom thou lovest,
and get thee into the land of Moriah; and offer him there for a burnt offering
upon one of the mountains which I will tell thee of" (Gen. 22:2).

Consider how great a sacrifice God asked Abraham to make. Never before or after did God ask this of anyone. God was always the giver. He used animal sacrifices to illustrate that there had to be shedding of blood for the forgiveness of sins (Heb. 9:22), but this was only foreshadowing His own sacrifice. Why would God ask this of a man?

This action isn't clearly explained in Scripture, but no doubt that one of the purposes for God doing this was to give us assurance. He would never ask more of us than what He was willing to give. If Abraham could sacrifice his son, then certainly God would do no less.

Our Lord Jesus used this same reasoning. In Luke 11:11-13, Jesus asked, *"If a son shall ask bread of any of you that is a father, will he give him a stone? or if he ask a fish, will he for a fish give him a serpent? Or if he shall ask an egg, will he offer him a scorpion? If ye then, being evil, know how to give good gifts unto your children: how much more shall your heavenly Father give the Holy Spirit to them that ask him?"*

Our heavenly Father's love for us certainly surpasses any earthly man's love and devotion to Him. Therefore, if Abraham, a mere mortal, could find the strength to sacrifice his son, surely God could do the same. The Lord was assuring us that He would make the ultimate sacrifice for our sins. God so loved the world that He would sacrifice His only begotten Son to redeem us back to Himself. Think on that! (AW)

JANUARY 20
DON'T TRUST YOUR EYES OR EARS
2 PETER 1:19

"We have also a more sure word of prophecy" (2 Pet. 1:19).

In the beginning of this chapter, Peter was reflecting on his experience on the Mount of Transfiguration. He was part of a select group of three who saw Jesus transfigured, His face shine like lightning, and His clothing radiate like the sun. He also witnessed Moses and Elijah appear and begin talking with the Lord. Peter emphasizes how He heard God speak to Jesus from the cloud and say, *"This is my beloved Son, in whom I am well pleased"* (2 Pet. 1:17). He also emphasizes that he saw the transfiguration of Jesus with his own eyes (verses 16 and 18).

I'm sure Peter's congregation felt blessed to have one of the original twelve disciples as their pastor. They felt especially privileged to have one of the three men who formed the inner circle of Jesus' friends. Peter was a special man for another reason. He actually saw Jesus transfigured and heard God speak from heaven.

But Peter tells them there is something more powerful than having an open vision or hearing God speak from heaven. It's having the Word of God in front of you. The Word is a more sure word. Not everyone has had a vision or heard God speak audibly. But everyone can have the Word of God!

The Word must be our final authority. If what we see contradicts the Word of God, we should go with the Word. If what we hear contradicts the Word, we should choose to go with the Word. Peter was simply reminding the people to place the Word of God as their highest priority in life. God has placed His Word above even His own name (Ps. 138:2).

Circumstances can never change the promises of God, but the promises of God can change circumstances. Heaven and earth will pass away, but God's Word will never change! (BY)

JANUARY 21
GOD'S KIND OF LOVE
1 CORINTHIANS 13:1-13

"Charity never faileth" (1 Cor. 13:8).

One of the first steps in receiving and releasing God's kind of love is to recognize the difference between human love and a true God-kind of love.

Man's corrupt nature doesn't have access to God's kind of love. God is love (1 John 4:8) and any man or woman who does not have God is separated from true love. Mankind has millions of songs, plays, movies, and stories about love, but many of them are not God's kind of love. Human love and God's kind of love aren't even in the same class. Basically, human love is selfish and God's kind of love is totally unselfish. Human love says, "I'll love you as long as you do what I want you to, or as long as I feel like it." God's kind of love is unconditional.

First Corinthians 13:4-8 lists the remarkable characteristics of God's kind of love. Few Christians fully appreciate how unique His love is. We often think that God loves us similar to the way we've been loved before, but that's not so. Our bad experiences often prevent us from accepting God's love. We lower God to our level and think His love is conditional and proportional to our performance. That's how everyone else loves us, but God's kind of love is different. It's like no other love you've ever experienced.

God's kind of love never fails, even when we do. God's love is unconditional. Since we didn't do anything to earn it in the first place, He doesn't withdraw His love when we don't deserve it. He loves us because He is love, not because we are lovable. Make the decision today to renew your mind in the area of God's kind of love. Ask the Lord to teach you anew what His love is all about. Then get ready for a revelation that will change your entire life! (AW)

JANUARY 22
GOD'S LOVE IS LONG-SUFFERING & KIND
1 CORINTHIANS 13:4-8

"Charity suffereth long, and is kind" (1 Cor. 13:4).

The first two qualities of God's kind of love recorded in 1 Corinthians 13 are that it's long-suffering and kind. As with each characteristic listed in this chapter, there are two ways to apply these truths. As Christians, we are to be long-suffering and kind to others, but this also describes the way God acts toward us. God is love (1 John 4:8), and the reason we can act in love toward others is because He first acted in love toward us (1 John 4:19).

Those who think the Lord is put out with them every time they do something wrong will be put out with others who do wrong to them. We give to others out of what we receive. What you are full of is what comes out (Matt. 12:34-35). Having a short fuse and being unkind toward others is a sure sign that you aren't full of God's love for you.

The Lord doesn't ask more of us than what He's willing to give. He wouldn't tell us to be long-suffering and kind to others, but then be short-tempered with us. No! The Lord is very long-suffering and kind in His dealings with us. Kindness and long-suffering are distinguishing characteristics of God's kind of love for us.

Do you believe that the Lord treats you kindly? If not, your conscience, which has been programmed by religion, is condemning you—not the Holy Spirit. Our heavenly Father is kinder and gentler in His dealings with us than any earthly father could ever be. If we can still love our children, regardless of what they do, then certainly God can love us infinitely more. God is your heavenly Father! Let Him reveal His kindness and long-suffering to you today. (AW)

JANUARY 23
GOD'S KIND OF LOVE DOESN'T ENVY
1 CORINTHIANS 13

"Charity envieth not" *(1 Cor. 13:4).*

God's kind of love is not envious. The dictionary defines *envy* as "discontented desire or resentment aroused by another's possessions, achievements, or advantages." A person who is discontent or resents others who have more things, talent, or a better job is a person who doesn't appreciate God's love for them. When we receive God's love for us, a supernatural contentment settles into our lives that cannot be affected by the desire for things. Discontentment is envy and is at the root of all temptation.

Take Adam and Eve as an example. Before the devil could get them to sin, he had to make them discontented. That was no small chore! How do you make people who are living in perfection dissatisfied? They had no needs. They had never been hurt or abused. They couldn't blame their actions on their dysfunctional family. However, the devil made them believe that they were missing out on something. He made two people, living in paradise, dissatisfied with perfection. That's amazing!

This shows us that contentment isn't a state of being, but a state of mind. If perfect people living in a perfect world could become discontented, then certainly imperfect people living in an imperfect world can be discontented regardless of how things are going. We must LEARN to be content in all states (Phil. 4:11). God's love will give us the contentment we desire.

Ask the Lord for a deeper revelation of His love for you today. Realize that your discontentment is really envy, and God's love is the antidote for this crippling attitude. Knowing that God Almighty—the King of the universe—loves you will keep you from being discontented and out of temptation. (AW)

JANUARY 24
GOD'S LOVE ISN'T BOASTFUL OR PROUD
1 CORINTHIANS 13

"Charity vaunteth not itself, is not puffed up" *(1 Cor. 13:4).*

The old English word *vaunteth* simply means "to boast." The *New International Version* translates this phrase as *"it does not boast, it is not proud."* In other words, those who are full of God's love don't think they are better than others.

I've been on the platform with a number of Christian celebrities. In some cases, these people have thought they were better than others. Some have demanded better rooms, better cars, better offerings and have said things like, "Don't you know who I am?" That's not characteristic of God's kind of love!

On the other hand, I was just recently with a television personality who is famous in both the secular and Christian realms. He showed the love of God that is in his heart. Because of poor weather, the crowds were a fraction of what was expected. Yet this man gave it all he had, just as if there were thousands there. He also ministered to the people individually, not just the pretty ones, but those who were hurting the most. He showed true humility, which spoke volumes to me of the work God had done in his heart.

Of course, the supreme example of humility is our Lord Jesus Christ. He was King of kings and Lord of lords, yet He regularly associated with the lowest of the lowest. It was this God-kind of love that compelled Him to do this, and if we have God's kind of love, we can do the same.

Are there people in your life that you feel are beneath you? Anything that's good in your life is a gift from God (1 Cor. 4:7). God's kind of love will compel you to share your gift with others. You don't have to descend to their level, but bring them up to yours with the love of Jesus. (AW)

JANUARY 25
GOD'S LOVE KNOWS HOW TO BEHAVE
1 CORINTHIANS 13

"*Doth not behave itself unseemly*" (*1 Cor. 13:5*).

One of the biggest lies the devil ever sold us is that love is an overpowering feeling that cannot be controlled. However, God's kind of love never acts in an inappropriate way.

Greek scholar Fritz Rienecker says, "Unseemly means to behave indecently or in a shameful manner." Love is tactful and does nothing that would raise a blush. This is because the Greek word translated *unseemly* literally means "an indecency; by implication, the pudenda" (which are the external genital organs of a woman). In other words, God's kind of love never bares itself in an indecent manner.

Therefore, those who seem so overwhelmed with love that they just can't control themselves aren't overwhelmed with God's love at all. That unseemly love is devilish. It's selfish and full of lust. The old line "We just love each other so much that we can't control ourselves" is more accurately rendered "We are so full of lust that we can't control ourselves!"

Understanding this will shine the light of truth on many of the lies that Satan brings our way. Anytime we are smitten with feelings for someone other than our mate, it's not God's kind of love. It will never act contrary to the Word. God's kind of love will never leave us either. Anytime we feel like love is gone, all that really happened is that lust has gone. God's kind of love never fails (1 Cor. 13:8).

Ask the Lord to help you redefine what true love is. Start with the assurance that God's kind of love is not a rush of hormones that'll get you in trouble. (AW)

JANUARY 26
GOD'S LOVE ISN'T SELFISH
1 CORINTHIANS 13

"*Seeketh not her own*" (*1 Cor. 13:5*).

Satan has tried to counterfeit every good thing God has given us. He has succeeded to a large degree in selling the world a corrupted, inferior type of love. Hollywood has been a big asset to the devil in this battle. They have portrayed an emotional, sensual lust as "love" that has little or no basis in reality. It causes people to long for some utopia where every sense is fully satisfied.

The most distinguishing characteristic of the true God-kind of love is that it's not selfish or self-serving. True love isn't getting what you desire, but is God's kind of love, which is selfless and giving. Just look at Jesus, the greatest example of God's kind of love that the world has ever seen.

Christ didn't come to this earth to satisfy Himself. Ultimately, He did receive great satisfaction by redeeming mankind back to Himself. But the act of Jesus becoming flesh was for us, not for Him. He left all the splendor of glory and came to dwell in the most humble surroundings. He left the adoration of all creation to live for thirty years in complete anonymity.

Although some praised Him during His ministry, He endured the scorn and ridicule of the religious establishment. Then He suffered the ultimate rejection of crucifixion and took all the shame that went with being a condemned criminal. Yet, Jesus did all of this because **"*God so loved the world, that he gave his only begotten Son*"** (John 3:16).

Use this total selflessness of God's true love as the acid test for your love. If you only love others when they fulfill your desires, then you need to reevaluate your motives. You may have bought a counterfeit. (AW)

JANUARY 27
GOD'S LOVE DOESN'T HAVE A SHORT FUSE
1 CORINTHIANS 13

"Is not easily provoked" (1 Cor. 13:5).

During a weeklong meeting in a church of about 600 people, I encountered a pastor who didn't understand the patience of God's love for us. I was teaching on the grace and long-suffering of the Lord toward us, and it set people free. However, it was obvious that he didn't like it at all.

This pastor led praise and worship each night and then would conspicuously walk down the aisle and right out of the church. I tried to explain and balance everything so that no one would think I was encouraging sinful living, but the pastor didn't stay for the messages. The last night of the meeting, I was desperately trying to penetrate his rejection.

He led a song that talked about how we should be loving and long-suffering toward others, forgiving them even before they ask for forgiveness. This was a song he wrote. Before he left the platform, I asked him if he really believed what he sang. I asked if that principle applied even to those who treated us badly over and over. He was adamant that we should always forgive in all circumstances. Then I said, "Isn't it strange that some people believe that God expects us to behave with more love than He shows toward us?" He got the point.

One sure test of God's kind of love is: Is it patient? God's love is always patient. As true as this is with our dealings with others, it's even more true of God's dealings with us. God will not instruct us to do something that He is unwilling to do. God is not easily provoked. He's not the one with a short fuse. Many people think God is short-tempered, but that isn't the truth. Meditate on God's long-suffering love for you, and let Him show you how patiently He loves you today! (AW)

JANUARY 28
GOD'S LOVE DOESN'T KEEP SCORE
1 CORINTHIANS 13

"Thinketh no evil" (1 Cor. 13:5).

Many years ago, Jamie and I sat down to have a "discussion." We felt like we needed to talk some things out. What we did was give each other a list of what we thought the other was doing wrong. Amazingly, this list went back years and included even the smallest acts. It became obvious to both of us that we'd been keeping a mental ledger of all the things we thought the other was doing wrong. We were keeping score of each other's errors.

This isn't God's kind of love. We were dwelling on evil. Therefore, we made a decision to quit keeping score. No more storing up all the things that hurt us so we could use them in our next "discussion." At first this was scary. It was like taking all the ammunition out of our weapons. But then we realized that we weren't each other's enemy and that we shouldn't have any weapons. God is our defense, and He can work on our mates better than we can.

We made a decision not to dwell on the things we dislike about each other but to choose only to think on the good and let God take care of the rest. It's amazing how much of a difference this has made!

Thinking on evil only gives fuel to the fires Satan wants to ignite within us. Thinking on the wrongs we suffer from others magnifies the offense until it becomes bigger than it actually is. The devil loves to take a small splinter-size offense, magnify it to the size of a baseball bat, and then beat our brains out with it. Don't let him do it!

Decide today to quit keeping score of all the offenses that come your way. Think instead on things that are pure, lovely, and of good report (Phil. 4:8). Then you'll enjoy His peace (Is. 26:3). (AW)

JANUARY 29
GOD'S LOVE DOESN'T REJOICE IN INIQUITY
1 CORINTHIANS 13

"Rejoiceth not in iniquity, but rejoiceth in the truth" *(1 Cor. 13:6).*

Rejoice means "to experience joy or pleasure." A great indicator of whether or not we are walking in God's love is to examine what gives us pleasure. God's kind of love only gets pleasure from things in line with His Word, which is truth (John 17:17).

Those who receive pleasure from things that are sin aren't full of God's love. It doesn't matter whether they're personally doing it or just watching others commit acts of iniquity. God's love is pure and evokes purity in everyone it touches. Therefore, it shouldn't give us pleasure to explore all the weird and perverse things that go on in the world today.

Talk shows that investigate every type of immorality known to the devil shouldn't be the type of thing that Christians derive pleasure from. Magazines and books that glorify relationships contrary to God's blueprint shouldn't be entertainment for believers. Movies that exalt values other than God's values shouldn't provide amusement for His children.

I'm not saying we must quit everything we're doing and be miserable. This is simply a thermometer for us to take our spiritual temperature. If we're rejoicing in iniquity, we need a healthy dose of God's love. Once we're full of God's love, nothing less will please us. His love will spoil us!

Ask the Lord for a revelation of His pure love for you today. Then let His love redefine what causes you to rejoice. (AW)

JANUARY 30
GOD'S LOVE CAN BEAR ANYTHING
1 CORINTHIANS 13

"Beareth all things" *(1 Cor. 13:7).*

Most people have unquestioningly accepted that there are restrictions on how far to go in loving others. It's like we build a fence and say, "Anything within this boundary I can take, but there are limits to what I can bear. After all, I'm only human!"

It is true that we are humans and humans have limitations. But it's not true that we are ONLY human and, therefore, cannot bear all things. The born-again part of us is supernatural and full of God's love, which can bear all things. Look at Jesus. He loved and prayed for forgiveness for the very ones who crucified Him. Stephen did the same thing. All believers are instructed to operate in this type of love (Eph. 4:32).

God's love doesn't have any limitations as to what it can bear, believe, hope, and endure. Its sustaining power is limitless. Those who say they can't bear any more are simply revealing that they haven't yet drawn on God's supernatural love. They've been loving out of their natural human love.

This message isn't intended to condemn, but rather to encourage us that there is an infinite supply of God's love within us that will never fail. All we must do is look beyond ourselves to the Lord and receive His supernatural love. God wants us to walk in His love more than we do. It'll happen if we believe.

Don't listen to your flesh, the devil, or other people who justify having limitations to how far you can love others. Instead, draw on the God-kind of love within you, which bears all things. If you let His love flow through you, you'll have an endless capacity to love others. (AW)

JANUARY 31
GOD'S LOVE BELIEVES ALL THINGS
1 CORINTHIANS 13

"Believeth all things" *(1 Cor. 13:7)*.

One of the great indicators of whether we are walking in God's kind of love is the level of faith we exhibit. Love begets faith. As this verse says, "[Charity] *believeth all things*" (brackets mine) *"Faith...worketh by love"* (Gal. 5:6). When we experience the love God has for us, faith comes a a natural byproduct.

Failing to walk in faith is actually failing to stay focused on the infinite love God has for us. If God Almighty is for us, who or what can be against us (Rom. 8:31)?

A young child in their father's arms isn't worried about anything. They trust their father completely and don't have a care in the world. They don't struggle to believe for their meals, clothes or future needs. Their loving father takes care of it all. That's the exact comparison Jesus made to encourage us to trust God for our needs (Luke 11:11-13). A loving relationship with our heavenly Father is the key to a life of faith.

If you have a problem trusting God in any area of your life, let that be an indicator, like the warning light on the dash of your car, that something is wrong. You don't try to disconnect the warning light. Instead, you fix the problem that caused the light to come on in the first place and then it'll automatically shut off.

Likewise, a lack of faith is a warning light that indicates you aren't properly focused on the love of God. Once you return to the place of intimacy with the Lord, where you're fully aware of His great love for you, faith will be so abundant that you can "believe all things." (AW)

FEBRUARY 1
GOD'S LOVE NEVER QUITS HOPING
1 CORINTHIANS 13

"Hopeth all things" *(1 Cor. 13:7)*.

Hopelessness is a terrible thing. God's Word says, *"Where there is no vision, the people perish"* (Prov. 29:18). Lack of hope is behind most, if not all, of the self-destruction we see in the lives of people today. Those who don't have a strong faith in the future throw today away without any consideration of the consequences. The destructive habits of people are rooted in despair or hopelessness. Jesus described this by the fool who said, "Let's eat, drink, and be merry" (Luke 12:19). Those who don't live with one eye on the future are headed for disaster.

Why is it that most of society is without hope? It's because God's love is the source of true hope, and there's a genuine famine in the world today of the truth of God's love for us. On the whole, religion tells us of God's holiness and our relative unworthiness, but the true love of God is not a reality in the hearts of most people—that is, most Christian people.

Luck and fate don't generate hope. It's only in knowing that a personal, loving God is working all things for our good (Rom. 8:28) that we can truly find hope. God's kind of love "hopes all things."

God has a perfect plan for your life. Regardless of where you are now—no matter how far off the track you may have strayed—God has a perfect course plotted for you to where you're supposed to be (Jer. 29:11). He loves you in spite of what you have or haven't done. As you believe this today, hope will spring up in your heart! (AW)

FEBRUARY 2
GOD'S LOVE ENDURES EVERYTHING
1 CORINTHIANS 13

"Endureth all things" *(1 Cor. 13:7).*

People are in a constant struggle to feel good about themselves. Yet it seems that life is full of pressures that repeatedly drive us to and beyond our limits to cope. We've all gone past what we know to be the boundary of a proper response. Our drive to maintain self-worth excuses our actions. We say, "There are limits. I'm only human. How much can one person bear?" Those who haven't yet tapped into God's limitless power supply will readily agree and let you off the hook for your selfish attitudes and actions.

But the truth is that where our limits come to an end, God's power just begins. The Christian is not abandoned to their own resources. God lives in every true believer, and He's placed His supernatural love in each and every one of us so we can "endure ALL things."

This truth isn't meant to condemn; it's a liberating truth that will set you free (John 8:32). The temporary solace that comes from giving up will soon be swallowed by the harsh realities that arise from inappropriate behavior. As the Apostle James said, *"The wrath of man worketh not the righteousness of God"* (James 1:20). Regardless of how good it may feel to give in to your limitations, that surrender will only bring you grief.

God's love will empower you with supernatural ability so that nothing will be impossible for you. You can change the things that can be changed, or endure the things that can't. Through Christ you can do all things. Let God's love strengthen you today! (AW)

FEBRUARY 3
GOD'S LOVE NEVER FAILS
1 CORINTHIANS 13

"Charity never faileth" *(1 Cor. 13:8).*

How could Paul say this? In his day, hatred, selfishness, oppression, and many other evils seemed to prevail. Paul experienced the sting of persecution and had administered it to others before his conversion. Certainly, he'd heard of the Christians who were burned at the stake and thrown to the lions by the Romans. In A.D. 70, the Romans completely destroyed Jerusalem, plundering everyone and everything in the city. Would Paul have changed what he wrote if these things had taken place before this letter to the Corinthians? Certainly not!

God is love (1 John 4:8) and God never fails. In our single frame view, it may appear that God doesn't always prevail, but that's not so. For example, take the persecution of the Christians in Paul's day. The 20/20 view of history shows us that many Romans embraced Christ and jumped into the theatre to die with the Christians who were being martyred. Christianity spread at a phenomenal rate under the persecution. In less than thirty years, the Roman world was evangelized. In just 300 years, the seemingly undefeatable Roman Empire was conquered by God's love, and Christianity became the official religion.

God never fails and His love never fails. Individuals may fail to respond to His love and thus bear the consequences, but love never fails. It will always prevail in the end. We just need to give it time. The Lord doesn't force everyone and everything into compliance, because it isn't time for that yet. Now is the time of mercy, when the Lord is long-suffering and gives everyone ample opportunity to repent (2 Pet. 3:9-10). As we act in love, we use the strongest force in the universe. History has proven the power of love. If we just believe and exercise patience, love will never fail us! (AW)

FEBRUARY 4
BE PREPARED
LUKE 14:28

"For which of you, intending to build a tower, sitteth not down first, and counteth the cost, whether he have sufficient to finish it?" (Luke 14:28).

"Be prepared" isn't just a slogan for Boy Scouts. Stewardship is preparation!

The word *budget* isn't a bad word. Many times when we hear people in the world say "budget" they're really saying, "Well, things are tight. We had to get on a budget." No, the reason things are tight is because they don't have a budget. If someone is a good steward, they'll have a budget. A budget is simply making preparation for needs that you know will occur. "Let's get back to the shouting stuff, brother." This will keep you shouting if you put it into practice. Satan will use everything he can to distract you from revival and more of God. If he can attack your finances successfully, it can affect your marriage, your health, and how you pursue God. If he's successful, you are then focused on "God, I need this. God, I need that." It becomes "I, I, I—me, me, me," rather than, "God, I praise you. God, I worship you." It will get your eyes off of God if you let it.

There are things that will wear out. Tires are a good example. It doesn't matter how much you plead the blood, pray, or read the Bible, the tires on your car will wear out. A good steward looks at their expected income, figures out how much new tires will cost, and then cuts that large amount into one-month or one-week slices. They pull that amount out each time they're paid and lay it up in store for when they need it. It's the same thing for clothes and other expenses.

It's not God's fault that some Christians must have a miracle every thirty days. They pay the rent, the light bill, and buy some food, but if there's any money left over—it's party time! They don't prepare and then, all of a sudden, they're calling everyone for prayer saying, "The devil's attacking me." To come out of that cycle of bondage, they're going to have to plan ahead. They can't continue to do what they've been doing and be successful. They must do something different. A good steward will budget for upcoming needs. It's been well said that failing to plan is planning to fail. Start where you are, make a plan, and stick to it. That way, you can shout the shout of victory and keep your sights where they're supposed to be—on God. (BN)

FEBRUARY 5
WILLING & OBEDIENT
ISAIAH 1:16-20

"If ye be willing and obedient, ye shall eat the good of the land" (Is. 1:19).

One Sunday a little boy in church was playing with his toy cars during the pastor's sermon. He kept standing up and making automobile noises during the preacher's message. The minister finally had enough and told the boy—right in front of the whole church—to sit down and shut up. The boy complied, but could be heard muttering under his breath, "I may be sitting down on the outside, but I'm standing up on the inside!"

We can all relate to this story. Every one of us has been forced into obedience at times, but that doesn't mean we did it with a willing heart. Yet in the kingdom of God, it takes both willingness and obedience to receive the goodness of God. First Corinthians 13:3 says that even if we make great sacrifices—but aren't motivated by love—it profits us nothing. The attitude behind the action is just as important as the action itself!

Certainly, every parent has witnessed their child obeying, but doing so with a bad attitude. It makes you want to say, "If that's the attitude you're going to do it in, just forget the whole thing!" God is our heavenly Father. Obedience is important to Him, but a willing heart is what brings Him joy (2 Cor. 9:7). God's blessings flow abundantly when we get our hearts and actions lined up so that we not only do what's right, but we do it with the right attitude.

Check your attitude. If your motives are wrong, don't quit doing what is right, but spend some extra time with the Lord until you get your attitude straight. Jesus didn't die for us out of duty. He was motivated by love. We should live our lives for Him out of love also. (AW)

FEBRUARY 6
IT'LL BE WORTH IT ALL
ROMANS 8:1-20

"For I reckon that the sufferings of this present time are not worthy to be compared with the glory which shall be revealed in us" (Rom. 8:18).

There have been terrible sufferings in this world. Even a casual glance at history will reveal sufferings so unspeakable that it challenges our ability to understand how God will ever wipe the tears away from some people's eyes (Rev. 21:4). But this verse assures us that God's reimbursement will be much greater than our expenditures.

Many things in life come only through much effort and hardship. Take, for instance, childbirth. By anyone's evaluation, nine months of pregnancy isn't all fun. And the actual birth process involves pain and suffering. Yet Jesus said it's all soon forgotten because of the joy that the child brings to the new parents (John 16:21). Athletes also endure suffering. However, all the afflictions of training are quickly swallowed up in the ecstasy of winning gold. The end result makes all the effort more than worthwhile.

That's the way it will be with us when we see Jesus. The worst injustice that any person in history has suffered is not even worthy to be compared with the glory that awaits those who love the Lord. Anyone who doesn't see it that way is empathizing more with the suffering than with the reward. It's so easy to feel the pain, but most of us have never had a glimpse of the glory that awaits us. Certainly none of us have fully comprehended how wonderful that'll be (1 John 3:2). Yet God's Word assures us that His provision is so infinitely greater than our need that there is no comparison between the two.

Take joy in the truth that whatever you may be suffering today will someday fade into oblivion as you experience God's limitless supply! (AW)

FEBRUARY 7
HOW DO WE HANDLE DISAGREEMENTS?
PHILIPPIANS 3:15

"If in any thing ye be otherwise minded, God shall reveal even this unto you" (Phil. 3:15).

Paul was addressing his favorite congregation, the Philippians. This group of people supported him with prayer, love, and finances when no one else would. As he was coming to the end of his prison sentence, he wanted to see no one else but the Philippians. We might consider them as close to a perfect congregation as possible. But what is a "perfect" congregation? It's certainly not one that makes no mistakes. Neither is it a group of people who agree on every teaching.

One Wednesday night as I was ministering, I asked the congregation how many of them disagreed with some things I had taught through the years. Every hand went up. I was a little disturbed. My ego was hurt. I thought maybe a few people might respond, but certainly not everyone!

Our Spirit-filled church is unique. It isn't united because of doctrine. The congregation is made up of Baptists, Methodists, Catholics, Presbyterians, and more. We're all united by the new birth and the baptism in the Holy Spirit. We all brought our pet doctrines with us when we became filled with the Spirit. Many of these teachings will not be corrected until we stand before the Lord at the judgment seat of Christ, no matter how well the pastor preaches otherwise. We are all going to disagree on certain issues until we get to heaven. No one has the corner on the market on every doctrine.

So what unites a church? Doctrine? No. Vision! Our vision is winning souls and meeting the needs of the body of Christ. Paul says, *"If in any thing ye be otherwise minded, God shall reveal even this unto you"* (Phil. 3:15). When we disagree, we should turn it over to the Lord, who will one day settle every issue. In the meantime, we can disagree without being disagreeable. We don't need to strive to make everyone believe as we do. We should endeavor *"to keep the unity of the Spirit in the bond of peace"* (Eph. 4:3). (BY)

FEBRUARY 8
INVENTION OR DISCOVERY?
ECCLESIASTES 1:1-11

"The thing that hath been, it is that which shall be; and that which is done is that which shall be done: and there is no new thing under the sun" (Eccl. 1:9).

Mankind often takes pride in its accomplishments, thinking that they are coming up with new inventions all the time. In reality, all inventions are just discoveries of God's laws that have existed since the beginning of time. Electricity isn't new. It's existed since the earth began. People just discovered how to harness and use it for their benefit. Likewise, travel by air isn't new. Birds have been traveling that way forever. People just recently discovered how to take the laws of nature that already exist and use them to fly.

This is also true in the spiritual world. We have experiences where the Lord touches us in a special way or gives us a new revelation. In reality, all we're doing is discovering things that are already ours in Christ. When we were born again, everything that God is and everything that God can do was deposited in our born-again spirits. We already have the fullness of God dwelling in us. However, we're in the process of discovering what God has placed in us and how to draw those things out into the physical world.

Experiencing God's love in a special way doesn't indicate the beginning of His love for us. He loved us before the foundation of the world. He sent His Son to die for our sins before we were even born. God's love for us is infinite and eternal. Our awareness of His love comes and goes, but His love is constant. Understanding this is one of the keys to staying full of God's love. God's love and faithfulness are always there. Discover them anew today! (AW)

FEBRUARY 9
THE LAW OF CONFESSION
MARK 11:22-26

"For verily I say unto you, That whosoever shall say unto this mountain,
Be thou removed, and be thou cast into the sea; and shall not doubt in his heart,
but shall believe that those things which he saith shall come to pass;
he shall have whatsoever he saith" (Mark 11:23).

The Lord emphasized *saying* four times in this verse alone, stating that we will have what we say. This can work for or against us. We can either have what we say (which enables us to change our circumstances) or say what we have (which makes us victims). Think about it—words are important!

Eleven times in Genesis 1, it's recorded that God speaks things into existence. When the Lord created the heavens and the earth, He spoke them into being. *"Through faith we understand that the worlds were framed by the word of God, so that things which are seen were not made of things which do appear"* (Heb. 11:3). God created everything—including us—by words. The universe was made through and is now held together by words (Heb. 1:3).

Words are keys that unlock the powers of the universe. When the words we speak are in line with God's Word, His power is released. If we agree with the devil and speak forth his thoughts of doubt, we unleash his power. *"Death and life are in the power of the tongue: and they that love it shall eat the fruit thereof"* (Prov. 18:21).

What words are coming out of your mouth? Are you saying what you have or what you want? If you learn the power of speaking positive words in faith, you can begin to change your life. Pray the prayer David prayed, *"Set a watch, O LORD, before my mouth; keep the door of my lips"* (Ps. 141:3). (AW)

FEBRUARY 10
THE POWER OF WORDS
GENESIS 11:1-9

"And the whole earth was of one language, and of one speech" (Gen. 11:1).

The unity of mankind was based on the fact that they all had one language and one speech. It is true that our words are often tools of the devil to divide us, but it's also true that there can be no unity without words.

At the tower of Babel, the Lord sought to divide the men on earth to restrict the things they could accomplish. The way He brought this about was to confuse their language. This was very effective. Hence, the people immediately stopped building the tower. In God's opinion—which is the only one that really counts—language was the key. God removed the key and the door was shut.

There are some things the Lord doesn't want us to prosper in, such as building the tower of Babel. But there are other things He definitely wants us to prosper in, such as love and unity with the brethren. The door to unity cannot be opened without the key of words!

In today's society, we have voluntarily opened ourselves to a barrage of words like no other generation. We are fed all the negative things happening all over the world in an instant of time, and we wonder why we're depressed. We are listening to depressing words! We must turn this situation around and start using positive, uplifting words to minister God's peace. The only pure source of godly words is the Word of God itself.

Let God's Word dominate your thoughts today, and use it to speak peace to others who have no peace. (AW)

FEBRUARY 11
IT'S TIME TO CHANGE DENOMINATIONS!
EPHESIANS 3:20

"Now unto him that is able to do exceeding abundantly above all that we ask or think, according to the power that worketh in us" (Eph. 3:20).

There are more one hundred dollar bills in circulation than there are one-dollar bills. I once heard someone ask, "Isn't it funny how one dollar looks so small when going to the grocery store, but so big when you take it to church?" Many Christians need to change denominations! God wants us to stretch our faith. He wants us to prove Him. You can't out-give God! It's just not possible. I want increase in my growth with the Lord, so I also want to increase my giving. I've decided that I don't want to be limited to ten dollars or a hundred. I don't want to limit God. I desire to increase to a thousand dollars, ten thousand, and beyond. But that won't happen until I change denominations.

Pray about it and ask the Lord. If you've been giving one-dollar offerings, bump it up to five. If you've been giving ten dollars, bump it up to fifty. Beloved, it's time to change denominations! (BN)

FEBRUARY 12
ACT ON YOUR FAITH
JAMES 2:14-26

"Even so faith, if it hath not works, is dead, being alone" *(James 2:17).*

On December 30, 1973, I hurt my back very badly. I experienced excruciating pain and couldn't straighten up. I could barely talk, and my shoulder blades were nearly touching each other. It was the night before I was to be ordained into the ministry, and all I could think about was what a terrible testimony this would be at my ordination!

I began to resist the pain and the devil by acting on my prayer of faith that I was healed. I did push-ups, deep knee bends, bent over and touched my toes, and anything else I didn't feel like doing. There was improvement, but I didn't have a total release until I was taking a shower and washing my hair to get ready for the service. It hurt terribly to bend my head under the spout, but I knew I was healed and was determined to act like it. In between the first and second rinse, all the pain left and I was completely normal.

Can you imagine a person in a burning building that believed they would die if they didn't get out but just continued to sit there? Of course not! Likewise, faith that doesn't have the proper corresponding actions isn't genuine faith at all.

A person who says they believe God for prosperity, but doesn't give, is deceiving themselves. A person who says "I'm healed," but continues to act sick, is killing whatever faith they have. A person who intercedes for someone, but then worries whether anything will ever happen, is not acting in faith. True biblical faith must be acted on. Therefore, act on what you believe today! (AW)

FEBRUARY 13
THE BLESSINGS OF UNITY
PSALM 133

"Behold, how good and how pleasant it is for brethren to dwell together in unity!
It is like the precious ointment upon the head, that ran down upon the beard,
even Aaron's beard: that went down to the skirts of his garments; As the dew of Hermon, and as
the dew that descended upon the mountains of Zion: for there the LORD commanded the bless-
ing, even life for evermore" *(Ps. 133:1-3).*

Only Christians—brethren—can truly dwell in unity. The world can come together, but they can't be unified. True unity is supernatural. It comes from the Holy Spirit. When two sinners come together, one plus one equals two. When two Christians come together, one plus one equals ten thousand (Deut. 32:30). The world adds, but the Holy Spirit multiplies!

David spoke of the goodness and pleasantness of Christian unity in verse 1 and the blessings of unity in verses 2 and 3. The blessings are twofold: *power and refreshment*.

First, it's like the oil that ran down the beard of Aaron to the skirts of his garments. Oil represents the *power* of the Holy Spirit. Aaron was the high priest. When the anointing oil was placed on his head, it ran onto his beard and down his garments to the bottom tassels. This is a type of the baptism of the Holy Spirit. On the day of Pentecost, the oil of the Holy Spirit was poured upon our great High Priest, Jesus (Heb. 1:9). It then ran down to the garments, the 120 waiting in the upper room that day. It has continued to flow throughout the church age and will one day reach the last tassel on the hem of the garment when the final person is born again. Jesus will then come back for His body, His church.

Second, unity is like the dew that descended on Mount Hermon. Dew speaks of supernatural *refreshment* that comes from the Holy Spirit. The Spirit not only comes to bring us power, but as Isaiah tells us, *"This is the rest...this is the refreshing."* He was referring to *"stammering lips and another tongue"* (Is. 28:11-12).

In an atmosphere of spiritual unity, there is power and refreshing. It is also in this moment of unity that the Lord commands blessings. No wonder we should strive *"to keep the unity of the Spirit in the bond of peace"* (Eph. 4:3). (BY)

FEBRUARY 14
YOUR FIRST LOVE
REVELATION 2:1-7

"Nevertheless I have somewhat against thee,
because thou hast left thy first love" (Rev. 2:4).

Many Christians cringe at this passage of Scripture. They know they don't love the Lord as they should, and this just reminds them of that. But the Lord wasn't speaking of returning to how <u>we</u> first loved Him, but returning to our revelation of how <u>He</u> first loved us. As the Apostle John put it, *"We love him, because he first loved us"* (1 John 4:19).

Often, preaching is centered around how we should love others. Although this is certainly appropriate, the greatest and most distinguishing characteristic of a true Christian is their love for the brethren (John 13:35). But we can't give away what we haven't received. Until we have a true revelation of how much God loves us, we can't genuinely love others. Trying to do so without a vibrant, experiential love within us is like trying to give someone a drink from a well that's run dry. It can't be done!

The Christian life is not just hard to live—it's impossible to live in our own strength. True Christianity is not us living for Jesus, but Jesus living through us (Gal. 2:20). Nowhere is this more apparent than in loving other people. The kind of love Jesus commands includes turning the other cheek (Matt. 5:39) and forgiving those who crucify us (Luke 23:34). This kind of love is humanly impossible, unless we walk in the supernatural love that only comes from God.

Therefore, loving others is the fruit—not the root—of God's love for us. As you return to the joy of understanding how much God loves you the way you did when you first received Christ, you'll love others more accidentally than you ever have on purpose! (AW)

FEBRUARY 15
UNBELIEF IS FAITH IN REVERSE
GENESIS 3:1-7

"And when the woman saw that the tree was good for food, and that it was pleasant to the eyes,
and a tree to be desired to make one wise, she took of the fruit thereof, and did eat, and gave also
unto her husband with her; and he did eat" (Gen. 3:6).

Have you ever thought about what unbelief really is? Unbelief is actually faith. It's just faith in something other than God and what He's said. When Adam and Eve ate the forbidden fruit, they were in faith. But their faith was in what the serpent said instead of what God had said. Their unbelief was just their God-given faith misdirected, causing them to believe a lie.

We are faith beings. God created us that way. We drive cars and ride on airplanes because we believe they will safely get us to our destination. If we believed we were going to die in transit, we wouldn't go. Faith governs our lives. We use faith every day. No one can function without faith. All of our actions are based on faith. But if we base our faith on things that contradict God's Word, we're in unbelief and using faith in reverse.

Therefore, unbelief is actually the power of faith working in a negative way. Just as faith is the power that releases God's ability (1 John 5:4), unbelief is the power that releases the will of Satan in our lives.

Therefore, realize that you do have faith and you use it every day in either a positive or negative way. Choose to direct your faith in the positive direction of God by basing it on the promises in His Word. (AW)

FEBRUARY 16
GOD'S WORD GIVES LIGHT
MARK 4:21-23

"And he said unto them, Is a candle brought to be put under a bushel, or under a bed? and not to be set on a candlestick?" *(Mark 4:21).*

Jesus had just given the parable of the sower sowing the seed. Then He interpreted it to His disciples. This teaching stressed the importance of God's Word in our lives. We can't bear fruit without putting God's Word in our hearts any more than a farmer can have a harvest without planting seeds. Then Jesus said that a candle must be put on a candlestick to shine its light. The Lord was still speaking about the importance of His Word.

"Thy word is a lamp unto my feet, and a light unto my path" (Ps. 119:105). Jesus was saying that God's Word is how He sheds light on all of our situations. Without the illumination of God's Word, we will stumble around in the dark. What's the purpose of having a light if we aren't going to use it? Why would anyone place a lamp under his bed or under a basket and block the light? That doesn't make sense. But that's exactly what we often do with the light that God's given us.

How many times have we neglected meditating on God's Word because of our busy schedules and just stumbled blindly through our day? The influence of God's Word in our lives is not a luxury we can do without. It's as essential as light in the midst of darkness! Light in the darkness enables us to function as if it were day, as long as the light is in a prominent place.

The focus of our hearts is the candlestick on which we set the light of God's Word. As we meditate on it day and night, there is no circumstance or secret that will not be clearly revealed to us through the light of God's Word (Mark 4:22). (AW)

FEBRUARY 17
THE GOD OF THE FEW
EPHESIANS 1:1; COLOSSIANS 1:2

"Saints and faithful brethren" *(Col. 1:2).*

This phrase opens both Ephesians and Colossians. It speaks volumes concerning the strategy of God. He doesn't look for many, but for few. He looks for quality, not quantity. Just like the U.S. Marines, God is looking for "a few good men."

In the Old Testament, God called the faithful few "the remnant." It was with an army of 300 that He defeated the multitudes of Midianites under Gideon's leadership. Gideon was looking for numbers, but God was looking for dedication. He's still looking for *"a man among them"* to pray for the nations (Ezek. 22:30).

Jesus looked for ways to slim down the multitudes that followed Him. He wanted a few who would stick with Him no matter what. Out of the seventy who followed, He had twelve. Out of the twelve, Jesus had three who were closest to Him. Yet out of the three, only one—John—stuck with the Lord when He was crucified.

Many times we look for great numbers in prayer. That's because our emotions are moved and we feel a greater anointing with larger numbers. However, God is still more impressed with a few in faith than a multitude in unbelief.

Just as in New Testament days, churches are filled with saints, but only a few are *"faithful brethren."* Although the Great Commission tells us to make disciples of all nations (Matt. 28:19), we're too busy making converts instead. Converts are many, but disciples are few. A disciple is one who continues to follow the Lord despite the circumstances. They are faithful no matter who else follows. Jesus said, *"If ye continue in my word, then are ye my disciples indeed"* (John 8:31). Continuing in God's Word sets you apart from the multitude of converts. It makes you more than a saint. It makes you a faithful brother (or sister) in Jesus. (BY)

FEBRUARY 18
LET'S JUST STICK TO SPIRITUAL THINGS
MATTHEW 6:21

"For where your treasure is, there will your heart be also" (Matt. 6:21).

It's been said that there have been a lot of hot arguments over cold hard cash. Some people get offended when a preacher starts talking about money. They'll think or say "Money? I'm here to hear about spiritual things, about the things of God." Well, if they're offended by men of God today, they'd certainly have been offended by Jesus! The New Testament speaks more about money than both heaven and hell combined. In fact, Jesus dealt with money in sixteen of His thirty-eight parables. Some of these same folks would say, "Talk about sin or anything else, but leave my money alone." Please bear in mind that when we talk about money, it's not your money or my money—it's God's money. Psalms 24:1 tells us that the earth is the Lord's and all it contains. That includes all the money. In 1 Chronicles 29:12 David prayed, *"Both riches and honour come of thee."* Even the Apostle Paul reminded the church in Colossians 1:16, *"For by him were all things created, that are in heaven, and that are in earth, visible and invisible, whether they be thrones, or dominions, or principalities, or powers: all things were created by him, and for him."* We cannot separate money, giving, and stewardship from our worship of God. It's a part of us and who we are.

When you love, you give—and your expression of that love is something tangible. Talk about love, Jesus gave Himself! Jesus said no one can be His disciple who does not give up all he possesses (Luke 14:33). There is a definite link between a person's heart and their pocketbook. Jesus said that where you put your money is where your heart truly is (Matt. 6:21). We can tell a lot about a person just by taking a look at their checkbook. A true gauge of whether we're being spiritual or not is in our giving. Focus today on being truly spiritual by putting God first in everything, including money. (BN)

FEBRUARY 19
YOU WILL HAVE WHATSOEVER YOU SAY
MARK 11:12-14, 20-24

"For verily I say unto you, That whosoever shall say unto this mountain,
Be thou removed, and be thou cast into the sea; and shall not doubt in his heart,
but shall believe that those things which he saith shall come to pass;
he shall have whatsoever he saith" (Mark 11:23).

One of the cardinal laws of faith is that we must speak our faith. When God created the heavens and the earth, He said *"Let there be..."* and there was (Gen. 1). We release our faith through our words. This not only works in the positive, but also in the negative. Jesus said we will have WHATSOEVER we say!

Most people are ignorant of this truth, or they don't believe it. They say things they wouldn't want to come to pass. But we will have WHATSOEVER we say. Instead of saying what they want, most people usually say what they have, thereby sealing their destruction. We need to learn the lesson that Jesus taught His disciples, to use our words to change our situation.

This is hard for people in the Western world to comprehend. We don't value words much any more. This is evidenced by how only written contracts hold any authority in our society today. But that's not the way it is in God's kingdom. Words are supreme. If we want to be successful in the kingdom of God, we must learn to live by God's principles. Words are important. Use them to your advantage! (AW)

FEBRUARY 20
BEWARE OF EVIL COMMUNICATIONS
1 CORINTHIANS 15:32-34

"Be not deceived: evil communications corrupt good manners" *(1 Cor. 15:33).*

Have you ever noticed that it's easier to gain weight than to lose it? It's also easier to destroy things than to build them, to get sick than to stay well, and to ruin a relationship than to maintain one. It seems that the things we desire are harder to come by than the things we wish to avoid. It's the same way with what we hear.

Values and attitudes that take a long time to build can be easily plucked by just a few words. Certainly, everyone has had their enthusiasm quenched by the disapproving words of someone else. Our words are important, but so are the words of every person we hear. To succeed in the kingdom of God, we not only have to watch what we say, but we must guard what we hear.

In our day and age, Christians are exposed to the negative words of this world as never before. Most of us pipe those words right into our homes and automobiles. In seconds, we're aware of all the negative things going on all around the world. Some people even listen to songs that wail about the miseries and sorrows of mankind for entertainment. Yet these words have power—negative power. They have power to depress and cause fear. We don't need that!

Think about the words you hear today. Do you really need or want what you're seeing and hearing? Probably not. Choose life instead of death (Deut. 30:19). (AW)

FEBRUARY 21
PRAY FOR YOUR WORDS
PSALM 141

"Set a watch, O LORD, before my mouth; keep the door of my lips" *(Ps. 141:3).*

David knew the power of words. He used them to praise the Lord personally and also established singers in the tabernacle who praised God twenty-four hours a day. David used words to draw the hearts of the people toward him and toward the Lord.

He also knew the power words have to destroy. He witnessed this firsthand from his son. Absalom spoke to everyone who came to his father, and stole their hearts away from David by his fair words (2 Sam. 15:1-6). No doubt, Solomon's statement in Proverbs 18:21—regarding death and life being in the power of the tongue—was a truth Absalom had heard his father utter many times before.

Words are powerful. But as the Apostle James said, *"The tongue can no man tame"* (James 3:8). That doesn't mean we're destined to destruction. He said no MAN can tame the tongue. We can't do it on our own, but God can.

This is what David was referring to in his prayer (Ps. 141:3). He was calling upon the power of God to do what he couldn't do in his own strength. Like David, we need to recognize the power of words and draw on the supernatural power of God to tame our tongues. Pray this prayer today, and watch the Lord miraculously intervene! (AW)

FEBRUARY 22
NOAH GAVE WHAT HE NEEDED THE MOST
GENESIS 8:20-22

"And Noah builded an altar unto the LORD; and took of every clean beast, and of every clean fowl, and offered burnt offerings on the altar" *(Gen. 8:20).*

The whole earth was flooded as a result of sin. All of humanity, as well as the vegetation and animals, were destroyed. There were precious few animals spared to repopulate the earth. Noah could have said, "Wow! God gave us the beasts for food now and we don't have very many left. I'd better ration them and make sure we'll have enough. They're all the food we have!" But he didn't say that. He gave. He knew that God kept them and that He was able to continually keep them. So Noah sacrificed burnt offerings to God.

For Noah to look at what he had as his provision when it was only a seed would have been a fatal mistake. A mistake that would not have only affected him but also his family and the whole human race! The fate of humanity really did rest in Noah's hands! (No pressure.) But Noah sowed what he needed the most. God only asks you to give what he wants you to have more of. You need to give the most when you have the least. He is no fool who gives what he cannot keep to gain what he cannot lose.

"For the eyes of the LORD run to and fro throughout the whole earth, to shew himself strong in the behalf of them whose heart is perfect toward him" (2 Chr. 16:9). God is just waiting for you to release your faith and to give as He leads without worry or fear. Then He can show Himself strong on your behalf.

If what you have isn't enough to meet your need, understand that it's just your seed. (BN)

FEBRUARY 23
ARE YOU CHASING YOUR TAIL?
COLOSSIANS 2:1-12

"And ye are complete in him, which is the head of all principality and power" *(Col. 2:10).*

Most of us have seen a dog chase its tail. It's amusing and puzzling at the same time. Why chase something you already have? I can't speak with authority as to what a dog really thinks, but it appears to me that a dog that chases its tail is the only one who can't see that it's already his.

Amazingly, Christians tend to do the same thing. We ask for joy, faith, healing, wisdom, etc., which according to God's Word, we already have. The Christian life is not a continual process of asking and receiving more from God, but it's a renewing of our minds to understand and appropriate what we already have in Christ. We are complete in Him!

Healing isn't "out there" somewhere. God's healing virtue is already inside of us. He doesn't have to come and place His mighty hand on us to heal us. *"By whose stripes ye <u>were</u> healed"* (1 Pet. 2:24, emphasis added). We just have to believe and manifest what we already have.

Faith isn't something that comes and goes in our lives. We were saved by faith (Eph. 2:8), and that faith becomes a fruit of our spirits (Gal. 5:22-23). But we must first pick the fruit to enjoy it. Faith is always in us. We just don't always take advantage of what we have.

Ask the Lord today for a revelation of what is really yours in Christ Jesus. Quit trying to get what you already have and enjoy your inheritance! (AW)

FEBRUARY 24
PHYSICAL HEALING
ISAIAH 53:1-5 & MATTHEW 8:16-17

"Surely he hath borne our griefs, and carried our sorrows: yet we did esteem him stricken, smitten of God, and afflicted" (Is. 53:4).

Physical healing is so prominent in Scripture—especially the New Testament—that there should be no debate about it, but there is. Many people interpret the promises concerning our healing to apply only in a spiritual sense. They believe scriptures such as Isaiah 53:4-5 are speaking of being healed spiritually.

The best way to interpret Scripture is by Scripture. If a particular passage is quoted and applied in another passage, then we have a very clear understanding of exactly what the Lord is saying. This happened with Isaiah's prophecy concerning the Messiah bringing us healing.

In Matthew 8:16, multitudes came to Jesus for healing and He physically healed every one of them. Then in verse 17, the Gospel writer said this happened *"that it might be fulfilled which was spoken by Esaias the prophet, saying, Himself took our infirmities, and bare our sicknesses."* This emphatically states that Isaiah's promise of healing was for our physical bodies. Praise the Lord!

Healing is just as much a part of the atoning work of Christ as is the forgiveness of sin. The Greek word used for *salvation* hundreds of times in the New Testament is *sozo*. It's also translated in reference to physical healing in Matthew 9:22, Mark 5:34, Luke 8:48, and James 5:15.

All faith for physical healing has to begin at the place of believing that it is God's will to heal us. The truth that this was part of the atoning work of Christ, as prophesied in Scripture, provides us with that foundation. (AW)

FEBRUARY 25
IT'S A DONE DEAL!
1 PETER 2:21-25

"Who his own self bare our sins in his own body on the tree, that we, being dead to sins, should live unto righteousness: by whose stripes ye were healed" (1 Pet. 2:24).

The last phrase of this verse is the same as Isaiah 53:4, with one important exception: It places our healing in the past tense. We have already been healed! This is a hard concept for some people to grasp. They cannot understand how they could already be healed if there is sickness in their bodies. So, one way to get around this is to say that this is speaking of spiritual healing. However, Matthew 8:17 made it very clear that the healing Isaiah was speaking of was physical, not spiritual.

The key to understanding this concept is relating it to the forgiveness of our sins. When were our sins forgiven? According to Scripture, they were forgiven when Christ died, long before we ever received it. Our prayers only enable us to receive what was already accomplished in the spiritual realm and bring it into physical reality. That's the way it is with healing.

Jesus has already accomplished our healing. The same virtue that raised Him from the dead is resident within every believer (Eph. 1:19-20). It's a done deal. All we must do is believe and give physical substance (Heb. 11:1) to what's already true in our born-again spirits. It's infinitely easier to release something that we already have than to try to get something that we don't have.

Start releasing your healing by confessing and acting on your faith instead of trying to use your faith to ask God to heal you. He's already done it! (AW)

FEBRUARY 26
ANOTHER REASON YOU NEED A PASTOR
DEUTERONOMY 1:38

"Joshua the son of Nun...shall cause Israel to inherit it" *(Deut. 1:38).*

Stop and think of as many things as you can that cause prosperity to come into your life. I'm sure you'll think of meditating on God's Word first. Next you'll remember to be a doer of the Word, walk uprightly before Him, and finally, to be a giver. All of these are found in God's Word and are a part of His plan of supernatural prosperity, but here's one you might not have thought of: *being a committed member of a church.*

Just as in Joshua's day, being submitted to a pastor, a leader, *causes you* to inherit the promised land of prosperity and blessing. A good pastor represents the leadership of Jesus in your life. Like following the Apostle Paul, to follow a good pastor is to follow Christ. Just like Jesus watches over His flock, the church, pastors watch over the sheep given to them. They are responsible for many areas of your personal life.

"Obey them that have the rule over you, and submit yourselves: for they watch for your souls, as they that must give account" (Heb. 13:17).

First, a pastor watches out for your soul. They teach God's Word so you'll be able to take authority over every thought that doesn't line up with God's will for your life. The care of your soul is not left with you alone but also with a shepherd—your pastor. They pray **"that ye may stand perfect and complete in all the will of God"** (Col. 4:12). Second, your pastor will one day give an account to God, not only for their teaching, but also for your spiritual growth. They are benefited by your submission to their teaching, but so are you. You'll be rewarded in heaven for your obedience to their revelations of the Word.

Not only will you be rewarded in heaven one day, but you'll also be prospered right here on earth. Your pastor will *cause you* to inherit the blessings of God! (BY)

FEBRUARY 27
SPIRITUAL DYSLEXIA
1 JOHN 4:7-21

"No man hath seen God at any time. If we love one another, God dwelleth in us, and his love is perfected in us" *(1 John 4:12).*

Dyslexia is when someone has a condition that causes them to see everything backwards. For instance, the word G-O-D looks like D-O-G to a dyslexic person. There's a big difference between God and a dog!

Likewise, there is a spiritual dyslexia that affects religious people, causing them to see the truths of God backwards. First John 4:12 is an example of this. They want God to dwell in them, so they try to love others, thinking that will cause His love to dwell in them. No! That's dyslexic! John was saying just the opposite.

Loving others doesn't cause God to dwell in us and love us. But having God dwell in us and experiencing His love will cause us to love others. Our acts of holiness don't cause God to love us, but experiencing His love causes us to act holy. This is the difference between religion and true Christianity.

Religion tells us what we must do to be right with God. True Christianity tells us that we are right with God through our faith in Christ and right actions just naturally follow. We can't walk in the Spirit by denying the flesh any more than we can bring light into a room by shoveling out the darkness. We must turn on the light to drive the darkness away. Likewise, we must walk in the Spirit to keep from fulfilling the lust of the flesh (Gal. 5:16).

You can't give away what you don't have! To set someone else free, you must be free. Let the Lord fill you with His love today, and you'll automatically love others. Walk in the Spirit, and you won't fulfill the lust of the flesh! (AW)

FEBRUARY 28
HE LOVED US FIRST
1 JOHN 4:7-21

"We love him, because he first loved us" *(1 John 4:19).*

It's amazing how we miss the truth of this simple and straightforward scripture. God doesn't love us for what we do—we love God for what He's done for us. All error in religion hinges on this point.

Everything that we do must be in response to God's love, not to obtain it. Any good deed, regardless of its merit, can be rendered unacceptable to God if our motives are to obtain His favor through what we do. The Lord doesn't relate to us based on our performance. Praise Jesus! God commended His love to us while we were still sinners (Rom. 5:8). He loves us because He is love, not because we're lovable.

Only when we appreciate this unearned, unmerited love of God can we truly love Him in return. God is love (1 John 4:8) and all love comes from Him. Love doesn't originate with us. We can only give love to the Lord after we receive it from Him.

Therefore, relax! We don't have to force ourselves to love God. All we must do is focus our attention on how much He loves us. As we begin to explore the depths of God's love for us, we'll automatically begin to love Him in return. It's inescapable! Instead of focusing on what you should be doing for the Lord, focus on what He's already done for you. Then love and appreciation will flow freely from your heart toward your loving Father. (AW)

FEBRUARY 29
EXPRESS LOVE BY YOUR ACTIONS
1 JOHN 3:13-19

"But whoso hath this world's good, and seeth his brother have need, and shutteth up his bowels of compassion from him, how dwelleth the love of God in him?"
(1 John 3:17).

I live in an area with one of the richest deposits of gold in the world. It's estimated that there is still twice as much gold in the ground as was ever mined. We have huge gold mines operating today. This has caused many people to try their hand at prospecting with the hope of striking it rich.

I remember when one of my Bible college students came running up to me and asked me to hurry out to his pick-up. He had the bed of his truck piled high with what he was sure was millions of dollars worth of gold. But it was just pyrite, or what we call "fool's gold." I couldn't help but laugh since I had tons of it on my property. Yet he was convinced he had hit the mother lode. It was weeks before he washed all that dirt out of his truck!

Many things look alike, but there's always a way to discern the precious from the ordinary. Gold is distinguished by the way it reacts to certain chemicals such as acid. *The acid test for true love is action.*

It's easy to say you love someone, but how do you treat them? That's the test that distinguishes God's kind of love from all counterfeits. Make sure you love the Lord and others today in Spirit and in truth, and treat them as Jesus would. (AW)

MARCH 1
NO CHILD OF GOD IS BETTER THAN ANOTHER
1 CORINTHIANS 12:15

"If the foot shall say, Because I am not the hand, I am not of the body" (1 Cor. 12:15).

This verse comes from an interesting part of 1 Corinthians 12. We have body parts talking to each other. Not only does the foot speak to the hand, the ear talks to the eye (verse 16). What we have is hidden parts speaking to visible parts. The foot and ear are not as readily visible to others as is the eye and hand.

If one part of your body could complain, it would be the foot to the hand: "I carry the weight all day. This man puts me into a sock, crams me into a shoe, and no one sees me. The hand is seen all day long. When was the last time this man bought me a ring or watch?" The ear could also complain about the eye. "I'm under this hair and no one can see me. The eye is right around the corner and everyone looks deep into it. When was the last time this woman washed back here? She buys eye makeup, but never ear makeup!"

This may all sound silly, but the body parts speak of the offices we all have in the body of Christ. Oftentimes, we complain because someone else is being shown all of the attention. "I serve in children's church and no one knows I'm back here. The music director is seen by everyone, and even the ushers get more attention than I do!" Just because you're not as visible in your ministry doesn't mean you are less important or not needed.

Would you rather lose your hand or your foot? Would you rather lose your sight or your hearing? When it comes to function, all of your body parts are equally important. The same is true with the Lord. God wouldn't want to lose the children's worker over the pastor. Both are equally important. Your ministry is just as vital to the body of Christ as the best-known evangelist, pastor, or teacher. (BY)

MARCH 2
THANK GOD THAT THINGS ARE AS GOOD AS THEY ARE!
PHILIPPIANS 4:6

"Be careful for nothing; but in every thing by prayer and supplication <u>with thanksgiving</u> let your requests be made known unto God" (Phil. 4:6, emphasis added).

I know of a gentleman in Fort Worth who found himself going through some tough times financially. He had two luxury cars and a nice home, but then he lost his job. During that time, he was able to keep his house, but unfortunately he lost both cars. Many people who find themselves in that kind of situation throw up their hands in discouragement or blame God, their job, or everyone else around them. They say, "Why me? I'm supposed to be a child of God. How could this happen?" Not this man. Although he had no car, he did have a bicycle. Refusing to blame God and give the devil the victory, this man took the garage door opener out of his car and attached it to his bicycle just before his car was repossessed. Every morning he would go out to the garage and get on his bike. He'd push the garage door button to open the door, ride out of the garage, push the button to close the door, and off he'd peddle to work. Every day he peddled that bike, and every day he thanked God he had a bike to get to work. He kept tithing, giving, and thanking God for what he <u>did</u> have instead of complaining about what he didn't. He went to work praising God that God was going to restore. He kept a P.F.A.—Positive Faith Attitude. It wasn't very long before that man didn't have to peddle to work anymore. He believed "new car cometh" and it did!

What do you need? Are you thankful for what you already have? Keep your switch of faith turned on, and thank Him that things are as good as they are. Be a faithful steward with what you have, and be faithful in giving your tithes and offerings. Sow in faith, believing, and you'll see your harvest come in. Throughout the day today, practice thanking Him for what you have and for what He's done in your life. Thanksgiving gets God's attention by showing that we know <u>all</u> our needs are met in Him! (BN)

MARCH 3
EXPERIENCE PRODUCES HOPE
ROMANS 5:3-5

"And patience, experience; and experience, hope" (Rom. 5:4).

There was a time in my life when I believed that God could miraculously supply my need, because that's what His Word promised (Phil. 4:19), even though I had never yet experienced such provision. However, the day came when I not only believed it, but my faith actually produced tangible results. I experienced what I believed.

That did something for me. I can't say it made me believe, because I was already believing. If I hadn't believed, I wouldn't have received (James 1:5-7). However, it strengthened my faith by giving me new hope. Before, my hope was that it could happen. Afterwards, my hope became that it would happen again and again. After seeing His provision many times, I've come to expect that God will always provide. Experiencing God's supply has generated new hope.

In the heart of someone who has consistently experienced God faithfulness, there abides a strength and depth of hope that a novice can't understand or appreciate. A person who has already built a home has a confidence and security that a first-time builder can't duplicate. They may be able to duplicate the performance of the seasoned builder, or possibly exceed it, but experience gives the veteran a definite edge.

There are no shortcuts to experience, but as the old saying goes: "Today is the first day of the rest of your life." Put God's Word to the test today, and begin enjoying the wonderful benefits of increased hope. (AW)

MARCH 4
BE SENSITIVE TO WHAT YOU CONSIDER
ROMANS 4:16-25

"And being not weak in faith, he considered not his own body now dead, when he was about an hundred years old, neither yet the deadness of Sara's womb" (Rom. 4:19).

People often overlook the key to Abraham's faith—his focus. Romans 4:19 reveals that when the Lord told Abram that he would have a child in his old age, he didn't even think about how elderly he and his wife were. All he considered was the promise of God, not all the reasons why it couldn't come to pass. This was the real strength of Abraham's faith. He totally focused on God's promise.

You can't be tempted with something you don't think (Heb. 11:15). Therefore, if we only think on the positives of God's Word, all we'll be tempted to believe is God's Word. Few Christians understand this, which is why they allow their thoughts to focus on things they should never consider. Then—after exploring all the negatives—they try to believe God and can't understand why their faith doesn't work. If Abraham had thought that way, his faith wouldn't have worked either!

To be strong in faith, we must be weak in unbelief. We cannot entertain thoughts that war against faith and still succeed. One of the keys to victorious faith is controlling our thoughts so our focus is constantly on the truths of God's Word. Ask the Lord to help you keep your mind and heart focused on His promises in the Word today. Then you'll find yourself strong in faith too! (AW)

MARCH 5
THE BLESSED HOPE
TITUS 2:11-15

"Looking for that blessed hope, and the glorious appearing of the great God and our Saviour Jesus Christ" *(Titus 2:13).*

The promise of the second coming of our Lord Jesus Christ is a great comfort. Regardless of how bad things get in this life, we have the promise that our Lord is coming again in total triumph and power.

While in basic training, I was often overwhelmed with all the ungodliness around me. My drill sergeants delighted in mocking God. They started every training session by having me stand in front of the company while someone blasphemed God, told a filthy joke, or shared what he had done with a local prostitute the night before. They did this to embarrass me and to try to provoke me. I remember the sergeant saying, "Preacher, I love to see you blush!"

At times, this all seemed too much. I longed for the Lord to come and just wipe them all out, but I knew that wasn't right. Then one evening as we were forced to march and my body and emotions were screaming, I looked up and saw one of the most gorgeous sunsets I've ever seen. This displayed the awesome power of God in such a way that all the corruption around me just vanished. The cursing of the vilest men couldn't stop God from showing His glory. Jesus was still the same and was on His throne, and there would come a day of reckoning (Matt. 12:36).

This is the hope that the second coming of our Lord produces. He's not deaf or blind as some people's actions suggest. He's just patient and waiting for the full harvest of souls to come in before He reveals Himself. At that time, every tongue will confess that Jesus is Lord, and the righteous will shine as the sun in its brightness. Our victory is nearer than we think. Hold on to that blessed hope! (AW)

MARCH 6
SEND IT AHEAD!
MATTHEW 6:19-21

"Lay not up for yourselves treasures upon earth, where moth and rust doth corrupt, and where thieves break through and steal: But lay up for yourselves treasures in heaven, where neither moth nor rust doth corrupt, and where thieves do not break through nor steal: For where your treasure is, there will your heart be also" *(Matt. 6:19-21).*

We live in a society that is concerned about things: buying the biggest and best house, driving the nicest car, and acquiring the latest gadget. But that is not the primary focus of the Lord, nor should it be for any believer. The Lord doesn't object to *us having things*, but He does object to *things having us*. God didn't say that money was the root of all evil. He said the *love* of money was (1 Tim. 6:10). That means putting money first in our lives above everything else.

The psalmist wrote, ***"Delight thyself also in the LORD; and he shall give thee the desires of thine heart"*** (Ps. 37:4). Jesus tells us to ***"seek ye first the kingdom of God, and his righteousness; and all these things shall be added unto you"*** (Matt. 6:33). The Apostle Paul told the Colossians ***"Set your affection on things above, not on things on the earth"*** (Col. 3:2). Our focus should be furthering the kingdom of God. If our bottom-line heart motivation isn't souls, we're not focusing on the right thing.

There is a record in heaven where we will have to give an account of everything that we do and say (Rom. 14:12). Matthew 6:20 instructs us to lay up treasures in heaven. So, every time we give to the Lord out of a pure heart, we're laying up a heavenly bank account and increasing our balance. Giving is making another deposit for eternity. And just like an earthly bank account, we can make withdrawals.

Consider giving as an opportunity to advance God's kingdom and enhance your heavenly bank account. Who knows you better—the teller at the bank or the recording angel of the bank of heaven? (BN)

MARCH 7
FAITH OPERATES EFFECTIVELY BY LOVE
GALATIANS 5:1-13

"For in Jesus Christ neither circumcision availeth any thing, nor uncircumcision; but faith which worketh by love" (Gal. 5:6).

The dictionary defines *work*, as used in this verse, as "to operate, or cause to operate, especially effectively." The driving force behind true biblical faith is God's kind of love. When we have a clear revelation of God's love for us, faith comes naturally. Faith is a byproduct of God's love.

Once a man argued with me that God doesn't heal all the time. His motivation for this belief was his twelve-year-old daughter who was quadriplegic and mentally retarded. He believed God made her that way. I shared scriptures, he shared scriptures, and we arrived at a stalemate.

Finally I asked, "What kind of father are you that you don't love your daughter enough to see her healed?" He became really mad and assured me that he'd do anything to see his daughter healed, even to the point of taking her place if that could happen. I responded, "And you think God loves her less than you do!"

He could argue doctrine, but when it came down to love, it's inconceivable that a God who not only has love but is love (1 John 4:8) would not use His power on our behalf. Those who don't believe that the Lord will act on their behalf are people who don't understand His love. Faith works when we know the great love God has for us.

Ask the Lord for a revelation of how much He loves you, and watch your faith come alive. (AW)

MARCH 8
FAITH IS BASED ON KNOWLEDGE
2 PETER 1:1-11

"According as his divine power hath given unto us all things that pertain unto life and godliness, through the knowledge of him that hath called us to glory and virtue" (2 Pet. 1:3).

Faith is an essential ingredient to life and godliness. And according to this key verse, faith is based on the knowledge of God.

Faith doesn't come by praying for it or by having others lay hands on you to receive more of it. Every born-again believer already has the faith of God in them (Rom. 12:3). Faith is resident in every believer's heart, but our heads must learn how to utilize it. We need to change our thinking to line up with the kingdom of God.

The way we do that is through studying His Word. The Apostle Paul said, **"So then faith cometh by hearing, and hearing by the word of God"** (Rom. 10:17). God's Word reveals His knowledge to us, which then releases His faith within us. Faith comes as the result of what we think.

If we think the wrong things, we'll get the wrong results. Those who continually live in poverty don't know or don't believe what God's Word promises them. That's true of deliverance, healing, joy, and whatever else we need that God has promised. God's people are destroyed for lack of knowledge (Hos. 4:6). The first step to faith and the victory it produces is obtaining the knowledge of the truth (John 8:31-32).

Make a commitment today to search out the knowledge of God through His Word. You won't be sorry and your life will change as your faith is released. (AW)

MARCH 9
GOD HAS ALREADY GIVEN EVERYTHING
2 PETER 1:3

"According as his divine power hath given unto us all things
that pertain unto life and godliness" (2 Pet. 1:3).

This simple verse can change your entire life. The revelation given here is simple, yet profound. God has already given us everything we need for our natural and spiritual lives. He will not make anything else. His divine power looked through the ages, saw everything we would need for life (natural life) and godliness (spiritual life) and made it ahead of time. When you received Jesus as your Savior, a storehouse was opened containing all you would ever need. It's almost blasphemous to think that we can face a need that will take God by surprise.

Our faith doesn't move God to supply, He has already supplied. Our study, prayer, faith, and trust in God moves us into a better position to receive what He has already given. God is never the problem—we are!

When the thief on the cross received salvation, Jesus told him they would be together in paradise that day (Luke 23:43). Adam and Eve were removed from paradise, but through Jesus, we are brought back into the garden. The angels that kept Adam and Eve out have welcomed us back. God put Adam and Eve into Eden after he finished the garden. Everything was created, then the man and woman were placed into it. God did not create a tree when the couple had a need. The trees were already made for every need they could possibly have.

God has done the same for us with our paradise, the garden of the New Birth. We were placed into this new life after God created everything we would need. We just need to wander through and find out what He's provided. Every tree is good. Because Adam and Eve sinned, they couldn't eat of the Tree of Life. Because we are born again, we're invited to eat of it. The Tree of Life is the Word of God (Prov. 3:18). Everything that pertains to life and godliness is made available to us through His Word, *"through the knowledge of him that hath called us to glory and virtue,"* through the *"exceeding great and precious promises"* (2 Pet. 1:3-4). (BY)

MARCH 10
LOVE IS THE KEY
ROMANS 13:8-10

"Love worketh no ill to his neighbour: therefore love is the fulfilling of the law" (Rom. 13:10).

If we truly loved others, we would never harm them. We wouldn't defraud people if we loved them as we love ourselves. There wouldn't be murder, divorce, theft, war, or prejudice if we lived in a world where everyone loved each other. What a wonderful place that would be!

Although this isn't the case, walking in God's love is still the best way to live. Since it takes two to make a marriage work, there's no guarantee that loving your mate will make them love you. However, it's certainly the most enjoyable way to live—regardless of the results! You can love others as yourself and they still may take advantage of you, but you can experience the joy of the Lord independent of what they do.

Life is complicated. It seems like there's so much we must remember to do. At times, it's like we're in a circus act trying to juggle our many responsibilities. We feel as if a disaster is bound to occur. It's frustrating and stressful!

But there's an easy way to simplify your life: Choose to walk in God's kind of love! Regardless of what others do, walk the love-walk. You won't have to worry whether you're doing everything right, love never hurts anyone. Therefore, as you walk in love, you'll walk free of offense and enjoy fellowship with God. Make the decision today to love your neighbor as yourself, and experience a new emotional freedom that only those who walk in love know. (AW)

MARCH 11
ABRAHAM BELIEVED IN HOPE
ROMANS 4:16-22

"Who against hope believed in hope, that he might become the father of many nations, according to that which was spoken, So shall thy seed be" (Rom. 4:18).

Hope seems to be lacking today. Many people intentionally resist hope because they don't want to face the disappointment that comes if their hopes are dashed. Their philosophy is: "Don't get your hopes up and you'll never be disappointed."

However, people who break away from the pack and accomplish great things are those who believe in hope. Abraham was one of these people. This verse says that he believed in hope. He knew the power of hope and wouldn't let it go. When Abraham was nearly a hundred years old and his wife was over ninety, he still held on to the hope of God's promise to give him a child. Although his faith gave him the victory, his hope kept his faith alive.

Where does hope come from? This verse says that Abraham's hope that he would become a father was according to the words God had spoken to him. The Holy Spirit constantly ministers hope to us as we meditate on the words God has spoken to us. God's Word releases His hope into our hearts. If we have no Word, then we have no hope. There's no other source for hope. The world doesn't give out hope, but actually destroys it by rampant pessimism.

Make a special effort to spend time listening to God's Word today, and let hope begin to work in your life. Let God paint a picture on the canvas of your heart of what you can be and do through His ability! (AW)

MARCH 12
SOW WHERE YOU WANT TO GO
1 KINGS 19:19-21

"And he returned back from him, and took a yoke of oxen, and slew them, and boiled their flesh with the instruments of the oxen, and gave unto the people, and they did eat. Then he arose, and went after Elijah, and ministered unto him" (1 Kin. 19:21).

Many people are waiting for their ship to come in, but they've never even sent out a rowboat! All things don't happen overnight, some things are long-range. Certain seeds take longer to grow than others.

In this passage of Scripture, the man of God—Elijah—came to Elisha and cast his mantle upon him. Elijah was beckoning Elisha to join him. By sacrificing his oxen, Elisha was sowing his livelihood. Then he sowed his very life by ministering to Elijah. He was sowing where he wanted to go. When Elijah was taken up to heaven in a chariot of fire, his mantle was passed on to Elisha (2 Kin. 2:11-14) who then also had a ministry of miracles. He was granted the desired double portion of Elijah's anointing (2 Kin. 2:9-10). You go where you sow!

My wife and I have invested in other people's housing. Through the years, we've helped ministers make house payments. Then God gave us our home at fifty cents on the dollar. Ultimately, it was supernaturally paid for. All of this was a result of sowing. It's line upon line, precept upon precept.

Giving is a way of life. I like the way missionary evangelist, Wayne Myers, said it, "I live to give." He's the first one I ever heard say that—and he does live to give! He made a large pledge to a Bible school and paid that pledge. Then he later pledged double that amount and paid that pledge as well. He's the first missionary that ever fought me for the lunch ticket. He and his wife are blessed because they're a blessing!

Giving isn't just in finances alone, although it's certainly that too. Invest in other people's children. Bless them, encourage them, and love them. You'll get the same seeds back. Again, you sow where you go, and you go where you sow. If you have a prodigal son, pray for someone else's prodigal son. God will recognize your seed and meet your need! *"Take heed what ye hear: with what measure ye mete, it shall be measured to you: and unto you that hear shall more be given"* (Mark 4:24). (BN)

MARCH 13
WE ARE SAVED BY HOPE
ROMANS 8:20-25

"For we are saved by hope: but hope that is seen is not hope: for what a man seeth, why doth he yet hope for?" (Rom. 8:24).

We receive more input from our eyes than from any of our other senses. Just think how drastically your life would change if you couldn't see. Therefore, it's easy to understand why we become so dependent on our physical sight. However, there are things we can't see.

In the kingdom of God, hope believes in things that have no physical evidence. Hope is a confident trust and reliance on God for results that can't be seen in the natural. Those who cannot break free from their senses, especially their sight, will never be able to operate in God's kind of hope.

How do we overcome what our eyes tell us? If our circumstances are contrary to what we know God wants us to have, how do we conquer the negative input? The answer is God's Word. Through meditating and acting on God's Word, we gain spiritual sight. We can see with our spiritual eyes. We do have spiritual senses. This is what Jesus meant when he said, *"He that hath ears to hear, let him hear"* (Matt. 11:15). We have spiritual ears and eyes that enable us to perceive things that are hidden to our natural senses.

But we must use our spiritual senses. We can't see with our physical eyes if they're closed. Likewise, our spiritual eyesight won't work if we're not open to the Spirit of God enlightening His Word. Those who aren't seeing their world through God's Word are spiritually blind. We don't want to be blind in our hearts! Open up your eyes through opening up your heart to God's Word, and then hope will surface. (AW)

MARCH 14
STRONG HOPE = STRONG PATIENCE
ROMANS 8:20-25

"But if we hope for that we see not, then do we with patience wait for it" (Rom. 8:25).

Have you ever noticed the patience that athletes possess? They only compete in the Olympics every four years, but they train incessantly. Some work their whole lives for one brief moment of glory. How can they do that? They have a strong hope and goal.

Athletes who want to win must deny themselves things that other people take for granted. There are special foods they eat and others they avoid. Practices and workouts require huge amounts of commitment, time, and effort. They work while others play. There are no summer vacations for those who "go for the gold." What is it that enables them to bind themselves to such a disciplined course of action? Their hope of winning the prize!

Likewise, in the Christian race, it's those who have a strong hope that are able to endure to the end. Christians without hope are like athletes who don't expect to win. They don't try very hard. Patience, which is a component of calm endurance, only operates in those who believe there is a payback for their efforts.

Moses was able to refuse the riches of Egypt and associate with the Israelites *"because he was looking ahead to his reward"* (Heb. 11:26, NIV). Those who succeed in the Christian life are those who have a strong realization of what awaits them. This enables them to keep on track all the way to the finish line. The Christian life isn't a fifty-yard dash, but a full marathon. The prize doesn't go to those who start well, but to those who finish well. Maintaining a strong hope will enable you to finish strong! (AW)

MARCH 15
THANKSGIVING MAKES US STRONG IN FAITH
COLOSSIANS 2:1-10

"Rooted and built up in him, and stablished in the faith, as ye have been taught, abounding therein with thanksgiving" *(Col. 2:7).*

This verse says we abound in faith through thanksgiving. The word *abound* means "to be plentiful in number or amount, to be copiously supplied." This English word actually comes from a Latin word meaning "to overflow." If we want our faith to abound, we need to be thankful!

Thankfulness increases our faith a number of ways. First, it takes our attention off the negative things that the devil is doing. You won't thank God very long if your mind stays focused on Satan's activity. It's important that we aren't preoccupied with the Enemy. Some people are so conscious of him that they panic at his every move.

Thanksgiving also causes us to think on the positive. As we turn from focusing on what the devil is doing, we must turn toward God and what He's already done. A person who chooses to operate in thanksgiving and praise is forced to take their mind off the problem and put it on the answer.

There's one more important aspect of thanksgiving. You don't give thanks for what you want, but for what you already have. To be able to thank God in the midst of a trying situation, you have to move into the realm of faith and see your need already met. In reality, all our needs have already been supplied in Jesus. It's only a matter of appropriating what we already have. Thanksgiving is an important part of this process.

Today, let thanksgiving guide your heart into the place of abundance where all your needs have already been supplied in Christ. (AW)

MARCH 16
HOPE KEEPS US FROM BEING ASHAMED
ROMANS 5:1-5

"And hope maketh not ashamed; because the love of God is shed abroad in our hearts by the Holy Ghost which is given unto us" *(Rom. 5:5).*

The word *hope*, as defined by Strong's concordance, means "to anticipate, usually with pleasure, expectation, or confidence." This verse reveals that the reason we can anticipate the future with pleasure and have positive expectations and confidence is because God's love has been shed abroad in our hearts by the Holy Ghost.

Therefore, we can say that hope is a result of experiencing God's love. Those who are short on hope don't understand His love for them.

Have you ever heard a young child confess, "I believe my father will not drop me. I believe he'll feed me today. I believe I'll have clothes to wear"? Never! A child simply rests in their father's love, and the hope that their needs will be met comes automatically.

Our heavenly Father is much greater and much more faithful than our earthly father, yet sometimes we worry that He won't supply our needs. The problem is with us, not Him. We need to focus on God's abundant and unconditional love for us, and then hope will swell up in our hearts. Once hope comes, our faith will be activated (Heb. 11:1) and our every need supplied. We will not be ashamed! (AW)

MARCH 17
HOW DOES FAITH REST?
HEBREWS 4:10

"For he that is entered into his rest, he also hath ceased from his own works, as God did from his" (Heb. 4:10).

Resting doesn't mean to sit down and do nothing. Plopping down in front of the television, eating some chips, and vegetating isn't God's idea of resting in our faith. To Him, resting includes being busy.

Rest in the Christian life is freedom from worry, anxiety, and stress. It's a relaxed enjoyment of each day as we work for the Lord.

Neither does resting mean to relax because you're tired. God doesn't want us to wear ourselves down working for Him and then need time off. There is no day off in the kingdom of God!

Our rest is compared to God. Can you imagine Him sitting down in front of a television eating chips? Does the Lord need to rest because He's tired? No, He's never tired, even though His responsibilities are never finished.

God rested on the seventh day because the work of creation was complete. His rest is an example to us. We rest because everything has been created or made for us. God hasn't failed to make anything we need or will ever need. Man and woman were placed into a garden that was complete. Adam could toil and dress the garden without a worry in the world. He could enjoy his labors. So can we enjoy our work in the garden of the New Birth.

Jesus entered a boat and commanded the disciples to go to the other side. He then laid down and went to sleep in the midst of a storm. The disciples worried, fretted, and even woke Jesus up, blaming Him for a lack of care for them. Jesus rebuked the storm and then rebuked the disciples (Mark 4:35-41). If Jesus could sleep through a storm, why couldn't they? The word was spoken and would come to pass. They'd make it to the other side. We too can rest in God's promises.

With the promises God has given us, we will make it through every trial in life. We can rest as Jesus did, knowing we're headed to the other side to set the captives free. True faith demands an attitude of peace. (BY)

MARCH 18
THE JUST *LIVE* BY FAITH
HABAKKUK 2:1-4

"Behold, his soul which is lifted up is not upright in him: but the just shall live by his faith" (Hab. 2:4).

The just don't use their faith occasionally, or only when they're in trouble. No! The just live by faith! This describes faith as a part of our life that is as essential as eating or breathing.

When my wife and I first started in ministry, we struggled financially. We often used the term "living by faith" to describe our condition. Indeed, it took a miracle each day to eat, pay bills, or buy gas for our car. Even though our faith has grown to a level now to where we walk in blessings and don't have to use it to receive food each day, we still live by faith. Our faith is what enables us to relate to God and thereby minister to others, which in turn produces finances to meet our needs. Our whole life is consumed with faith!

You don't have to be a minister to live by faith. Everyone needs to fellowship with the Lord daily, which takes faith. We need to recognize God as our Source, and not rely just on our jobs. We need to depend on the Lord to handle the pressures of family and work that confront us every day. We need to walk in faith not just for ourselves, but for others. The people we encounter each day need the Lord. You have other people's miracles on the inside of you that can only be released as you live by faith.

Make a conscious decision to live by faith today. If all your needs are met, believe God to help someone else. As you practice living by faith daily, your faith will grow. And then when you're in need, you'll be ready to receive by faith. The just live by faith! (AW)

MARCH 19
FAITH COMES BY HEARING
ROMANS 10:13-17

"So then faith cometh by hearing,
and hearing by the word of God" (Rom. 10:17).

This verse doesn't say that faith comes by having heard. The word *hearing* is a present tense word and is continuous. Hearing is an action that is currently taking place.

Faith that comes from God's Word is like the energy we receive from food. We don't have to eat every moment of every day, but we can't live off the food we ate a year ago. The food we eat today fuels us for a relatively short period of time. Likewise, faith that comes from God's Word has to be appropriated on a regular basis. We can't cram when we're in the midst of a trying situation and expect faith to work any more than a student can just study the night before an exam and expect to score 100 percent.

The food we ate as a child isn't just gone; it was used to increase and nourish bones, muscles, and body tissue. We still benefit from that food today but constantly need a fresh supply to exist. In the same way, time we've spent in the Word, which produced faith, is not lost. It's become a part of who we are and provides a structure for our spiritual growth on which we'll always be building. However, faith for today must come from our current relationship with the Lord, which includes meditating on His Word.

There are many analogies that can be drawn between our body's need for food and our heart's need for faith. Certainly, one of the clearest comparisons is that we don't just eat once a week. Therefore, we need to be in God's Word more than just once a week. Seven days without studying God's Word makes one weak! (AW)

MARCH 20
THOMAS & THE CENTURION'S FAITH
MATTHEW 8:5-13, JOHN 20:24-29

"Jesus saith unto him, Thomas, because thou hast seen me, thou hast believed: blessed are they
that have not seen, and yet have believed" (John 20:29).

When I first became aware that the Lord did miracles today, I realized that I'd missed out on the supernatural in my Christian life. That made me want to make up for lost time by immediately receiving everything I could. I heard about visions, dreams, and angels appearing to people—and I wanted some of that! So I started praying for these things to happen to me. However, the Lord used scriptures like the verse above to stop me in my tracks.

Jesus said that the greatest faith He'd ever seen was a faith that didn't have to see to believe. This faith was in the Word of God alone (Matt. 8:10). In contrast, He told Thomas that he had believed because he had seen, but there is a greater blessing on those who believe by faith and not by sight. This means that we'll walk in a greater degree of faith the more we're directed solely by God's Word.

That settled it for me. I wanted God's best. I knew that without faith, it was impossible to please Him, and I wanted to operate in the highest form of faith. That's not to say I refuse visions and dreams—I've had both—but they are no longer my focus. God's Word is enough. If the Lord chooses to use an angel or some other means to speak to me, I'll listen, but I no longer require it. God's Word needs no additional confirmation. God's Word is the absolute authority in my life. It's good to desire the faith of the centurion that made Jesus—the Author and Finisher of our faith—marvel. (AW)

MARCH 21
YOU'VE MILKED THIS COW LONG ENOUGH!
GALATIANS 6:9

"And let us not be weary in well doing: for in due season we shall reap, if we faint not" (Gal. 6:9).

Many years ago, we started a little church in an old Post Office building on Berry Street in Fort Worth, Texas. Those were days of small beginnings for us. I was the pastor, youth minister, singles' minister, janitor, and yard man. We bought an old building and fixed it up to be a nice little chapel, all by the grace of God. I was hungry for God and crying out, "Lord, as long as it's right and as long as it works, I'll do whatever it takes, but we've got to have a move of God!" He answered that prayer and sent a group of young hippies to launch us into a revival that totally turned our church around. Praise God! We grew and finally we were using everything we could get our hands on. Then God opened up the opportunity for a beautiful building in downtown Fort Worth.

As impossible as it seemed, we came downtown in 1976. But in the process, we assumed someone else's indebtedness with the purpose of buying the building. We left Berry Street with 300 people and got downtown with about 200. When we left, we sowed our church to a young congregation who never could've purchased even that small facility. After twelve years, we just walked away and blessed them with our equity and stayed on the bank note. We let them have a break that we didn't have in the beginning, so that they could just take over a beautiful little chapel out on Berry Street. You know, when I look back and see some of the steps we've taken, it scares me. But God is faithful! At that time, I think we would have charged hell with a dry water pistol! When you have a word from God, you don't sweat the small stuff.

Then the balloon note on our beautiful downtown church property was coming due. It had to be paid, or we'd forfeit the whole property. A gentleman in our congregation came forward one Sunday morning and asked what he could do to help me. I told him our situation. That gentleman went to the bank where we had our account, put his cowboy hat on the desk, shook hands with the bank president and said, "This preacher needs a loan. You've milked this cow long enough, it's time to feed it a little bit." The banker laughed and asked how much money we needed. We got our loan. It was God. It wasn't me, it wasn't the man in the cowboy hat, and it wasn't the banker. It was God!

All of our lives are spent sowing seeds—our words, our actions, our smiles, our finances. We may not have money, but we can give something that helps somebody. To tithe is what God said to do, but our giving is where we get into the blessing and the return. (BN)

MARCH 22
VOICE-ACTIVATED FAITH
HEBREWS 11:1-6

"Through faith we understand that the worlds were framed by the word of God, so that things which are seen were not made of things which do appear" (Heb. 11:3).

God created the world and the universe by faith. And that faith was released by the words He spoke. There are eight times in Genesis 1 that God spoke things into existence. Everything physical that we see around us was formed by words. Faith is always voice activated!

King David said in Psalm 116:10, *"I believed, therefore have I spoken."* Paul quoted this statement of David in 2 Corinthians 4:13 and referred to it as a *"spirit of faith."* Therefore we can see that the true spirit of faith speaks.

Jesus spoke to the fig tree in Mark 11:13-24 and it obeyed. His disciples were amazed, but He explained to them that anyone with faith could do the same thing. Three times in verse 23, Jesus linked our operating in faith to the words we speak. Most people say what they have and continue to have more of the same. Instead, we can say what we are believing for, and it'll come to pass when we speak in faith. Say what we already have or have what we say—the choice is ours!

You may think your words don't matter that much, but they do. Jesus said that what's in your heart in abundance will come out of your mouth (Matt. 12:34). You can tell what you really believe by the words you speak. If you're pessimistic, your words will reveal it. If you are full of faith and hope, your speech will certainly coincide.

What words are you speaking? If you realize that your words aren't filled with faith, don't just change your words. Change your heart and your words will follow suit. Words are the gauge of the heart. (AW)

MARCH 23
DEATH OR LIFE?
PROVERBS 18:16-24

*"Death and life are in the power of the tongue: and they that love
it shall eat the fruit thereof"* (Prov. 18:21).

This verse says that the tongue has the power of death or life. Notice that it didn't say there was also a multitude of nonproductive vain words. No! *Every* word we speak releases either life or death. There is no middle ground. Jesus said in Matthew 12:36, *"But I say unto you, That every idle word that men shall speak, they shall give account thereof in the day of judgment."* We need to watch our words!

James said that the tongue is like a bit in a horse's mouth or a rudder on a ship that steers the vessel (James 3:3-4). We wouldn't get in a vehicle that we didn't have the ability to steer. That's suicide! Likewise, a person who has no control over their words is headed for destruction.

There are many distinguishing characteristics between human beings and the animal creation. Certainly, one of the most important differences that sets us apart is our ability to speak. That gives us creative power like God. God spoke the world and the universe into existence. We speak our own environments into existence by the words we say.

With this creative power comes responsibility. Our words have the power to bless or curse, to give life or release death. Sadly, the majority of people are using the negative power of their tongues instead of the positive. We need to pray the prayer of David that says, *"Set a watch, O LORD, before my mouth; keep the door of my lips"* (Ps. 141:3).

Ask the Lord to show you the power of your words today, and then use it to bless God and man. (AW)

MARCH 24
THE FIG TREE
MARK 11:13-24

*"And Jesus answered and said unto it, No man eat fruit of thee hereafter for ever.
And his disciples heard it"* (Mark 11:14).

This is an amazing story. Jesus was hungry and He saw a fig tree that already had leaves, which led Him to believe it had figs. But that wasn't the case. There were no figs. In response, Jesus cursed the fig tree with His words, saying, *"No man eat fruit of thee hereafter for ever."*

Jesus talked to the fig tree. This verse says, *"Jesus answered and said unto it."* That means the fig tree had been talking to Him. Some people think this is weird, but things talk to us all the time. Your checkbook tells you that you don't have enough money to make it. Your body tells you that you're sick. Situations speak negative things to us without saying a word. Most of us pick up on these negative comments and speak them right out of our mouths, thereby giving them power over our lives.

Jesus did the right thing. He used His words to silence the hypocrisy of this fig tree. It professed fruit by having leaves, but it didn't possess it. It had spoken something to Him that it couldn't deliver. Jesus said that it would never yield fruit to anyone ever again—and it didn't! It immediately died at its roots, and its death was visible the next day (Mark 11:20).

His disciples were overwhelmed with this miracle and questioned Him about it. He said that this was the power of words. Anyone who speaks in faith, without doubting in their heart, will have whatsoever they say. This works in the positive or negative.

Whenever a negative circumstance starts speaking to you today, talk back to it in faith, and watch the situation change. (AW)

MARCH 25
GOD'S WAY OF TALKING
ROMANS 4:16-25

"(As it is written, I have made thee a father of many nations,) before him whom he believed, even God, who quickeneth the dead, and calleth those things which be not as though they were" (Rom. 4:17).

Paul was speaking about God's dealings with Abram. The Lord appeared to Abram and told him that he would give him children, and they would become so numerous that they would number as the sand on the seashore or the stars in the heavens (Gen. 15:1-6). Then years later, the Lord reassured Abram of His promise and, as a token, changed his name to Abraham, which means "father of a multitude."

God called Abram the father of a multitude when he didn't even have the promised son yet. That's what Paul was referring to when he said, *"God...calleth those things which be not as though they were."* God speaks what He believes, not just what He sees.

In Genesis 1:3, God said, *"Let there be light: and there was light."* But it wasn't until the fourth day of creation that God created the sun, moon, and stars (Gen. 1:14-19). He spoke light into existence before He created the sun. That's not the way we do things, but it's how God operates.

If we want godly results, we need to learn to talk like God. Instead of speaking about what you have, use your faith to speak about what you're believing. There is creative power in your words. Speak about the things that aren't manifest in the physical yet as though they were, and if you are speaking in faith, they will come to be. (AW)

MARCH 26
THE TRUTH & THE FACTS
JOHN 17:17

"Thy word is truth" (John 17:17).

Do you remember Sergeant Friday on *Dragnet?* "Just the facts, ma'am." God would rather hear from you, "Just the truth." There's a great difference between the truth and the facts!

Many Christians want to confess God's Word, but they're afraid they are lying. "How can I say I'm healed when my body is still sick? Isn't that lying?"

We live in two worlds, the natural as well as the spiritual. We are in the world, but not of it. We are residing in the earth, but we're citizens of heaven. We are standing presently on the earth, but we're seated spiritually in heavenly places with Christ Jesus. We are an outward man, and we are also an inward man. The earthly kingdom will not change the kingdom of God, but the kingdom of God can change this earthly kingdom.

Even in this natural world, circumstances change. The rain is falling, but the clouds will clear away. The night is dark, but the sun will shine tomorrow. We even have a greater hope in God's promises.

If our bodies are sick, that's a *fact*. The Word says we are healed. That's the *truth*. The facts will never change the truth, but the truth will change the facts. Facts can change, but the truth will never change. Whether you are sick or well, the Word will always say, *"By whose stripes ye were healed"* (1 Pet. 2:24). Whether you are in abundance or lack, God's Word will always say, *"Beloved, I wish above all things that thou mayest prosper"* (3 John 2).

It is quite acceptable with God to look at and address the facts of your life, as long as the truth remains preeminent. Moses, David, Paul and others spoke of problems, sickness, and the trials of life, but they didn't allow these to shipwreck their faith. You too can continue to trust in God's Word, and your circumstances will change. The truth will change your facts! (BY)

MARCH 27
PLANT A SEED!
PROVERBS 11:24-25

"There is that scattereth, and yet increaseth; and there is that withholdeth more than is meet, but it tendeth to poverty. The liberal soul shall be made fat: and he that watereth shall be watered also himself" (Prov. 11:24-25).

During a challenging time in our ministry, when God worked out our financing for our church facility, the bank said, "We'll handle the financing on the upper part of the property for you if you'll sell the lower part." I thought it was like checkers or chess. What do you do? You survive. We bought it for $600,000, and we sold it for $850,000, with the stipulation that we had guaranteed parking rights for the church and that they would make it into a parking lot with improvements. Little did I know, one stipulation cost them contracts with major hotel chains and a few others. Every other year or so, we would try to buy it back. One day we went over to Dallas to see what they would sell the parking lot for, and they said at that point it would be seven million dollars! Oh, but God was working.

For almost thirteen years, every time I'd turn the corner to come to the church, that property would laugh at me, but I'd say, "In the name of Jesus, Isaac, you're on the altar, but you're coming up off that altar!" I had remembered the faithfulness of God and how He had miraculously brought us from tiny beginnings to that church as we stood in faith on Isaiah 41:10.

We were in a meeting down in Florida and that church desperately needed to buy some property. We pledged $5,000. It was a hard $5,000, but we paid it. Listen, we've discovered something—what you make happen for someone else, God will make happen for you. We invested in another church's property when we desperately needed our own. But thank God for the power of planting seed. God answered our need.

One day the bank set up a meeting with us, and the real estate agent said, "I'm Jewish and I don't know if you understand this, but this property has been like a Jonah to us." I told him I thoroughly understood. He continued, "Would you make us an offer?" I thought awhile and then, with boldness from the heart of God, said, "I'll tell you what we'll give you: $100,000, and we'll close any time you want." They looked at each other, gathered their papers, and walked out. Thirty days later, they called back and said, "We've been in this business for a long time and don't understand this." Hallelujah! We bought back Isaac off the altar for $100,000 and still have him today! Remember, when you talk to God about a need, He'll tell you to plant a seed. (BN)

MARCH 28
GOD'S WORD GIVES US HOPE
ROMANS 15:1-4

"For whatsoever things were written aforetime were written for our learning, that we through patience and comfort of the scriptures might have hope" (Rom. 15:4).

People look for hope in many different places. Some consult horoscopes or fortunetellers, while others look to spouses, friends, or government agencies. This verse makes it clear that the Scriptures are where our hope comes from. Of course, God is the God of all hope (Rom. 15:13), but God uses His Word to deliver His hope to us.

Still, many people choose to learn everything the hard way. They don't want to believe God's Word until they've personally experienced victory. But if they don't believe the Word, they won't experience victory. It's a Catch-22. So what's the solution?

Any problem we face—and even worse problems—have already been encountered by someone in the Bible. The Scriptures graphically record the struggle and victory of those who trusted God. That gives us hope. If God is truly not a respecter of persons (Rom. 2:11), then what He's done for others, He'll do for us. We can live vicariously through the lives of Bible characters and have hope for situations we've yet to encounter.

We don't have to wait until we're in a crisis and under pressure before we try to gain hope. Through the pages of Scripture, we've already "been there and done that" and received the hope and faith necessary to bring us through our situation. We don't have to prove God anew every time trouble comes. God has already been tried and proven countless times. We can benefit from others as we draw on their experiences. It's much better to learn at someone else's expense! (AW)

MARCH 29
HOPE CAUSES REJOICING
ROMANS 12:9-15

"Rejoicing in hope; patient in tribulation; continuing instant in prayer" (Rom. 12:12).

Hope is what causes us to rejoice. Yet 1 Peter 1:8 says, *"Yet believing, ye rejoice with joy unspeakable and full of glory."* Which is it that causes us to rejoice—faith or hope? The answer is both. Hope is just future tense faith. Hope is believing God for something that's not presently manifest. Faith is believing God to bring something into manifestation now (Heb. 11:1).

So, hope is faith. It's just faith that has a future fulfillment. If we really believe that God will supply what we hope for, we'll rejoice.

If I were to promise you that one year from today I would deposit $1,000,000 in your bank account, and you believed it, you'd rejoice. Likewise, if we really believe the promises God gives us, we'll rejoice. Those who don't rejoice don't believe.

Expectant joy is a sure sign of hope. Just as you can distinguish real gold from other look alike metals by its characteristics, you can distinguish real hope by its rejoicing. If rejoicing is not present, then real hope isn't there either.

Our emotions are like the tail of a dog. The tail isn't the dog itself, but you can sure tell what's on the inside of a dog by watching its tail. We can learn a lot about ourselves by checking our emotions. Are we rejoicing? If we have true biblical hope, we will! (AW)

MARCH 30
GOD IS A GOD OF HOPE
ROMANS 15:8-13

"Now the God of hope fill you with all joy and peace in believing, that ye may abound in hope, through the power of the Holy Ghost" (Rom. 15:13).

God is a God of hope. With God nothing is impossible. This is foreign to our finite thinking, but there is no situation in which God doesn't have an answer.

Picture the children of Israel at the Red Sea. It looked impossible, but only to those who failed to consider that God could part the sea. Envision Daniel in the lions' den. His accusers thought there was no way out for him, but they didn't know God. Remember the Hebrew children in the fiery furnace? How much more impossible can you get than that? Yet God made a way. Look at the resurrection of Lazarus, Jesus walking on the water, and thousands of other examples in Scripture with God doing the "impossible."

God is a miraculous God! Therefore, there's always hope for those who trust in Him. Regardless of where you are now or what situation you find yourself in, God can chart a course for you back into the center of His perfect will. No one is too far gone, and no situation is too desperate for His miraculous intervention!

The first step out of a desperate situation is to hope. Before we can totally believe, we must hope. Faith only produces what we hope for (Heb. 11:1). Hope comes from the promises of God. Embrace the hope that God can turn your situation around, and be encouraged in your heart today. Find a parallel circumstance in the Word to what you're presently facing and recognize that God is no respecter of persons. If He came through for others, He'll come through for you! (AW)

MARCH 31
HOPE CAUSES PURITY
1 JOHN 3:1-3

"Every man that hath this hope in him purifieth himself, even as he is pure" (1 John 3:3).

Every time the Apostle Paul preached grace, the question arose, "Are you saying that I can sin because I'm under grace?" Paul dealt with that question three times in his writings (Rom. 3:8; 6:1-2a, 15; Gal. 2:17) with the resounding answer, "God forbid!" Certainly that is not what Paul was communicating.

This verse makes it very clear that every born-again person who has the hope of the resurrection is seeking to purify himself even as Jesus is pure. That doesn't necessarily mean they're accomplishing that goal, but it's a goal nonetheless.

There are many things that can make the grace of God have no effect in our lives and thereby keep us in bondage to sin. But it's also an irrefutable fact of Scripture that those who are truly God's children now have a new nature and desire to live a life that pleases Him. This is one of the distinguishing characteristics of true Christians.

This is the same reasoning that Jesus used when He said, *"For ye know not what hour your Lord doth come"* (Matt. 24:42). Keeping the coming of the Lord in view affects our actions. Those Christians who aren't living a pure life have forgotten the love of God and the promises that will be fulfilled at His second coming. Today, remember that this world and everything that affects you is temporary and will fade into obscurity at the appearance of our Lord. (AW)

APRIL 1
HOPE LESSENS SORROW
1 THESSALONIANS 4:13-18

"But I would not have you to be ignorant, brethren, concerning them which are asleep, that ye sorrow not, even as others which have no hope" (1 Thess. 4:13).

The hope of being reunited with loved ones who have died puts the believer in a different situation than those who don't have that hope. To the unbeliever, death is final. There's no way to bridge the gap between the living and the dead. Those who die are lost forever. And forever is a long, long time.

Yet for the believer, death is just a temporary separation. We have the hope of seeing our loved ones again in the resurrection and dwelling with them forever in the glory of God. This hope disarms the ungodly sorrow of the world. A Christian may still miss someone who has died, but it's not the same sorrow as the world, which is hopeless. That type of sorrow produces death (2 Cor. 7:10).

Anyone can handle separation as long as they know it's not permanent. We see our children off to school, our mates off to work, and our friends leave for vacation. It would be illogical to grieve as if they had died, when they're gone just for a little while. Likewise, those who believe in the resurrection will see their loved ones again, if they are Christians.

Make sure you view all your situations through hope today. Just as the sorrow of losing someone you love is diminished through the hope that you'll see them again, so the pressures of everyday life are lessened through the hope that God's promises are true. Every negative situation in your life is only temporary. Praise the Lord! (AW)

APRIL 2
HOW DO YOU VALUE JESUS?
JOHN 12:1-9

"Then took Mary a pound of ointment of spikenard, very costly, and anointed the feet of Jesus, and wiped his feet with her hair: and the house was filled with the odour of the ointment" (John 12:3).

The ointment Mary anointed Jesus with was very costly. That's because the spikenard plant it came from grew in the Himalayan Mountains at elevations above 11,000 feet. Since this ointment had to be transported over 6,000 miles to Palestine, it was more expensive than gold. Many scholars believe that Mary's gift was worth more than one year's wages. That would be more than $30,000 today!

Judas Iscariot was greatly offended to see Mary bestow such wealth and affection on Jesus. If this same thing were to happen today, many modern Christians would be offended too. However, we must remember what Jesus did for her. This was the Mary who, along with her sister Martha, had known Jesus for a long time. They had entertained Him in their home while she hung on His every word (Luke 10:38-42). Greatest of all, Jesus raised Mary's brother from the dead.

How do you put a price on seeing your dearly loved brother rise from the dead? No amount of wealth is worth a human life. Mary's lavish affection for Jesus was consistent with what He'd done for her. The problem was that Judas didn't value Jesus as much as Mary did. Just a few days later, he accepted thirty pieces of silver to betray the Lord. That was less than half the amount of Mary's ointment!

What value do you place on Jesus and what He's done for you? Your answer will determine whether you become a Mary or a Judas. Make sure you value Jesus more than anything else in your life! (AW)

APRIL 3
WHERE'S YOUR HEART?
JOHN 12:1-9

"This he said, not that he cared for the poor; but because he was a thief, and had the bag, and bare what was put therein" (John 12:6).

Judas' attitude still lives in the hearts of many people today. It's human nature to put self and personal gain above everything and everyone else. No one desires their greed to be known, but most want what they want when they want it. They just become more skilled in concealing their true motives.

Politicians trumpet their programs as the answers to the problems of society when in truth, many of them only adopt causes in order to get elected. Many employees only serve their employers because of how it will benefit them personally. Marriages fail every day because of a greater love for self than for one's mate. Many ministers do tremendous damage because they're seeking to build their own kingdoms under the guise of building God's kingdom.

Self-love seems all pervasive and inescapable, but there is an antidote. There is a way to live above the grasp of self. You can't just not love self. You must love someone else more than yourself.

Mary loved the Lord more than her own life. Jesus had done everything for her and her family, and she was willing to give liberally of all she had, to lavish praise and honor on Him. In contrast, Judas only thought of what he could have done for himself with the money that ointment could've brought. Mary loved Jesus more than self. Judas loved self more.

Which is it with you? You can readily identify where your love lies by where your praise goes. Are you constantly praising Jesus? If not, start denying yourself today by praising God for all His love and faithfulness. (AW)

APRIL 4
IT'S ALL DIRT!
LUKE 16:13-15

"And he said unto them, Ye are they which justify yourselves before men; but God knoweth your hearts: for that which is highly esteemed among men is abomination in the sight of God" *(Luke 16:15).*

Everything man desires comes from the dirt. Jewelry is and always has been a big business. Lots of people like to wear fine jewelry. We even buy it as special gifts for loved ones, or to commemorate and celebrate special events. But think about it, gold is from the earth. It's dirt. The gold that men prize so highly on earth is used for road metal in heaven. And did you ever notice those stones that we set in the gold? Diamonds are rocks—old, compacted dirt. It's all dirt! Have you heard the saying "Not worth the paper it's printed on"? Well, contrary to popular belief, money is made of cloth, not paper. It's actually called "rag" and is made from a form of cotton. At any rate, money comes from cotton, which grows out of where? The dirt. Food comes from the earth too. There are a lot of people driving cars today, aren't there? I do. So does almost everyone else I know. Well, cars are from iron ore, which is taken from the dirt. What about the seats in those cars? Many people like leather interiors. Those leather seats are the skins off a dead cow! Are you partial to furs? Minks are rodent hair coats. Oh, don't forget houses, they're totally made of dirt. They're just bigger, better mud huts. Are you seeing a pattern here? It's all dirt.

All these things are great, but let's keep them in proper perspective. There's nothing wrong with having nice things, but God knows the heart. These physical things that are highly esteemed and sought after by people are just dirt. Before you pass up a chance to sow into the kingdom of God in exchange for some "thing," just remember and say to yourself, "It's all dirt!" (BN)

APRIL 5
WHEN GOD ROLLED UP HIS SLEEVE
ISAIAH 53:1

"Who hath believed our report? and to whom is the arm of the LORD revealed?" *(Is. 53:1).*

God is compared to us as human beings in many places in Scripture. He's said to have feet, eyes, and ears. That's because we're made in His image—both spiritually and physically.

We're told in Psalm 8:3 that God created the universe with His fingers. What an incredible thought! Your fingers are not known for much strength. Yet with little effort, God used His fingers to create an infinite amount of galaxies, planets, and star systems.

Hebrews 1:10 tells us that God created the earth with His hands. There's more strength in your hands than in your fingers. It took more power for God to create the earth than it did the universe. God took time to mold the earth, shape it, and prepare it for His crowning creation—mankind. This tells me the greatest place in the universe—next to heaven—is earth. Heaven and earth continually work together.

Yet, Isaiah 53:1 reveals that the work of redemption took the arm of the Lord. This verse begins an entire chapter on the redemptive work of Jesus on the cross. It took more power to redeem one sinner than it did to create the universe and the earth. God had to roll up His sleeve to redeem us from Satan's curse and Adam's fall. When God raised Jesus from the dead, it took ***"the exceeding greatness of his power"*** (Eph. 1:19).

Anyone can look into the night sky and see the work of God's fingers. The stars and planets are visible to all. Anyone can also look at the earth, the mountains, the oceans, and the animals that live here and see the work of God's hands.

However, only those who put their trust in what Jesus did on the cross can see the work of God's arm. *The arm of the Lord is revealed to those who believe the report!* (BY)

APRIL 6
DO YOU MAGNIFY THE LORD?
LUKE 1:41-55

"And Mary said, My soul doth magnify the Lord" *(Luke 1:46).*

God is who He is, regardless of our opinion. Doubting God doesn't diminish who He is. So what does it mean when the Bible says that Mary magnified the Lord? The word *magnify* means "to make greater in size, extent, or effect; enlarge." How do we do that? How can we make God greater? What can we possibly do or say that has any effect upon God?

Our soul functions like a pair of binoculars. When we focus our hearts on the Lord through praising Him, God looks bigger than any problem. However, when we focus on our problems, it's like turning the binoculars around and looking through the big end. *Our problems look bigger than God. Our souls enlarge whatever or whomever we focus our attention on and decrease what we neglect.*

As Mary praised the Lord, God increased in size, extent, and effect in her life. She was able to believe Him for the greatest miracle to have ever taken place up until that time.

Of course, God is greater in size, extent, and effect than any problem we face, regardless of what we do. It's not a matter of who God is that determines our victory or defeat. It's our perception of who He is that controls our experiences. God is always the same for all of us, but different people receive different results because of how big they perceive Him to be.

If you want God's best in your life, you must magnify Him in your soul, above all else. You do that by focusing your soul on God. Meditating His Word and praising Him by faith for His promises will magnify the Lord and shrink your problems. Let Jesus be big on the inside of you today! (AW)

APRIL 7
WHY SEEK THE LIVING AMONG THE DEAD?
LUKE 24:1-9

"And as they were afraid, and bowed down their faces to the earth, they said unto them, Why seek ye the living among the dead?" *(Luke 24:5).*

The angel asked the women at the tomb, **"Why seek ye the living among the dead?"** That's a great question!

The women who came to the tomb that resurrection morning were seeking Jesus, but they weren't seeking a living, victorious Christ. They were grieving because the Jesus they were seeking was dead.

Likewise, we often seek a dead God. We don't phrase it that way, of course, but that's what it amounts to. We pray and talk about how big and impossible our problems are, just as if God was dead. We forget, or don't believe, that Jesus overcame ALL the problems of this life. We say things like, "The doctor told me I'm going to die!" What does this mean to the person who's already conquered death? It's nothing to Him. If we pray to the risen Christ, then death won't overwhelm us either.

When the women at the tomb believed that Jesus was alive, all their sadness turned to joy. That's the way it will be with us too when we start relating to a risen Christ who has put all our enemies under His feet. It's not enough to just seek Jesus; we need to seek the risen Lord Jesus. We need to recognize that Jesus is Almighty and start treating Him as such.

It doesn't glorify the Lord to fall apart like a two-dollar suitcase every time something bad happens. We have access to Him who has all power in heaven and earth. We need to come to the risen Christ and expect resurrection power to flow into our situations. Let true joy arise in your heart today as you seek the Jesus who has conquered death and hell. (AW)

APRIL 8
DO YOU REMEMBER GOD'S WORD?
LUKE 24:1-9

"And they remembered his words,
And returned from the sepulchre" (Luke 24:8-9).

The women who came to Jesus' tomb were greeted by two angels who asked, **"Why seek ye the living among the dead?"** (verse 5). Then the angels reminded them how Jesus had prophesied that He would rise from the dead on the third day. It wasn't until they remembered His words that they quit seeking a dead Jesus and started looking for the living Christ. Just think, a vision of angels announcing the resurrection of Jesus didn't turn these women around, but the words of Jesus did.

Peter said that the written Word of God is a more sure word of prophecy than even an audible voice or a visible manifestation (2 Pet. 1:16-20). We often think that if something supernatural would just happen, then we would believe. This example shows us differently.

The spectacular gets our attention, no doubt, but faith only comes from God's Word (Rom. 10:17). God's Word is what we need. More specifically, we need faith in God's Word. The Lord has given us exceedingly great and precious promises, but our unbelief still causes some of us to mope around as if Jesus didn't come out of the tomb. Our unbelief negates the power of Christ's resurrection in our lives.

Meditating on God's Word causes faith to come and doubt to go. It causes us to look for a God who is alive and able to handle any problem we have. Jesus was resurrected before these women knew it. Until they knew it, sorrow filled their hearts. If sorrow is filling your heart, it's because somehow, you've been blinded to the victory that the resurrection produces. Believe Jesus is alive and Lord over all your circumstances today and you'll see the difference it makes. (AW)

APRIL 9
DO YOU RECOGNIZE JESUS?
LUKE 24:13-35

"And it came to pass, that, while they communed together and reasoned,
Jesus himself drew near, and went with them" (Luke 24:15).

Two of Jesus' disciples were walking to a city called Emmaus. They were sad as they traveled, not because their hearts were evil and their deeds were bad, but because they were thinking about Jesus. They were even pondering the reports they'd heard of a resurrected Christ, but they were in unbelief. They wanted to believe, but reason wouldn't let them.

At that moment, Jesus joined them, but they didn't recognize Him. The very one whom they loved was with them and they didn't know it. How could this be? If they could have perceived Christ being with them, all their questions would have been vanquished and their sorrow would've turned to joy.

This same story is recorded in Mark 16:12-13. In this account, Mark said Jesus appeared to these two disciples **"in another form,"** but that didn't mean He looked different. Later that day, Jesus told His disciples to behold the nail prints in His hands and feet (Luke 24:39-40). He looked the same, but was in a spiritual body. The natural man can't discern spiritual truth with the physical senses. Spiritual reality must be spiritually discerned (1 Cor. 2:14).

Likewise, the Lord is always with us. He never leaves us, but we often miss Him. We fail to perceive His presence because we look through the eye of reasoning instead of looking through our hearts by faith. The disciples on the road to Emmaus recognized Jesus when He broke bread with them (Luke 24:30-31). It's when we have communion with the Lord by faith that our eyes are opened to His presence. Look through your eyes of faith today at the one who's promised never to leave you nor forsake you (Heb. 13:5). (AW)

APRIL 10
WHAT'S UNDER YOUR CLOTHES?
2 SAMUEL 6:14

**"David danced before the LORD...and...was girded with
a linen ephod"** *(2 Sam. 6:14).*

King David personally brought the Ark of the Covenant back to its rightful home among the people of God in Jerusalem. David not only walked ahead of the ark, he danced in front of all the city's citizens. His wife watched from a window and was filled with wrath as her husband—*the king*—took off his prestigious robe and was dressed as a common priest. There were many priests, but only one king. How could her husband be so callous toward her feelings to dress and act as a common priest? David couldn't be recognized among the other priests. He no longer looked like a king. He'd left the throne and joined the people.

When we come to church, we are meeting the family of God and joining the royal priesthood. We need to take off our kingly robes and shed the attitude of our worldly positions so we can look and act like the priests we are. Leave your banker's clothing at home. You aren't an attorney or an investment counselor when you come to church. Neither are you a janitor or a waiter at a restaurant. Every person who is a child of God is dressed in a linen ephod. When we come to worship, we all look alike to God. The banker stands beside the janitor, praising the Lord together. This is the place where we worship God with all our might—singing, shouting, and dancing.

Church on earth is a type of the throne room in heaven. One day we'll all stand before the Lamb of God as the redeemed of the ages and will praise Him forever. There will be no white or blue-collar section, no rich or poor, but all priests rejoicing before the Great High Priest—Jesus. Why wait until then? Let's start now! (BY)

APRIL 11
YOUR RESOURCES OR GOD'S?
2 KINGS 4:1-8

**"And Elisha said unto her, What shall I do for thee? tell me, what hast thou in the house? And
she said, Thine handmaid hath not any thing in the house,
save a pot of oil"** *(2 Kin. 4:2).*

This woman was in a desperate situation: Her husband had died, and she was unable to meet her financial obligations. If you couldn't pay your debts back then, you became the slave of the person you owed—and the creditor was coming to take her two sons away as slaves.

This woman's husband had been one of the prophets associated with Elisha. So she appealed to him for help. Elisha had been her husband's friend and mentor. Therefore, she looked to him for aid. However, Elisha refused to take responsibility for this woman's prosperity and put the issue back in her court. It wasn't a matter of what he had, but what did she have?

Many people would think this showed a lack of compassion on Elisha's part. Why didn't he just give her money out of his own pocket? There could be many answers to that question, but certainly one of the reasons was that Elisha's resources were limited. Even if he could have met this woman's need, there were others, and their needs exceeded his ability. Therefore, he was correct in pointing her to the Lord to get her needs met.

It's true that we should do what we can with what we have, but we'll never be able to meet the needs of everyone. It's actually doing others a disservice to make them dependent on us for their supply. God should be everyone's Source. Instead of Elisha helping her temporarily, he gave her a permanent solution to her problem. He taught her to use what she had and trust God to bless it. (AW)

APRIL 12
LITTLE IS MUCH WHEN GOD IS IN IT
2 KINGS 4:1-8

"And Elisha said unto her, What shall I do for thee? tell me, what hast thou in the house? And she said, Thine handmaid hath not any thing in the house, save a pot of oil" (2 Kin. 4:2).

By anyone's evaluation except God's, this poor widow's resources were woefully inadequate to meet her needs. Her tiny bit of oil was worth only a pittance, certainly not enough to get her out of debt and the impending slavery of her children. Reason would say her situation was hopeless. But faith said, *"With God all things are possible"* (Matt. 19:26).

The widow knew she had this oil. She's the one who told Elisha about it. No doubt, she had taken a complete inventory of all her assets and had dismissed them as insufficient to meet the need. *But little is much when God is in it!* She had failed to factor into her equation what God could do with what she had. The man of God opened her eyes to the possibility of what God could do, and she acted in faith. She not only met her present need but had enough left over to live off for the rest of her life.

Like this widow, we often fail to see the potential of what God has given us. We look at ourselves and what we have only in human terms. We fail to factor in the anointing. With God's blessing, a few fish and a couple of pieces of bread can feed thousands. But first, we must take that step of faith.

This woman's oil didn't multiply until she had borrowed the vessels and began to pour out what she had. She prepared for increase and then began to give. As she gave of what she had, the power of God multiplied it back to her abundantly.

Everyone has something. What do you have? It may seem too small to do any good, but give what you have to God in faith and watch it grow. (AW)

APRIL 13
MIRACLES SPROUT FROM SEEDS
2 KINGS 4:8-37

"Let us make a little chamber, I pray thee, on the wall; and let us set for him there a bed, and a table, and a stool, and a candlestick: and it shall be, when he cometh to us, that he shall turn in thither" (2 Kin. 4:10).

The raising of this widow's son from the dead is one of the greatest miracles recorded in the Bible. Everyone would love to see God's miracle working power displayed in their lives like this. Yet miracles don't just happen; there are reasons why some people receive them and others do not.

If it was only up to God, then all of us would have miracles. God loves the whole world, and His power is extended to us in grace. The reason why few experience the miraculous power of God is because few cooperate with Him. Electricity doesn't flow through wood, and miracles don't come to those who haven't planted for them.

This woman recognized God's anointing on Elisha and she blessed him. This wasn't just her desire; it was God working through her to bless His servant, Elisha. This woman yielded to God's leading, thereby sowing a seed into her future. She gave what she wasn't obligated to give and that put her in a position to receive a blessing by being a blessing.

This isn't to say that she earned this miracle. No! None of us at our best deserve God's favor. Our unbelief can stop God's blessings, and our yielding allows them to flow. There's a reason why this woman's acts of kindness toward Elisha were recorded. They were the seeds for the miracle she received!

Are you planting seeds today for the miracles you'll need tomorrow? Tomorrow will come. Your need for God's intervention in your life will also come. Get ready today by planting seeds of God's love in someone else's life. (AW)

APRIL 14
WHAT'S YOUR MOTIVE?
2 KINGS 4:8-37

"And he said unto him, Say now unto her, Behold, thou hast been careful for us with all this care; what is to be done for thee? wouldest thou be spoken for to the king, or to the captain of the host? And she answered, I dwell among mine own people" (2 Kin. 4:13).

Have you ever noticed that giving to others causes them to want to give back to you? Buy a friend's lunch sometime. I'm confident they'll say something to the effect of, "I'll get it next time." This is just a law of God.

This woman had built an extra room on her house and furnished it just for Elisha. He appreciated it and wanted to bless her back. When asked what could be done for her, she didn't have any request. Elisha offered her favor with the king or the top general in the land, but she didn't accept it. She never did make a request. This says volumes.

This woman wasn't kind to Elisha just so she could get something from God. She didn't give to get. However, she also wasn't so religious that when God wanted to bless her, she refused His blessing out of false humility. She accepted His gift. But the motive behind her gift was totally unselfish. She gave expecting nothing in return. There's a lesson for all of us here.

Our giving should be with pure hearts of love for God and those to whom we give. We shouldn't be giving just to get something in return. Our giving should be selfless. Yet the law of God says that when we give, it will be given back to us good measure, pressed down, shaken together, and running over (Luke 6:38). Our seeds of giving will produce increase and we should receive it so that we can give even more. But our motives must always be pure.

Give like this woman gave—with a pure heart of love for others! (AW)

APRIL 15
SHUT THE DOOR
2 KINGS 4:8-37

"And she went up, and laid him on the bed of the man of God, and shut the door upon him, and went out" (2 Kin. 4:21).

This woman was in a terrible situation. Her only son had just died a tragic death. All of us have experienced enough tragedy that we can imagine what she must have felt. This was a special child too, a direct miracle of God, which made the loss even greater.

What do you do in a crisis like that? Sadly, most of us tend to nurse our problems. We indulge grief and rehearse the tragedy over and over in our minds. We don't let go. We don't cast the care of the situation over on the Lord as He commanded us to (1 Pet. 5:7). We become dominated by our affliction.

To this woman's credit, she carried her son up to the man of God's room and left him there. She shut the door on him. That's hard to do. But there was really nothing better that she could've done. Sitting there holding her dead son wouldn't have changed anything. So she did what she had to do. She left the dead behind and went for help.

Have you experienced some hurt that still controls you? Are the memories of your tragedy never really out of your thoughts, regardless of what you're doing? You need to take that pain to God and leave it there. Shut the door on it, and then get on with what you must do. Don't let grief paralyze you!

If this woman hadn't torn herself away from her son, she would've lost him forever. She had to travel twenty miles one way to reach the man of God and get her miracle. She couldn't have done that carrying a dead body with her. She had to let go to take hold of her miracle.

Make sure that all your care is cast on the Lord today. Shut the door on it, and get on with what you must do to believe God! (AW)

APRIL 16
IS IT WELL WITH YOU?
2 KINGS 4:8-37

"Run now, I pray thee, to meet her, and say unto her, Is it well with thee? is it well with thy husband? is it well with the child? And she answered, It is well" (2 Kin. 4:26).

This was a woman of great faith. Her only son had just died and yet when Elisha asked how it was with her, her husband, and her son, she said, *"It is well."* That's awesome!

What if you had just lost your only son and someone asked you how you were doing? How would you answer? Would you praise God and say "It is well," or would you speak forth all your hurt? Your answer to that question is the reason you receive from God the way you do.

This woman had shut the door on her problem and was believing for a miracle. She hadn't let the grief of her situation swallow her, because she hadn't accepted it as being final. Faith gave her a different perspective on her problem than what other people would've had. Because of her faith, all was well.

Some people look at confessions of faith like this as lies. They see it as denying reality. That's not it at all. People of faith don't deny what exists; they just aren't limited only to physical truth. They realize the potential available through God and speak forth their faith. They supersede natural truth with greater spiritual truths.

What have you been speaking? Open up your spiritual eyes, and see what God has promised you. Then speak that into reality. If you're focused on what God says, then regardless of what may happen, it really is well with you. (AW)

APRIL 17
WHAT ARE YOU WAITING FOR?
PSALM 1:1-3

"Whatsoever he doeth shall prosper" (Ps. 1:3).

A few conditions are laid out before this verse is given. God will allow us to make our own decisions when we meet the guidelines of verses 1 and 2. First, we are not to walk in the counsel of the ungodly. God's children have been redeemed from the world and the advice of it. We are in a new kingdom with a new level of counsel—God's Word. God knows our problems and the source of them. He can give counsel that will always work.

Second, we are not to stand in the way of sinners. This means a life free from sin. How can we win sinners to the Lord if we live and act as they do? They know they're having problems and are looking for answers to bring them out. Our lives should be a louder witness than our voice.

Third, we are not to sit in the seat of the scornful. Bitterness and anger are not luxuries we can afford. Joy is a choice we are to make and walk in daily. To rejoice in the Lord is a command (Phil 4:4). Therefore, it must be a choice, not a feeling that comes and goes.

Our delight must be in the law of the Lord, and we must meditate in God's Word day and night. This will cause our roots to grow deep, our leaves to never wither, and our fruit to remain.

Then God says, "Whatever you do will prosper." What a remarkable thought—God trusts you. If your life is pleasing to the Lord and you have prayed for direction, but gotten nothing, perhaps God is saying, "You decide what's best and I'll back it!" Many times you don't need a green light or a red one. No light at all means proceed. If you make a mistake, God will be there to guide. (BY)

APRIL 18
START WHERE YOU ARE WITH WHAT YOU HAVE
MATTHEW 25:21

"His lord said unto him, Well done, thou good and faithful servant: thou hast been faithful over a few things, I will make thee ruler over many things: enter thou into the joy of thy lord" (Matt. 25:21).

Tithing—giving God ten percent of all your increase—is foundational to living a prosperous life. It's the starting point. We also need to give above the tithe. An important thing to remember is to start where you are and give, stretching a little bit and mixing it with faith. This is a faith situation based on God's Word. It's not a gimmick or a multilevel type of thing. It's God's promise and it receives His blessing—every time.

The only time in my life when I didn't tithe was in the early days when my wife, Joy, and I were just married. The bills were high and money was scarce. When I was an associate minister, I once took a night job to try to catch up, but we couldn't. We just kept getting further and further behind. One day, Joy said, "Bob, are we tithing?" Thank God for a godly wife. I wasn't trying to withhold my tithe. I intended to make it up, but it seemed like there was no way. That's where we learned that you start where you are and be faithful. Thank God, He brought us back out!

I remember one week recently that we _gave_ more in that week than we _made_. The key is to start where you are and mix it with faith. Not too long ago, I was going through some old financial records. I was surprised that we still had them. It was really interesting to me to see that there was a time when we were just married that my wife and I gave one-dollar offerings. A dollar fifty would've been like five or ten dollars today! That's all we could do at the time. It was also interesting to see the progression over the years of offerings going up to four dollars, and then five. That was a lot to us! I think of how a hundred dollars would've been a week's salary when we were associate ministers.

Can you see the progression? Do what you can where you are, and stretch a little. It takes awhile sometimes, but put some seed in the ground. Some seed comes up real quick, but others take more time. We have some seed coming up now that we planted twenty years ago!

Be diligent. Start where you are with what you have. If you can't give money, give your time, give love, give clothes—whatever. Just get some seed in the ground, and watch God's Word work in your life! (BN)

APRIL 19
LITTLE & BIG FAITH
ROMANS 12:1-3

"God hath dealt to every man the measure of faith" (Rom. 12:3).

If I were serving soup in a buffet line and used the same ladle to serve everyone, then the ladle would be THE measure that I served. Therefore, everyone I served would receive THE same measure. In like manner, the Lord only dishes out faith with one measure. We all have the same measure of faith.

Someone might ask, "Then why did Jesus speak of big and little faith?" There are four different instances in the Gospels where the Lord spoke of little faith (Matt. 6:30, 8:26, 14:31, and 16:8) and two where He spoke of great or big faith (Matt. 8:10 and 15:28). From these statements, many conclude that some people have more faith than others. That's not so. According to the above verse, we all have been dealt *"the measure of faith."*

Every born-again believer has been given the same amount of faith. It's just that some people use a lot of faith and others only a little. The different degrees of faith are only different degrees of usage, not different amounts.

Understanding this, simplifies the process of getting faith to work. We don't need to ask God for more faith. We just need to learn how to use what we have. The first step in getting our faith to operate is to acknowledge that we have as much faith as anyone. There is only one measure of faith. Failure to understand and believe this truth is a sure way to limit yourself to little faith. Break away from little faith thinking today, and begin recognizing what's already yours in Christ. (AW)

APRIL 20
FAITH WITHOUT WORKS IS DEAD!
JAMES 2:14-26

"Even so faith, if it hath not works, is dead, being alone" *(James 2:17).*

If I told you the building you were sitting in was on fire and you would die unless you did something, you'd do something. I can't imagine anyone saying "Yes, brother Andrew, I believe you" and yet not move. Different people might react differently, but they would all act. True biblical faith always produces action.

This concept is often taught and applied to the spiritual realm, but it's usually misunderstood. People mistakenly think that actions produce faith, but that's incorrect. Faith comes from God through His Word (Rom. 10:17). True biblical faith can be distinguished from any counterfeit by the actions it produces. If our actions are consistent with what God's Word teaches, then we have the real thing.

Our actions indicate what we really believe in our hearts. We can deceive others and even ourselves into thinking we're in faith when we aren't. But our actions don't lie. Although minor fluctuations may occur, our consistent actions reveal the overall belief of our hearts.

If your actions reveal that you aren't in as much faith as you thought, don't try to change your actions. Change your heart and your actions will follow. That's the way God made you. What you truly believe will manifest itself in your actions. (AW)

APRIL 21
YOU CAN SEE FAITH
MATTHEW 9:1-8

**"And, behold, they brought to him a man sick of the palsy, lying on a bed:
and Jesus seeing their faith said unto the sick of the palsy;
Son, be of good cheer; thy sins be forgiven thee"** *(Matt. 9:2).*

What does faith look like? Faith itself is like the wind. You can't see the wind, but you can see the effects of it. You can see things that are being blown by the wind. Likewise, you can't see faith. But by their actions, you can see those who are moving in faith.

For Jesus to see the faith of these men meant that He saw their actions. Specifically, they climbed on the roof, took the roof off, and lowered the sick man down right in front of Jesus and in the presence of an antagonistic crowd. They were sure to be criticized by the religious leaders and would also be in trouble with the owner of the house whose roof they had just removed. They must have believed that what they were going to receive was worth the price. They believed their friend would be healed!

These men could've just believed that Jesus could heal their friend but not do anything about it. If they hadn't acted on their faith, it wouldn't have done their friend any good. Their faith without any action would have produced nothing. Actions are a vital part of faith. Faith without corresponding action is not faith at all (James 2:17).

What kind of actions would show true biblical faith in your situation? Is that the way you're acting? If not, why? Is it because you don't have true biblical faith yet? Determine in your heart today to walk in real trust and reliance on God. Then watch your actions change. (AW)

APRIL 22
IS YOUR HEART SICK?
PROVERBS 13:12

**"Hope deferred maketh the heart sick: but when the desire cometh,
it is a tree of life"** *(Prov. 13:12).*

When I was in the sixth grade, I competed in a spelling bee. I was determined to win that competition, so I diligently studied for weeks. I knew every word in the book by heart. The day of the competition came and I was ready. I told everyone—including the teachers—that I was going to win. Therefore, they gave me the very first word to spell. It was the word *Rhine*, as in the Rhine River. I confidently spelled r-h-i-n-e, which was correct, but I failed to capitalize the letter "r." Therefore, I was the first one eliminated.

I was humiliated and frustrated because I knew every single word they gave and could've easily won that contest, if I had just capitalized the letter "r." My heart was sick. I lost all desire to excel in spelling. In my sixth grade mentality, I actually vowed to never study spelling again. Bad idea!

When my hope was high, I was ecstatic. When my hope was dashed, I was hurt, bitter, and angry. I went on to become one of the worst spellers in history. Just recently, I've confronted it and begun learning how to spell again. It's taken me thirty years to get over that day!

Is your heart sick because of some disappointment? Maybe your hurt is more serious than mine, but the results are the same. You may have lost your will or your hope to try, but don't let it haunt you another day. Go to the Lord, and let Him give you new hope. Life without hope isn't God's kind of life. (AW)

APRIL 23
THE HOPE OF HEAVEN
1 CORINTHIANS 15:12-23

"If in this life only we have hope in Christ, we are of all men most miserable" *(1 Cor. 15:19).*

This seems like a very peculiar statement to many Christians. After all, what if there was no life after death? Christianity would still be a great way to live. That's definitely true. However, Paul must have been speaking of the unique problems Christians experience which can only be offset by the hope of a better life to come.

For instance, salvation will cost you some of your best friendships and relationships. Those who were on board with you before you became a Christian jumped off as you made your abrupt turn toward the Lord.

And then, there is the area of increased expectations. Before you became born again, you didn't believe for much. Therefore, you weren't disappointed as often. After realizing that God is real and His power is available to you in your everyday life, your expectations soared. Not experiencing what you're believing for can become a recipe for disaster. Unbelievers find solace in that everyone they know is as miserable as they are and that that's just the way it is. Believers know that all things are possible with God. Therefore, they become discontent with a life that's less than what Jesus provided.

If we as believers focus on what Christianity costs us, then we can get as discouraged as anyone. The hope of our salvation is so far beyond anything we can imagine that it makes all the effort in this life fade in comparison. We must keep an eye on the prize that's set before us to prevent us from growing weary in the race. Think about the wonders of spending eternity in the presence of Almighty God. Let that thought encourage you to hold your course in this life today. (AW)

APRIL 24
THE HOPE OF *HIS* CALLING
EPHESIANS 1:15-23

"The eyes of your understanding being enlightened; that ye may know what is the hope of his calling, and what the riches of the glory of his inheritance in the saints" (Eph. 1:18).

Notice how Paul prayed that we'd know the hope of HIS calling. We're carrying out the call of Jesus, not our own. Great peace, hope, and faith are the results of knowing that we're fulfilling God's call and not just doing our own thing.

In 1969, an Army recruiter came to my home to show me all the advantages of volunteering for the Army rather than being drafted. I told him I could save him a lot of time if he'd listen to me. I explained that the reason I was 1-A was because I had quit school. He agreed. Then I shared how the Lord specifically directed me to leave the university and that I was in His hands. If God wanted me drafted, I would be, and if He didn't, I wouldn't be. The recruiter started laughing and said, "Boy, I can guarantee that you'll be drafted!"

That really made me mad. I told him that if it was God's will for me to stay at home, then neither he, nor the United States Government, nor all the demons in hell could draft me. He thought I was crazy. Sure enough, I received a draft notice in the next day's mail. When I went to Vietnam, I knew in my heart that I was there because of my obedience to the Lord. This gave me a confidence that others didn't have, and a hope and faith that the Lord was responsible for taking care of me.

Are you living your life in direct obedience to what God has called you to do? If you are, then you should enjoy the hope of His calling. (AW)

APRIL 25
NO HOPE = NO GOD IN THE WORLD
EPHESIANS 2:8-22

"That at that time ye were without Christ, being aliens from the commonwealth of Israel, and strangers from the covenants of promise, having no hope, and without God in the world" (Eph. 2:12).

It's a terrible thing to be without God. That will be the true torment of hell. The physical suffering, as bad as that'll be, is nothing compared to being cut off from God for eternity. This verse says that without God, there is no hope. Therefore, being hopeless is very similar to living in hell.

On the other hand, with God there's always hope. Hope is one of the characteristics of God that enables us to face any situation. If the doctor's report says you're going to die, there's hope. If your bank statement says you are broke, there's hope. If your boss says you're fired, there's hope. If your mate says they're leaving, there's hope. No situation is hopeless with God!

Even if some circumstance of life does overcome us, we have the assurance from God that we'll spend eternity with Him in perfect health, love, and harmony. We can't lose for winning! We have the ultimate victory assured to us by God Himself. Hope should be the banner of every Christian. As surely as we have passed from death to life, we have passed from hopelessness to hopefulness.

However, this hope must be appropriated. It doesn't just come automatically. Just like faith, hope comes from the scriptures (Rom. 10:17 and 15:4). Hope is the calm assurance that God is greater than whatever threatens us. We receive this assurance as we spend time in the presence of the Lord, allowing Him to assure our hearts. Let hope arise in your heart by spending time with your Father today. (AW)

APRIL 26
TRUE LIVING IS A LIFESTYLE OF GIVING
ACTS 20:35

"I have shewed you all things, how that so labouring ye ought to support the weak,
and to remember the words of the Lord Jesus, how he said,
It is more blessed to give than to receive" (Acts 20:35).

We must catch the concept that giving is all about our lifestyles. I've seen people who live to take. Takers are miserable people. The real joy is when you've sown and you see that seed coming up. Not all of giving is money. We must also remember what God saves us from having to spend. Begin to see that everything you do is planting a seed. In due season, you'll reap.

I watched my mother. She was a tither all of her life. My father's health declined and his hospitalization was terminated, leaving her with several thousand dollars worth of medical bills when he died. I watched mother take her Bible and say to God, "I've always been a tither and a giver." Every medical bill was paid when my mother died, and she had money in the bank. I've watched that principle of giving. We're setting an example for our own family and our own children. My mother taught me that if you'll tithe, God will always take care of you. *If you put God first, you'll have God's best.* That's the greatest inheritance a person can have! She didn't leave me a lot of money, but she left me a gold mine of truth. (BN)

APRIL 27
GOD SPEAKS TO US THROUGH CREATION
PSALM 19:1-6

"The heavens declare the glory of God; and the firmament sheweth his handywork" (Ps. 19:1).

The physical creation all around us is awesome. Man has never fully appreciated the wonder in the simplest actions of God. Take for example the sunrises and sunsets.

The sun rises and sets with such precision that almanacs can predict its exact arrival and departure down to the minute, years in advance. The Lord created this world in such a way that the rising and setting of the sun is spectacular. It's like a trumpet calling attention to the glory and faithfulness of God. There are no words to adequately describe the beauty when the rays of the sun first appear on the clouds in the early morning, or leave us late at night.

Yet, these events often go unnoticed or unappreciated by the vast majority of people. There is no language that doesn't understand this speech, but our preoccupation with ourselves makes us deaf to the obvious. The Lord speaks to us through His creation, but few listen.

Regardless of how dark your situation may be, a dawn is coming for those who trust in God, just as surely as the sun will rise in the morning. Regardless of how hard your labor may be, a time of rest is coming, just as surely as the sun sets each day and people go to sleep. Nothing that man can do can change the rising and the setting of the sun. Nothing that man can do will change the faithfulness of God to His children. The Lord has given us reminders of His love and faithfulness every day. They're all around us. Look for them today! (AW)

APRIL 28
THE HOPE OF GLORY
COLOSSIANS 1:19-29

"To whom God would make known what is the riches of the glory of this mystery among the Gentiles; which is Christ in you, the hope of glory" (Col. 1:27).

It's easy to focus on all of our problems. Sickness can demand our attention. Family issues, stress at work, and a multitude of other things vie for our concentration every day. Regardless of what's happening to us in the natural, our spiritual condition never changes. Once we're born again, the Spirit of Christ comes, dwells in us (Rom. 8:9), and never leaves (Heb. 13:5).

Directing our thoughts to the indwelling presence of Christ is one of our strongest weapons against hopelessness, depression, fear, and unbelief. As we become totally convinced that Jesus is in us—in all of His power, love, and authority—how can anything or anyone prevail against us? *"The LORD is on my side; I will not fear: what can man do unto me?"* (Ps. 118:6).

Most Christians have knowledge that Christ dwells in them, but it's not an experiential knowledge that impacts them on a daily basis. In reality, what they see with their physical eyes seems more real to them than the unseen spiritual truths. Yet, the reality of Christ in us should overwhelm any and all of our physical problems.

The benefits of having God Almighty living in us are not automatic; we must appropriate those benefits by focusing our thoughts on Christ in us, instead of the problems around us. The Lord wants to guide you into this new way of thinking. He wants to show you the riches of the glory of this mystery. Receive His help today by dwelling on the truth that Christ—in all His splendor—is in you today and every day. He will never leave you (Matt. 28:20). (AW)

APRIL 29
GIVE SACRIFICIALLY—RECEIVE SUPERNATURALLY
2 SAMUEL 24:24

"And the king said unto Araunah, Nay; but I will surely buy it of thee at a price: neither will I offer burnt offerings unto the LORD my God of that which doth cost me nothing. So David bought the threshingfloor and the oxen for fifty shekels of silver" (2 Sam. 24:24).

David refused to offer a sacrifice to God that didn't cost him something. He wanted it to be meaningful—dear to him. There is a time for sacrificial giving. A sacrifice is giving something highly valued for the sake of one considered to have a greater value. Isaac sowed in the year of famine and reaped a hundredfold that same year (Gen. 26:1 and 12). That was a miracle! Giving sacrificially demonstrates our complete trust in God as our Provider and the one who prospers us.

This is supernatural and the mind can't grasp it. The natural mind cannot receive it and will fight you. *"__The carnal mind is enmity against God: for it is not subject to the law of God, neither indeed can be__"* (Rom. 8:7, emphasis added). It's baffling how you can give more when you're seemingly already in lack and come out ahead? Well, God's way is not always logical to what our way would be. God's ways are not our ways (Is. 55:8-9). His ways are higher—better—than ours. We must choose to operate in God's way.

When you learn how to give sacrificially, you'll begin to receive supernaturally! (BN)

APRIL 30
WAIT A MINUTE. BACK UP!
LUKE 6:38

"Give, and it shall be given unto you" (Luke 6:38).

"Why have I given through the years and seen so little in return?" As a pastor, I've heard this statement many times. Dedicated tithers and givers have struggled with little or no harvest in their financial lives. "Doesn't the Bible say if we give, it'll be given back to us?" Yes it does.

But let's back up a bit and get a running start at verse 38. The thought begins in Luke 6:35. This teaching starts with *"love...your enemies."* Love toward friends is not often difficult, but love toward our enemies takes a great deal of faith. This is the true love of Jesus. He loved His enemies so much, He died for them.

Second, we're told to *"do good."* This is the production of good works. Our light is to be seen by the world, not just God Himself.

Third, we are told to *"lend, hoping for nothing."* How many people out there owe you? You loaned them something and they've never given it back. Forget it. Forgive them. God will take care of you.

Next, we are to *"be...merciful"* (verse 36) and *"judge not"* (verse 37). Instead of rising up with a critical attitude, be merciful to those who have spitefully used you. This can be tough.

"Condemn not" and *"forgive"* are the next commandments (verse 37). Your mouth and your heart are connected in this thought. Let your attitude and words be gracious as you forgive others.

Let's put this all together and find out God's plan for prosperity. *"Love...your enemies, do good, lend, be...merciful, judge not, condemn not, forgive...give, and it shall be given unto you; good measure, pressed down, and shaken together, and running over, shall men give into your bosom"* (Luke 6:35-38). (BY)

MAY 1
A LIVELY HOPE
1 PETER 1:1-9

"Blessed be the God and Father of our Lord Jesus Christ, which according to his abundant mercy hath begotten us again unto a lively hope by the resurrection of Jesus Christ from the dead" (1 Pet. 1:3).

Jesus is our hope (1 Tim. 1:1) and Jesus is alive! Therefore, we have a living hope.

The tombs of Buddha, Mohammed, and every other religious leader of the world are still occupied today, but Christ's is empty. Jesus isn't there. He was resurrected because He is greater than death, and *"through death he might destroy him that had the power of death, that is, the devil"* (Heb. 2:14). Jesus not only gave us a last will and testament with great promises and provisions, but then He rose from the dead to become the executor of His own will. This ensured it would be administered properly. What a Savior and what a salvation!

The Resurrection is the hinge on which all the claims of Christianity swing. Jesus is the only person who rose from the dead to validate His claims. No one else has ever compared to Jesus in this respect. This puts Him in a category all by Himself. The Resurrection literally separates God from men.

Therefore, the promises Jesus gave us are different from all other promises. They come with a warranty enforced by the guarantor Himself. God watches over His Word to perform it. God's Word is backed by His personal integrity. Therefore, our hope in His promises is alive since He is alive. (AW)

MAY 2
ARE YOU HOT?
2 CORINTHIANS 4:7-18

**"For which cause we faint not; but though our outward man perish,
yet the inward man is renewed day by day"** *(2 Cor. 4:16).*

I remember when my sixth grade teacher heated a metal gas can. Once it was very hot, he put the lid on securely, making it airtight, and set the can on his desk. The whole class watched as it began cracking and popping. Then, right in front of our eyes, the can was crushed without anyone touching it!

Hot air occupies more space than cold air. When the air inside the can was hot, it equaled the atmospheric pressure. As it cooled, the air condensed and formed a partial vacuum inside the can. That's when the normal atmospheric pressure crushed it.

What an awesome illustration of everyday life! We all face pressures. However, if our lives are full of the presence of God, these pressures are no problem. It's only when we have a partial vacuum in our hearts that daily pressures affect us. Those who seem overwhelmed by everyday life have cooled off in their relationship with the Lord and are no longer full of God.

Life hasn't become worse or more stressful in our modern times as some proclaim. Life has always been tough! Think about those who fought in World War II. What about those of you whose parents just a few generations ago were slaves? What about the Great Depression? Most of us have never experienced hardships like these people did. Yet, it seems there is more depression, suicide, and heartache today than then. The difference isn't the pressures outside but the vacuum inside. Get full of the love, faith, and hope of God, and normal, everyday pressures won't be a problem! (AW)

MAY 3
MUSTARD SEED FAITH
MATTHEW 17:14-21

"And Jesus said unto them, Because of your unbelief: for verily I say unto you, If ye have faith as a grain of mustard seed, ye shall say unto this mountain, Remove hence to yonder place; and it shall remove; and nothing shall be impossible unto you" *(Matt. 17:20).*

Why did Jesus compare our faith to that of a mustard seed? For one thing, a mustard seed is the smallest of all herbal seeds. It's tiny! The Lord was making the point that you don't have to have "big" faith to receive miraculous results. Pure faith is what moves mountains. An unopposed faith will work every time.

Most Christians have the concept that it takes "big" faith to get results. How big was your faith when you were born again? None of us were spiritual giants before we were saved. We didn't spend weeks or years studying and praying to build our faith. God knocked at the door of our hearts and we responded. That's faith! The biggest miracle you'll ever believe for is to be born again. Everything else pales in comparison.

So the faith you used for salvation is sufficient for any other need you'll ever have. It's not the amount of faith you have that counts but the purity of your faith. A lack of faith isn't the problem for Christians—it's the presence of unbelief hindering their faith. Unbelief is an opposing force to faith. A little unbelief will negate a lot of faith.

Unbelief comes through listening to the devil in the same way that faith comes through listening to God (Rom. 10:17). It's not good enough just to build your faith; you must also decrease your unbelief. Turn away from the things that increase your doubts today and *"only believe"* (Mark 5:36). (AW)

MAY 4
UNBELIEF IS THE PROBLEM
MATTHEW 17:14-21

"And Jesus said unto them, Because of your unbelief: for verily I say unto you, If ye have faith as a grain of mustard seed, ye shall say unto this mountain, Remove hence to yonder place; and it shall remove; and nothing shall be impossible unto you" (*Matt. 17:20*).

Notice what Jesus didn't say. He didn't say the disciples' problem was their "little" faith. Instead, he said the problem was their unbelief.

If you hitched a team of horses to a wagon, they could pull it under normal circumstances. But if you hitched another team of equal strength to the back of the wagon to pull in the opposite direction, then even though there'd be great force exerted on the wagon, the net effect would be zero. The wagon wouldn't move, because the two teams counterbalanced each other.

In like manner, faith and unbelief are opposing forces. Often, the reason why our prayers are unanswered isn't because we have "little" faith but because we have unbelief. We ought to be just as concerned about decreasing unbelief as we are about increasing faith.

Imagine two wall-mounted thermometers side by side, one measuring unbelief and the other faith. Most Christians would try to get the faith thermometer to register larger than the unbelief one. A simpler approach is to just pull the plug on unbelief. In the absence of unbelief, a mustard seed amount of faith is more than enough to get the job done.

Instead of just feeding your faith, learn to starve your doubts. Unbelief must be fed to survive. Starve your unbelief by focusing all your attention on God and His Word today! (AW)

MAY 5
GOD'S CONCEPT OF GIVING WILL WORK ANYWHERE!
ACTS 10:34-35

"Then Peter opened his mouth, and said, Of a truth I perceive that God is no respecter of persons: But in every nation he that feareth him, and worketh righteousness, is accepted with him" (*Acts 10:34-35*).

God's Word works! His way works! It'll work for preachers, it'll work for housewives. It'll work for businessmen, teenagers, and children. It'll even work for missionaries. God's concept of giving will work for anyone anywhere!

I've seen it work in Calcutta, India. One of the greatest lessons I ever learned was with Dr. Mark Buntain and his great mission work there. I saw tithes and offerings working in the middle of leprosy and disease. The most prosperous people I saw there were givers. Calcutta has long been known as a decayed civilization. At that time, when the airplane door opened, the stench would just knock you back. It was so intense that many ministers would come, stay in the only decent hotel, and then take the next plane out. They simply couldn't handle it. I saw Dr. Buntain teach the people tithing. Out of that church came some of the most outstanding, creative people in all the world—educators, neurosurgeons, doctors, even the assistant chief of police for all of Los Angeles County.

God's concept of giving will work anywhere when people put feet to their faith. Start with what you have, and reach out and stretch a little further in faith. If it'll work in a third-world nation, it will work for you! (BN)

MAY 6
HOPE IS OUR ANCHOR
HEBREWS 6:13-20

"Which hope we have as an anchor of the soul, both sure and stedfast, and which entereth into that within the veil" (Heb. 6:19).

The purpose of an anchor is to hold something in place. It gives stability. That's what hope does for the soul.

Our souls are the mental and emotional part of our beings, and a soul without hope in God is doomed to drift away from the Lord. Just as surely as a ship will drift without an anchor, our souls will float away from the Lord without a strong hope. Hope is our anchor.

Notice where our hope is anchored: *"within the veil."* That's a reference to the temple and specifies the Holy of Holies, or the part of the temple where God dwelt. The Holy of Holies was also where the Ark of the Covenant was, which contained the tablets on which the Ten Commandments were written. The Word of God was *"within the veil."* Therefore, having our hope anchored *"within the veil"* is having our hope anchored in the Word of God.

Our hope comes from God's Word (Rom. 15:4), and apart from His promises, there's no sure place to anchor our souls. Our hope must be placed securely in God and not in the temporal things of this life. Putting our confidence in anything but God's Word is a sure way to drift from where He wants us to be.

Seek out the promises of God's Word. Personalize them and let your soul begin to hope for their fulfillment in your life. Strengthen your hope by keeping your focus on the promises every day. You'll find your hope will keep you anchored to the Lord, regardless of the storms of life. Every ship has an anchor. Every soul has hope. It just has to be put in the right place. (AW)

MAY 7
WE HAVE HOPE BECAUSE OF GOD'S GRACE
2 THESSALONIANS 2:13-17

"Now our Lord Jesus Christ himself, and God, even our Father, which hath loved us, and hath given us everlasting consolation and good hope through grace" (2 Thess. 2:16).

Hope is a confident expectation of good. How is it that we can hope when there's so much bad in this world? Casual observation of the world around us shows us that not every story has a happy ending. The evening news is full of real-life accounts that war against hope. What makes us think that things will go any better for us? What makes us special? The answer: God's grace!

Grace is God's ability that is available to us on an unearned, undeserved basis. The reason Christians have hope in a hopeless world is because we have access to God's ability through faith. The Lord doesn't have any limitations on what He can do, except our faith. We are the only ones that limit God's intervention in our affairs. Satan can't do it. People can't stop God. We're the only ones who stop the Lord from working on our behalf through our unbelief.

Notice that I didn't say we stop God from moving through our lack of holiness. It's not our actions that determine the outcome, but our beliefs. We have access to God's grace through faith (Rom. 5:2). All we must do is believe more in the ability of God than in the ability of Satan and man. It's God's grace that enables us to do this.

The Lord doesn't give us what we deserve; He gives us what we believe. If we can believe that God is a good God, who only wants us to prosper, then we can have prosperity, regardless of what others have. It's the grace of God that gives us hope. Focus on His grace today, and let hope abound in your heart. (AW)

MAY 8
OUR HOPE IS IN GOD
1 PETER 1:10-21

"Who by him do believe in God, that raised him up from the dead, and gave him glory; that your faith and hope might be in God" (1 Pet. 1:21).

Our world looks for hope in many different places. Even among Christians, we often misdirect our hope toward politics or people. Just look at the reactions of many believers when things go wrong. At the public exposure of a few Christian leaders, panic swept through many in the body of Christ. I received letters from people who said they would never trust any preacher again. There were people who swore our country was doomed after an election that showed that character and moral values weren't important.

Such reactions reveal that these individuals' hope wasn't in God but in people. A person whose hope is in God is never dismayed at what happens around them. Regardless of what the conditions are in the world, there's always reason to hope if our hope is in God.

The early church had no political power. They were persecuted mercilessly, yet within 200 years, one-tenth of the Roman Empire was Christian because of the hope they saw in believers. Paul rejoiced in prison and prevailed because his hope was in God. Most of the Christians throughout history would love to be in our situation. We enjoy more freedom and opportunity than nearly all the Christians that have ever lived. Do we have more hope? Not really. Why? Because many Christians today have switched their hope from God to the government or to charismatic leaders.

Certainly, we need to pray for godly leaders. But regardless of who's in leadership, God is always on His throne. Make sure your hope is in Him alone. (AW)

MAY 9
WHO MOVED?
1 JOHN 1:7

"If we walk in the light, as he is in the light, we have fellowship one with another" (1 John 1:7).

Do you want to know where Jesus walks? He always walks in the light. This light is God's will. The light is also God's Word. If we want to be successful, we need to walk in God's will and God's Word. This way, we'll always be walking beside Jesus.

When we walk in God's light, we have fellowship with God the Father and Jesus. God's desire is not only to have sons and daughters but friends. God wants to talk with us and have us talk with Him. The Greek word for fellowship is *koinonia*. It's more than just speaking to one another; it's intimate fellowship—conversation between close friends.

Jesus is always in the light. He never moves. We're the ones who move in and out of the light. Sin removes us from the light of fellowship. Forgiveness of sins brings us back. *"If we confess our sins, he is faithful and just to forgive us our sins, and to cleanse us from all unrighteousness"* (1 John 1:9). This brings us out of the darkness and back into the light of His presence.

An older couple was driving down the road one day. The wife was next to the door on her side and a great distance stood between her and her husband. Who knows how many years ago this began. A young couple drove around them. They were sitting so close together they almost looked like one person. A small tear came down the cheek of the older woman as she remembered the days she and her husband were young and in love. She remarked to her husband, "Do you remember when we used to sit that close to each other?" He replied, "I haven't moved."

Are you wondering why you and the Lord aren't as close to each other as you once were? Just remember, He hasn't moved. (BY)

MAY 10
THE MASTER KEY & THE MASTER GIVER
JOHN 3:16

"For God so loved the world, that he gave his only begotten Son, that whosoever believeth in him should not perish, but have everlasting life" (John 3:16).

Giving is the master key that unlocks the door to the blessings and the heart of Almighty God. God is a giver. He gave His best—and gave it with no promise of anything in return. If I really love you, I'm willing to give if I know where and how to give. The biggest giver in the universe is God. He's the one who set the example for us. The Bible shows more examples of this truth: the widow who gave her last bit of meal and oil, the woman who broke the alabaster box and poured the precious ointment on Jesus' head, etc. There are many examples, but God truly is the prime giver.

Love is being willing to give your best, asking nothing in return except faith in the seed that you plant. Even giving love to another person is sowing. You sow mercy, you reap mercy. You sow love, you reap love. You sow help, you reap help.

Each day I purpose in my heart to be a giver. It's a response to the goodness of God for all the love and mercy He's poured out on me. Not because of my own goodness, but as it says in 1 John 4:19, *"We love him, because he first loved us."* He is the Master giver. (BN)

MAY 11
WHERE DO YOU STAND?
PROVERBS 3:1-8

"Trust in the LORD with all thine heart; and lean not unto thine own understanding" (Prov. 3:5).

A man once fell off a cliff. In desperation, he clawed at the air and succeeded in grabbing a small bush growing out of the rock. It stopped his fall, but still left him in a precarious position. He started yelling for help in hope that someone would hear him and come to his aid.

Finally, when his strength was almost gone, he heard a booming voice say, "Let go!" No one was around, but the voice came again saying, "Let go!" The man asked, "Is that you, God?" The Lord said, "Yes, it's Me. Trust Me. Let go." After a long pause, the man asked, "Is there anyone else up there?"

Faith is somewhat like that. It's letting go of anything and everything that we're clinging to and putting our total trust in God. True faith doesn't have "Plan B" or "Plan C." There are no safety valves or nets to catch us if God doesn't come through. Faith can't be just another weapon in our arsenal that we use if everything else fails. True faith is commitment.

Just as Peter stepped out of the boat onto the water at Jesus' command without a life preserver, we must also step out in faith on nothing but the promise of God's Word. That's not unreasonable. He created everything we see by His Word (Heb. 11:3), and He's still holding it all together by the same (Heb. 1:3). God's Word is the parent force. Certainly, the parent is greater than the offspring! God's Word will still be standing long after this physical world is dissolved.

Faith is standing on nothing but God's Word. Where do you stand? (AW)

MAY 12
WHAT ARE YOU STANDING ON?
MATTHEW 14:22-33

"And he said, Come. And when Peter was come down out of the ship,
he walked on the water, to go to Jesus" (*Matt. 14:29*).

It looks like Peter walked on the water, and indeed this verse says he did. However, you can't walk on water. It won't support your weight. In reality, Peter was walking on the word of Jesus. The Lord told Peter, *"Come."* That one word, spoken by the Creator Himself, had enough power to enable Peter to walk on water. Peter wasn't just walking on water—he was walking on God's Word!

The Word of God is more sure than anything physical we see around us. Jesus said, *"Heaven and earth shall pass away, but my words shall not pass away"* (Matt. 24:35). God's Word is more stable than the mountains or the oceans. We should be more assured of our footing when we are standing on God's Word than when we're standing on firm ground. For God's Word to fail, God would have to fail—and that's never going to happen!

How do you stand on God's Word? You act in faith on what He's told you. In Peter's case, that meant getting out of the boat and walking on the water. He couldn't have stayed in the boat and said, "I'm trusting You, Jesus. I'm acting on Your word." Peter had to do what Jesus said. It's the same with us.

If you really trust Jesus, then do what He tells you to do. Don't listen to the guys in the boat. It'd have been crazy for them to get out on the water. They weren't the ones the Lord told to *"Come."* You must have a word to stand on from God.

What has the Lord told you to do? Do it and let God's Word hold you up! (AW)

MAY 13
CHECK WHAT YOU'RE SOWING!
GENESIS 1:11

"And God said, Let the earth bring forth grass, the herb yielding seed,
and the fruit tree yielding fruit after his kind,
whose seed is in itself, upon the earth: and it was so" (*Gen. 1:11*).

Sowing and reaping is a foundational biblical principle. God told Noah, *"While the earth remaineth, seedtime and harvest, and cold and heat, and summer and winter, and day and night shall not cease"* (Gen. 8:22). If you want to grow wheat, you don't plant corn seeds. It's the same with your giving, because *giving is sowing*.

We've sown in helping many ministers get their own cars. Then the Lord gave us a brand-new car—totally unexpected. I've sown shoes and received shoes. I've sown suits. Whatsoever a man sows, that shall he also reap. This is a positive for the believer. *If you don't want it coming back, don't sow it!*

We've assisted small churches in desperate situations with their payments. We've sown to help other churches, ministers, and people in general. We've sown into helping individuals with medical bills in a time of need. It's built my faith and my confidence that, really, whatever I need, I know that my God will supply. We're givers, not takers!

"Ye have sown much, and bring in little; ye eat, but ye have not enough; ye drink, but ye are not filled with drink; ye clothe you, but there is none warm; and he that earneth wages earneth wages to put it into a bag with holes. Thus saith the LORD of hosts; Consider your ways" (Hag. 1:6-7, emphasis added). The Israelites were setting up nice comfortable homes for themselves, while the house of God was lying in waste. The good news is, they repented and God restored them.

If we judge ourselves, we will not be judged. It's good from time to time to give ourselves a spiritual checkup. Remember, if you don't like what you're reaping, check what you're sowing. When we make sure that we put God first, we can be sure that all our own needs will be taken care of in the process (Matt. 6:33). (BN)

MAY 14
HUMAN FAITH VS. GOD'S FAITH
EPHESIANS 2:1-10

"For by grace are ye saved through faith; and that not of yourselves:
it is the gift of God" (Eph. 2:8).

The faith we use to become saved is not human faith. It doesn't come from us but rather is a gift from God. We were so destitute that we couldn't even believe the Gospel on our own. God had to impart His supernatural faith into our hearts so we could believe the good news of our salvation.

Sitting in a chair you've never sat in before or riding on a plane that you haven't inspected are often used as examples of faith, but that's human faith. It's based on sensory knowledge. If you saw a four-legged chair with three of its legs leaning to one side, you wouldn't sit in it if you had any sense. What if I asked you to sit down in a chair that you couldn't see? You couldn't do that with human faith.

Human faith can't believe what it can't see, taste, hear, smell, or feel. Yet, when it comes to salvation, we must believe in things we can't see. We can't see God or the devil, heaven or hell, yet we believe in all these things when we become born again. Where does that faith come from? It's the gift of God.

God's faith comes through His Word (Rom. 10:17). That's the reason we must hear God's Word in some fashion to be born again. The faith that every Christian has isn't just human faith, but a supernatural God-kind of faith. If we use it the way God uses His faith, it'll accomplish for us as it accomplishes for Him. Don't limit the power of faith today. Believe BIG! We have a BIG God, and we have His supernatural faith! (AW)

MAY 15
NEVER LOSE YOUR CONFIDENCE
2 CORINTHIANS 5:6

"Therefore we are always confident, knowing" (2 Cor. 5:6).

How would you like to have an everlasting confidence? Or, as this verse says, be *"always confident"*? Confidence isn't a feeling. It's not an assurance based on circumstances. Things going your way shouldn't be a reason for confidence. If confidence is based on circumstances, then sometimes you'll be confident and other times you won't. How can you be confident always?

This verse goes on to tell us how *"knowing"* brings confidence. Confidence is based on knowledge. What you know brings you confidence. The Bible doesn't give you confidence. Knowing the Bible gives you confidence. Jesus didn't tell us the truth would make us free. He said knowing the truth would make us free.

Because you can know at all times, you can be confident at all times. You can be confident when you're hungry or when you have plenty to eat. You can be confident when you have money or when you don't know where your next penny is going to come from. When your confidence is in the Lord and His Word, you can be confident He'll come through. You may not know where the food or money is coming from, but you have confidence it will arrive. It's knowing the faithfulness of God that is your confidence.

David gave us a look into his own confidence when he said, *"I have been young, and now am old; yet have I not seen the righteous forsaken, nor his seed begging bread"* (Ps. 37:25). When we're cared for by the Lord and taken care of by His faithfulness, we can boldly declare, "I will not be forsaken nor left begging bread." Confidence will remain at all times as an eternal stabilizer in our lives. (BY)

MAY 16
DON'T FORGET!
PSALM 103:1-22

"Bless the Lord, O my soul, and forget not all his benefits" (Ps. 103:2).

In May 1991, I was sitting on a church platform just minutes before I was to minister. The final song was "How Great Thou Art." I suddenly had a flashback to May 1961, when I was a twelve-year-old boy sitting at my father's funeral. That auditorium was packed with over 500 people singing my father's favorite song, "How Great Thou Art." I vividly remember what I was thinking then. I wasn't in tears, because I really hadn't yet comprehended what had happened, but I knew something had taken place that would alter my life forever.

The minister spoke of victory and hope, which seemed to be so contrary to the situation. That song also appeared to be out of place. Yet in my heart, it struck a chord. I felt faith arise. So I prayed and said to the Lord, "If You really are so great, then protect me and direct the rest of my life."

I hadn't thought about that prayer for thirty years. Yet that song brought all that back to my remembrance in an instant. I was overwhelmed with the faithfulness of the Lord to answer such a simple prayer by a twelve-year-old boy. He did exceedingly, abundantly above anything I had asked or even thought!

Remembering the faithfulness of God has been a vital part of my faith. Good memories stir us up (2 Pet. 1:13). The Lord commanded us not to forget, because He knows we will if we don't make a deliberate effort to remember.

All of us have uttered prayers—whether spoken requests or just desires—that we've forgotten, but God hasn't. Only eternity will reveal the true faithfulness of God. Yet in the meantime, we need to make an effort to remember the goodness of the Lord. Today let the Holy Spirit bring back to your remembrance instances of God's faithfulness to you. You'll be blessed! (AW)

MAY 17
CHRIST IS OUR HOPE
1 TIMOTHY 1:1-17

"Paul, an apostle of Jesus Christ by the commandment of God our Saviour, and Lord Jesus Christ, which is our hope" (1 Tim. 1:1).

Most of us turn to the Lord in hopeless situations. We know hope comes from God and we run to Him when we're in trouble. But sadly, as soon as our seeking the Lord begins to pay off and our situation improves, we often transfer our hope back to carnal things. We begin to hope because our circumstances are looking better. That's laying a foundation for disaster!

Actually, that's not putting our hope in God at all. That's finding our hope (or confidence) in circumstances. We only use God to get our situations back in the positive and then we're on our way.

Jesus is not just the source of hope when everything in our lives goes bad; He's our hope at all times, good and bad. We must realize that Jesus does more than just give us hope. He is our hope. Every good thing that we anticipate in the future is found in Him.

True hope doesn't come from circumstances. It comes from a person—the Lord Jesus Christ. Therefore, those who have Jesus as their only hope have an advantage over those who see Him as the one who gives them hope. True hope is a result of a relationship with Christ.

Putting all our hope in Jesus makes our hope steadfast. He's always the same (Heb. 13:8), and those who have all their hope in Him always have the same hope. Those whose hope comes from circumstances fluctuate with situations. Where is your hope? If it's in Jesus, you'll still be hoping in the face of hopeless situations. Put your hope in God today! (AW)

MAY 18
THE FULL ASSURANCE OF HOPE
HEBREWS 6:10-20

***"And we desire that every one of you do shew the same diligence
to the full assurance of hope unto the end"*** *(Heb. 6:11).*

There are different levels of hope. There is "hope" and there's "an assured hope." Then there is ***"the full assurance of hope."*** We need to settle for nothing but the best! Therefore, how do we attain this full assurance of hope?

According to this verse, diligence is a key to developing a fully mature hope. The dictionary defines *diligence* as "long, steady application to one's occupation or studies; persistent effort; assiduity." In other words, hope develops with a steady, constant application of it in our lives.

Our society has become spoiled with an instant mentality. We have instant coffee, instant oatmeal, and instant potatoes. Just about everything can be microwaved today. If it's not instant, we don't want it. You can't microwave hope. You can only achieve the full assurance of hope by using it consistently every day over a period of time.

How can we attain to this type of diligence? What is the key to patience? The context of this verse gives the answer. Abraham's hope was in the promise of God. It was the Word of God that gave Abraham a strong hope. Even though it was impossible for God to lie, He swore with an oath to Abraham to emphasize how unchangeable His promise was. We have the same promises from God that Abraham had—and many more. Clinging by faith to the promises in God's Word produces diligence in us.

Lay hold of the hope that God has given us through His Word, and don't let go until you have the full assurance of hope. (AW)

MAY 19
LAY HOLD ON HOPE
HEBREWS 6:10-20

***"That by two immutable things, in which it was impossible for God to lie,
we might have a strong consolation, who have fled for refuge to lay hold upon
the hope set before us"*** *(Heb. 6:18).*

Every believer has good reason to hope. God is for us, so who can successfully be against us (Rom. 8:31)? God has given us His Word that He is on our side. He's even sworn with an oath to further assure us! What more could we want? But this hope doesn't come automatically. It doesn't just grab us. We must ***"lay hold"*** of it.

Strong defines *lay hold* as "to use strength, i.e. to seize or retain." It takes effort to lay hold of hope, which is precisely the reason so few people have a strong hope—it's too much effort. There's a misconception that we just pray and ask God to give us hope. If hope comes, then God answered our prayer. If it doesn't come, then we must pray again harder. That's not it!

In 1 Samuel 30:6, David was in trouble. His city had been raided and burned, and his wives and children were taken captive along with those of all his men. David and his men cried until they had no more power to weep. Then—to top it all off—his men spoke of stoning him. Most of us would consider that a hopeless situation. David didn't just pray and ask for help, he encouraged himself in the Lord! He began to lay hold on hope by reminding himself of God's promises and praising Him that what He had promised, He would perform. It was just a matter of hours until David regained, with interest, everything the enemy had stolen, and just a couple of days until he was anointed king.

We need to show some strength and lay hold of the hope of God's Word. There is no shortage of God's power, just a shortage of people who have taken hold of it by hope and faith. (AW)

MAY 20
LOOK & LIVE
NUMBERS 21:8

"And the LORD said unto Moses, Make thee a fiery serpent, and set it upon a pole: and it shall come to pass, that every one that is bitten, when he looketh upon it, shall live" (Num. 21:8).

Why do we complicate what God has made simple? We often want to construct seven steps to answered prayer, five steps to healing, six levels of faith, or four doors to salvation.

Jesus taught in parables to make difficult teachings simple. He told stories so unlearned multitudes could understand the simplicity of reaching God. Jesus thanked His Father for hiding the profound teachings of Scripture from the naturally wise of this world and revealing them to people of childlike faith (Matt. 11:25).

Throughout the Word, faith is compared to simple functions. In Isaiah 55:1, faith for salvation is compared to eating and drinking. Everyone can eat and drink. It requires little human effort. Moral and immoral, fat and skinny, male and female, educated and uneducated, babies and adults, black and white—people can eat and drink. In other words, salvation is for *whosoever will*. It's religion that adds works to the simple plan of God. We want them to believe in Jesus, but we also want them to give money. This limits salvation to those with means. We also want people to be water baptized and join our church. These things are fine, but in no way make us saved. We are simply to *"taste and see that the Lord is good"* (Ps. 34:8).

To demonstrate how simple divine healing is, Moses commanded the people to look at the brass serpent and they'd be healed. How difficult is it to look? A doctor once told me that the opening of the eyelids requires the least amount of physical effort in the body. What a beautiful picture of faith for healing. Faith is the only thing we can do without doing anything! (BY)

MAY 21
WE DON'T GET WHAT WE DESERVE
1 CORINTHIANS 15:10

"By the grace of God I am what I am" (1 Cor. 15:10).

Pastoring a church can be a very challenging occupation. There are wonderful people in the congregation, but there are also many others who try your patience.

One such lady approached me after a church service and told me how she'd seen me in public not living up to my own preaching. I don't remember exactly what the circumstance was, but I had said something or did something that was contrary to what I had preached in church. She let me know what a hypocrite I was for not living what I preached and that she planned to go to another church that had a more "spiritual" preacher. She ended her reprimand by telling me, "You don't deserve to be in the pulpit!"

I replied, "You're right, I don't deserve to be in the pulpit. And you don't deserve to sit in the congregation either." She was stunned. I continued, "If we hung a sign outside of the church that said 'All Deserving May Enter,' no one could come. We're all here by the grace of God!"

I'm not called into the ministry because I am perfect. God called me as I am because His call is by grace. *"But when it pleased God, who separated me from my mother's womb, and called me by his grace"* (Gal. 1:15). I don't take advantage of God's grace by looking for every opportunity to sin. I strive with everything in me to live a life pleasing to God. But if you followed me around every day, you'd probably find me sinning at times and not living up to God's Word.

I'm not anointed to live it, but I am anointed to teach it. When I leave the pulpit, I must put the same effort into living the Christian life as everyone else. I don't have time to follow my congregation home to see if they're living it or not. I have a full-time job just looking after myself—as do they. The Holy Spirit is the only one who follows each of us home. The one who called us by grace watches over us! (BY)

MAY 22
THE STEWARDSHIP FACTOR
LUKE 12:42-44

"And the Lord said, Who then is that faithful and wise steward, whom his lord shall make ruler over his household, to give them their portion of meat in due season?" (Luke 12:42).

Stewardship is an important factor when talking about prosperity. Start where you are, do what you can, and keep doing it. If you don't take care of what you have, how can God bless you with something better?

Many people are poor stewards. They don't take care of their homes or automobiles. I believe if you're a good steward of what you have and keep it clean, then you're a candidate for God to give you something better. The following testimony of a precious family in our church is a real-life stewardship success story!

"We bought a car back in the '80s and kept it because we don't like car payments. Over time, we put 178,000 miles on it. The window fell down into the door when you tried to use it and the air conditioning had died. When I went to the car wash, I had to stuff a rag in the window to keep from being drenched. I had to keep it washed because I remembered pastor said that you can't expect God to give you something better if you don't take care of what you already have. I really desired a particular kind of station wagon, and I found one that was the exact color I wanted. The dealership did an evaluation on our car, but the bluebook only went back to 1986—ours was an '84. It was only worth $250, but they gave us $500! All this time we had been sowing and trying to work the principles we'd been taught at church. We kept giving because it was the right thing to do and we believed the testimonies that came forth. We also refused discouragement from the Enemy.

"We sowed our car money in a particular Sunday morning offering as the Lord led us. People don't know that. The salesman asked if we could put about $3,000 down. After we got back in the car, my husband prayed. He said, 'Lord, You are no respecter of persons. If You want us to have that car, You're going to have to make a way.' The next day after church, a couple came up to us and said they felt impressed to give us a check. It was for $3,000—the exact amount of the down payment! The salesman was also able to find a company that would finance it for a longer period of time. The payments are what we wanted, and included life insurance too! The car is a 1995 model and has a twelve-month, 12,000 mile bumper-to-bumper warranty, which is unheard of for a used car. God is so good!"

Yes, God is good. Remember, Luke 12:43-44, *"Blessed is that servant, whom his lord when he cometh shall find so doing* [being a good steward]. *Of a truth I say unto you, that he will make him ruler over all that he hath"* (brackets mine). (BN)

MAY 23
BLOOM WHERE YOU'RE PLANTED!
2 KINGS 5:1-14

"And the Syrians had gone out by companies, and had brought away captive out of the land of Israel a little maid; and she waited on Naaman's wife" (2 Kin. 5:2).

The healing of Naaman's leprosy is one of the greatest things the Lord did through Elisha. Yet this never would've happened if it hadn't been for a young servant girl who informed Naaman's wife about God's healing power. Without her speaking out, no miracle would have taken place.

This is especially meaningful when you realize that this young girl was an Israelite who'd been captured during a Syrian raid and taken back to Syria as a slave. The Hebrew word used for *maid* in this verse means "a young girl from the age of infancy to adolescence." This means she certainly wasn't out on her own yet. She was taken from her parents. It's possible that her parents were killed by the Syrians or made slaves themselves. She could've been bitter and chosen not to tell Naaman about God's healing power. Leprosy in those days was considered by many to be God's judgment on sin. She could've thought, *It serves him right!* She could've even been praying for his death as vengeance.

Instead, she showed concern and compassion for her master. Apparently, she'd forgiven him and gotten over any bitterness. This allowed God to use her as an instrument to touch the highest-ranking general in the Syrian army. No doubt, many Syrians came to faith in the Lord because she had moved on with her life.

We can't change the past, but we can affect the future for ourselves and others. Regardless of what situation you find yourself in, bloom where you're planted. It's possible that the very ones you have grievances with would respond to the touch of God if you reach out to them. Give someone God's love today! (AW)

MAY 24
GO ALL THE WAY
2 KINGS 5:1-14

"Then went he down, and dipped himself seven times in Jordan, according to the saying of the man of God: and his flesh came again like unto the flesh of a little child, and he was clean" (2 Kin. 5:14).

Elisha's actions and instructions were strange. What was he trying to accomplish?

For one thing, Naaman hadn't really humbled himself before the Lord yet, which is a very important part of faith. Jesus said that no one can believe who is seeking the honor that comes from men more than the honor that comes from God (John 5:44). Naaman was too impressed with himself. That's why Elisha didn't even bother to go out and see him.

This incensed Naaman. He headed back to Syria in a rage. Elisha hadn't responded to him as his position deserved. Besides, he thought any Syrian river was better than the Jordan in Israel. Naaman definitely had a pride issue, but his servants prevailed on him to give the prophet's instructions a try. Need often drives people to do things they wouldn't otherwise do. So Naaman humbled himself and dipped in the Jordan River.

Nothing happened the first or the second time. His healing didn't come gradually. He was still a leper after dipping six times in the Jordan. But on the seventh time, his flesh was completely restored. Just think: Naaman's pride almost caused him to miss his miracle!

Are there issues of pride in your life that have kept you from doing what God has told you to do? If so, humble yourself and obey. Don't do it halfheartedly. Your deliverance will come when you go all the way! (AW)

MAY 25
PASSIVE & ACTIVE FAITH
MARK 5:24-34, JOHN 5:1-9

"And he said unto her, Daughter, thy faith hath made thee whole; go in peace, and be whole of thy plague" (Mark 5:34).

There's a dramatic contrast between the faith of the woman who had the issue of blood and the man who was lame at the pool of Bethesda. Both desperately wanted to be healed. The man at Bethesda was feeling hopeless because he didn't have anyone to help him into the pool. However, the woman had an active faith that reached out and took God's healing. The woman acted while the man sat and waited. Both were healed, but there was a big difference!

Jesus told the woman that HER faith had made her whole. That's an amazing statement! It wasn't Jesus' faith that produced her miracle, but her faith. This woman was able to receive when Jesus wasn't physically there, because her faith was active. However, the man didn't have the kind of faith that produced on its own. Jesus had to encourage him to get him to believe. Unless this encounter changed him, the man would've had to have someone else encourage him the next time he was in trouble.

An active faith is full of energy and action. It's a faith that's felt so strongly that it compels the individual to act. A passive faith is one that only acts on the encouragement of others. One is dependent on what's happening around them, while the other depends only on God. One's easily discouraged, while the other will not be denied.

Which kind of faith would you rather have? The choice is yours. Both of these individuals were the way they were because of choices. Both were in hopeless situations, but they had totally different responses. Choose to stir up your faith today so that it's active instead of passive! (AW)

MAY 26
FAITH THAT MOVES MOUNTAINS
MATTHEW 21:18-22

"Jesus answered and said unto them, Verily I say unto you, If ye have faith, and doubt not, ye shall not only do this which is done to the fig tree, but also if ye shall say unto this mountain, Be thou removed, and be thou cast into the sea; it shall be done. And all things, whatsoever ye shall ask in prayer, believing, ye shall receive" (Matt. 21:21-22).

What is different about "mountain moving" faith? For one thing, God's kind of faith understands and uses authority. Notice that Jesus said we should speak to the mountain. Most people are praying to God about their mountain, but the Lord said we should speak directly to it. This reflects our God-given authority.

Once I had a toothache that bothered me for two weeks. I prayed and asked God to heal it many times. As I was traveling, I listened to a tape where the minister was talking about speaking to the mountain instead of speaking to God. It dawned on me that I hadn't done that. I hadn't used my authority. I was asking God to do something that He told me to do!

When I got to my hotel, I looked in the mirror, stuck my finger into my mouth, pointed to my tooth and said, "You are healed in the name of Jesus! Pain, leave right now!" In less than ten minutes, all the pain was gone and I never had another problem with that tooth.

"Mountain moving" faith believes that God has already provided healing for us. It speaks directly to the problem (mountain) instead of speaking to God about the problem. Use your God-given authority, and speak to your mountain today. If you believe, it'll move! (AW)

MAY 27
SOME ADULT CONVERSATION
I CORINTHIANS 14:2

"For he that speaketh in an unknown tongue speaketh not unto men, but unto God" (1 Cor. 14:2).

When you speak in tongues in prayer or worship, you speak to God. That's a powerful statement! What could you possibly say to interest the Creator of the universe? For one thing, your mind could have nothing to do with the conversation. When you pray with tongues, your understanding is unfruitful (1 Cor. 14:14). That means the words come directly from your human spirit to God. The Holy Spirit empowers your words and puts you on a conversation level with God Himself!

When I was a child, my mother couldn't wait for me to speak. She wanted to find out what was inside my head. At the proper age, I began to put sentences together and she found out what I was thinking. My vocabulary consisted of cookies, milk, Mickey Mouse, and toys. My mother told me she wanted adult conversation so bad that she would often go to the neighbor's house just to talk on an adult level. My mother was so happy to see my father come home from work each day. She'd talk and talk and talk to him, seeking adult conversation. She was very glad when I grew up enough and learned how to carry on an adult conversation.

What about God? I'm sure He's happy when we approach His throne to ask Him to meet our needs. He's also happy when we come into His presence with praise and worship. But when all of our prayers and praise are in English, He must think they sound a lot like cookies, milk, Mickey Mouse, and toys. He must breathe a sigh of relief when we're filled with the Holy Spirit and begin to speak in tongues. Suddenly, we're talking to God on His level. He must say, "Ahh, some adult conversation!" (BY)

MAY 28
SHUT UP & GET OUT OF THE WAY!
2 KINGS 6:24-7:20

"Then a lord on whose hand the king leaned answered the man of God,
and said, Behold, if the LORD would make windows in heaven,
might this thing be? And he said, Behold, thou shalt see it
with thine eyes, but shalt not eat thereof" (2 Kin. 7:2).

This famine in Samaria was so severe that people were eating dove's dung—and some had even eaten their own children! The king held Elisha responsible because he'd captured the Syrian army but let them go (2 Kin. 6:22-23). The king was intent on killing the prophet, but Elisha gave a prophecy that within twenty-four hours, there would be such abundance that food would be cheap.

One of the king's servants laughed at Elisha's prophecy and basically said that even God couldn't do a miracle like that. Elisha responded by saying that it would happen and the servant would see it but that he wouldn't partake of the blessing because of his unbelief. It came to pass exactly as Elisha prophesied. The miraculous provision took place, but that servant was trampled to death by the people rushing after the food.

It's easy to say that God can do anything, but when push comes to shove, most people don't really believe it. We all have limits that we put on God. Just like this unbelieving servant, our unbelief keeps us from partaking of the miracle.

Ask the Lord to help you take all the limits off what He can do. As you're in the process of increasing what you can believe God for, at least use enough common sense to not speak forth your unbelief. And certainly don't get in the way of those who do believe. They just might trample your unbelief to death. (AW)

MAY 29
HOW LONG WILL YOU KEEP DOING THE SAME THING?
2 KINGS 7:3-11

"There were four leprous men at the entering in of the gate: and they
said one to another, Why sit we here until we die?" (2 Kin. 7:3).

These lepers were in a terrible situation. There was a famine in the city of Samaria because of the Syrian blockade. The situation was so bad that people actually cannibalized their own children. These lepers would certainly be the first ones to die. They were outcasts because of their disease. Since they wouldn't be fed at the expense of others, what were they to do? Something had to change. They decided to go out to the Syrians and ask for mercy. The worst thing that could happen was that they'd be killed.

Many people would call that crazy—they were taking too big a risk. *True insanity is to keep doing the same thing and expect different results.* If things continued as they were, death was certain. These lepers made a wise decision that not only resulted in their own salvation but the deliverance of the entire city.

They had an advantage over other people because they didn't have much of a life. They were cut off from society and were already dead in a sense. These lepers had nothing to lose and no fear of loss. Courage flourishes in the absence of fear!

Are you stuck in a rut? Are you still doing the same thing that hasn't worked in the past but expecting different results? Maybe it's time for you to take a radical step and try something different. What have you got to lose? Probably less than you think. You may fail, but failing to try is the worst failure of all. However, you just might experience a great deliverance like these lepers did. (AW)

MAY 30
HAVE YOU TOLD SOMEONE?
2 KINGS 7:3-11

"Then they said one to another, We do not well: this day is a day of good tidings, and we hold our peace: if we tarry till the morning light, some mischief will come upon us: now therefore come, that we may go and tell the king's household" *(2 Kin. 7:9).*

There are many parallels between this situation and ours today. Just like the people in Samaria, people today are starving to death spiritually. Our own sins have surrounded us and are choking the life out of us. Like the Samaritans who were eating dung and their own children to stay alive, this desperate situation causes many to do things they'd never do otherwise.

Certainly every one of them prayed to God for deliverance. However, when God answered their prayers, they didn't know it immediately. They continued in their hunger and despair for a time when there was an abundance of food just outside the gates.

These four lepers were the ones who discovered their redemption. They rejoiced at their own deliverance but in a short time remembered the others who were still starving. Feeling responsible to share their discovery, they brought the good news back to the city.

These lepers could've kept the news all to themselves. Remember, the people in the city had rejected them. This would've been a great opportunity to get even, but they knew that was the wrong thing to do. People's lives were hanging in the balance.

If you know Jesus and the forgiveness He brings, then you've been delivered from a fate far worse than starvation. Others need to know who and what you know. Don't keep the good news to yourself! (AW)

MAY 31
NONE WALKS THIS WAY ALONE
1 JOHN 3:16-17

"But whoso hath this world's good, and seeth his brother have need, and shutteth up his bowels of compassion from him, how dwelleth the love of God in him?" *(1 John 3:17).*

"There is a law that makes us brothers. None walks this way alone. All that we send into the lives of others comes back into our own." (Anonymous)

Our whole lifestyle is giving—our time, our talent, our words, our thoughts, even kind deeds. I'd rather err on the side of generosity than be stingy. If you think the only time to give is at an offering in church, you've missed it. Look around! There's always somebody who's worse off than you are. Rather than looking at what we think we lack, why not look at how we can bless someone else? If you can't sow money right now, sow time. Find some things in your house, and give them to someone who'd be blessed by them: clothes, pictures from your wall, cleaning supplies. Why not have them over for dinner? Lunch? Sow into someone's marriage. Why not baby-sit a couple's children so they can spend time together? What you have or what you can do will bless somebody.

We need each other. I've said it before and I'll say it again and again: Partners catch more fish. On any given Sunday, there is enough money to meet every need. Calvin Coolidge said it well when he said, "No person was ever honored for what he received. Honor has been the reward for what he gave." (BN)

JUNE 1
OPEN YOUR SPIRITUAL EYES
2 KINGS 6:8-23

***"And he answered, Fear not: for they that be with us are
more than they that be with them"*** *(2 Kin. 6:16).*

This is an amazing statement by Elisha! At that moment, he and his servant were surrounded by thousands of Syrian troops. I'm sure Elisha's servant thought he had finally blown a fuse. How could the prophet say such a thing? Wasn't this a lie? It depends on what you believe about reality.

To those who think that the only truth and reality is what they can see, taste, hear, smell, and feel, then Elisha did lie. That's all there is to it. Those who have this limited vision also think that anyone who believes something to be true when their five senses "prove" it isn't is a liar.

However, there is more to reality than what we can perceive with our peanut brains and its limited capacities. Elisha went on to pray that the Lord would open his servant's eyes. He wasn't talking about his physical sight but was praying for the Lord to let his servant see into the spiritual world. The young man's spiritual eyes were opened and he saw thousands of horses and chariots of fire on the mountains surrounding them.

Elisha wasn't trying to make something that was untrue become true by confessing it. He was speaking truth, but it was a spiritual truth that couldn't be proven by scientific methods. If you include the spiritual realm, there were more with Elisha and his servant than with the Syrian army. If you include the spiritual realm, there's always victory for you in Jesus, regardless of what your physical eyes currently see!

Ask the Lord to open your spiritual eyes today so you can see the awesome provision that has already been made for your every need. If you can see it by faith, you'll eventually see it with your physical eyes too! (AW)

JUNE 2
ARE YOU A PLODDER?
COLOSSIANS 1:7

"Epaphras...who is for you a faithful minister of Christ" *(Col. 1:7).*

Have you ever heard of Epaphras? He was the pastor of the church at Colosse. Let me tell you what's missing in this verse. We are not told the size of his congregation or the number in his youth group. We don't know if he had a cell group program or a traditional Sunday school. This is what churches are known for in our day. We're only told one thing about Epaphras—he was faithful. His name wasn't well known in the ancient world. If Paul hadn't mentioned him, we probably would never have heard of him ourselves. None of this seemed to matter to Epaphras, because he remained faithful.

A faithful person is a plodder. Without a lot of outside inspiration, a plodder keeps moving each day, driven by the Word of God in their heart. We are told we'll reap in due season if we faint not. A plodder is one who will not faint. They never seem to give up. Unlike many others, they don't gain great amounts of ground at one time. Yet, when others have given up and thrown in the towel, the plodder is still going.

Many begin a race. Beginning is easy, but finishing is difficult. Many who begin with a flash will never make it. They bask in the limelight of popularity, but when it fades, so does their stamina. The plodder draws from the wells of inspiration they have in their own heart. They've developed a personal relationship with God and will continue whether anyone stands with them or not. They know that God will never leave nor forsake them.

The important thing is not who starts, but who finishes. Finishing is much more difficult. That's why many are at the starting line, but only a few cross the finish line. God's not so interested in how many begin with Him. He's more interested in how many finish. This is reserved for the plodder. Remember, the one who won the race was the tortoise, not the hare. (BY)

JUNE 3
GOD HAS NEVER HAD ANYONE QUALIFIED WORKING FOR HIM YET!
1 KINGS 19:1-21

***"And after the earthquake a fire; but the LORD was not in the fire:
and after the fire a still small voice"*** *(1 Kin. 19:12).*

Many times we think we have to do everything just right to have God bless us, but the Scriptures certainly don't present that. David sinned greatly, yet he was the man after God's own heart. Moses failed, as did Abram, and just about every other mighty man of God. *The truth is that God hasn't had anyone who was qualified working for Him yet.* It's always by God's grace that He uses any of us!

Take Elijah for example. Here he was in such despair that he asked God to kill him. He thought he was the only one left serving God when the truth was that there were thousands who were faithful to the Lord. He had led a revival just days earlier where the whole nation turned to God. In just that short amount of time, Elijah had slid into self-pity and begged God to let him quit.

The Lord spoke to Elijah in a still small voice and told him to do three things. One was to anoint Elisha to take his place as prophet. That was the last thing the Lord told Elijah to do, but it was the first thing he did. As it turns out, it was also the only thing he did. He never anointed Hazael to be king over Syria nor Jehu to be king over Israel. He simply ignored two-thirds of the things that God had audibly told him to do!

Was that the end of Elijah? No. I think we can safely say that was a turning point, and he never did fulfill God's true potential for his life, but the Lord still used him. Elijah is one of only two people in the Bible who never died. He was actually caught up into heaven in a whirlwind (2 Kin. 2).

Do you think that the Lord is through with you because you've failed Him? Take courage from Elijah. Regardless of your failures, you can still walk with God in a powerful way! (AW)

JUNE 4
GOD HAS AN ECONOMY AND YOU CAN GET IN ON IT!
PSALMS 35:27

***"Let them shout for joy, and be glad, that favour my righteous cause:
yea, let them say continually, Let the LORD be magnified,
which hath pleasure in the prosperity of his servant"*** *(Ps. 35:27).*

A long time ago, before one of our church staff members was on staff, he saw how the Gospel of Jesus Christ changes financial disasters. His wife brought him to the church just two days after he received salvation. He was born again, but his checkbook wasn't. One of the first things he remembers was hearing me say, "God has an economy, and you can get in on it!"

He and his wife began to tithe and they also began to give. He asked, "How can I tithe? I owe thousands and thousands and thousands of dollars to the IRS. I owe bankers and banks, friends, and family." God told him, "Put Me first." They decided to honor the Lord with their finances. He reasoned that if God can save and deliver him, then He can sure take care of a little money—or a lot of money! This man was so under the barrel that anything he got would have to come from God. He figured it up one day and found that he'd have to pay $650 per month until he was seventy years old in order to get out of debt—and he was only thirty-two at the time!

Finally, God told him that if he would get his eyes off of his lack and put them on His abundance, He would get them out of that mess. They purposed to get out of debt and quit spending money. They tithed for two years and it seemed like nothing was happening. When you can't see something happening in the natural, it's happening in the supernatural. He was in the real estate business. God brought him favor and real estate clients in a time when the market was severely hurting. In less than twenty months, God paid off every bit of that debt!

There are things we can do to get in on God's economy. We tithe, we give, and we always put God first. (BN)

JUNE 5
FAITH COMES FROM GOD'S WORD
GENESIS 3:1-6

"Now the serpent was more subtil than any beast of the field which the LORD God had made. And he said unto the woman, Yea, hath God said Ye shall not eat of every tree of the garden?" (Gen. 3:1).

Notice how Satan tempted Adam and Eve. He didn't approach them through a mammoth and try to force them to submit. He had no power or authority against them. His only avenue was deception, so he used the most subtle animal God had created.

The devil initiated the whole temptation by challenging God's Word. That's because faith comes from the Word (Rom. 10:17). There is no other source. Therefore, there's no way we can please God if we don't believe what He says (Heb. 11:6). Our actions are simply the result of what we believe (Prov. 23:7). Satan challenged the authority of God's Word and went right to the source of their faith.

Notice that the serpent spoke to the woman. Adam was there too (verse 6), but the temptation was directed toward Eve. That's because she didn't receive God's command directly. The Lord told Adam not to eat of the tree before Eve was created (Gen. 2:16-18). The woman was more susceptible to doubt because God's Word was secondhand to her. Maybe Adam didn't repeat it exactly. Maybe he misinterpreted God's reasons for denying them access to this tree.

From this example, we learn that God's Word must be believed regardless of the reasons against it. We must personalize what the Lord says through His Word. It's not good enough to say, "Well, Adam said..." We need to meditate on the Scripture until it becomes God's personal Word to us. Adam and Eve would not have sinned if they hadn't disbelieved God's Word. It's the same with us. (AW)

JUNE 6
THE ORIGINAL SIN
GENESIS 3:1-21

"And the serpent said unto the woman, Ye shall not surely die" (Gen. 3:4).

A casual reading of the account of Adam and Eve's transgression would lead you to believe that their sin was eating the forbidden fruit. But that was only the action their sin birthed. Their real sin was unbelief.

Before they ever ate the fruit from the Tree of the Knowledge of Good and Evil, they quit believing God. The Lord told them that if they ate of that tree, they would die, but the serpent told them they wouldn't. They chose to believe the devil and disbelieve God. That was the real sin—they didn't believe God.

Our actions are simply byproducts of what we believe. People act wrong because they believe wrong. No one can consistently act differently than what they believe. Instead of trying to control our actions, our focus should be on controlling our beliefs. Then our actions will follow.

What we focus our attention on is how we affect our beliefs. That's the reason brainwashing works. If a person hears anything long enough, they start to believe it. *"Faith cometh by hearing, and hearing by the word of God"* (Rom. 10:17). Faith doesn't come by having heard, but by present-tense and repeated hearing.

So, if we want to act right, we need to believe right. The way we believe right is to get our brains washed by the cleansing water of God's Word (Eph. 5:26). There is no such thing as being "totally objective." Whatever or whomever we listen to the most is going to control our beliefs. Make sure you're focused on the Lord! (AW)

JUNE 7
TEMPTED JUST LIKE US
HEBREWS 4:15

"For we have not an high priest which cannot be touched with the feeling of our infirmities; but was in all points tempted like as we are, yet without sin" (Heb. 4:15).

Have you ever pondered the temptation of Jesus? How could He really have suffered the temptations that come with marriage when He was never married? How could he have suffered the temptation of drug addiction when He never encountered cocaine? There are many pressures we battle that He never did.

However, God's Word plainly says that Jesus was tempted in all points just like we are. This underscores the truth that our actions ARE NOT where temptation actually takes place. It's in our beliefs that the battle rages. Jesus was tempted to disbelieve God exactly the same as we are, but He never did. The things Satan tempts us with aren't the true issues. All of his devices are simply bait to get us to bite the hook of unbelief.

Too often, the church argues against sin on the basis of the physical consequences it produces. For instance, homosexuality is wrong because of the disease it produces. What if they find a cure for AIDS? Would that mean that homosexuality would no longer be wrong? Of course not!

As bad as the consequences of our actions are, the real root of sin is the rejection of God's Word. This takes place in our hearts long before we act it out. A homosexual rejects the biblical and intuitive truth that God made the first couple male and female. That's the true sin—rejecting the truth—regardless of what does or doesn't happen as a result of our actions.

The conception of sin is unbelief in your heart. Keep your heart pure and in faith with God and you won't have to worry about your actions. (AW)

JUNE 8
WHO ARE YOU?
MATTHEW 4:1-11

"And when the tempter came to him, he said, If thou be the Son of God, command that these stones be made bread" (Matt. 4:3).

The real temptation of Jesus was not to turn the stones into bread but to disbelieve His Father about who He was. Satan said *"If thou be the Son of God,"* then do these things (Matt. 4:3, 6). God had just spoken to Jesus in an audible voice saying, *"This is my beloved Son, in whom I am well pleased"* (Matt. 3:17). Yet the devil wanted Jesus to do something to prove who He was. Satan was trying to move Jesus' faith off of what God said and onto what Jesus could do. The devil was probing Jesus to see if He had any doubt about who He really was.

This may seem amazing to you, but Jesus could have doubted that He was the Son of God. Christ had to increase in wisdom and stature (Luke 2:52). He was Lord at His birth and, in truth, existed before the earth was formed. In fact, He'd actually formed the earth, but His physical body had a beginning and His physical mind was subject to doubt just as ours are.

Jesus accepted by faith that He was God manifest in the flesh. Of course, Joseph and Mary shared with Him the miraculous events of His birth, and no doubt, the Holy Spirit reassured Him in many ways. But the point is that Jesus' physical mind accepted who He was by faith.

Satan tried to deceive Jesus with the same temptation he used on Adam and Eve. He got them to disbelieve what God said about them, and they took the forbidden fruit in order to become more like God. Adam and Eve bit, Jesus didn't. Why? Because He stood in faith on every word of God. Like Jesus, we must live by every word that God has spoken to us. What has the Lord said to you? (AW)

JUNE 9
ARE YOU WORRIED?
MATTHEW 6:25-28

"Take no thought for your life, what ye shall eat, or what ye shall drink, nor yet for your body, what ye shall put on...Behold the fowls of the air...Consider the lilies of the field" (Matt. 6:25-28).

When Christ told us not to worry about the necessities of life, He gave us two examples. Jesus was sitting on a mountain with His disciples and said, *"Behold...Consider."* He said this because birds were overhead and lilies surrounded them. Their object lesson was right in front of their eyes.

Do birds worry? How about flowers, do they fret? No! Birds don't read the paper, watch the news, or look for stock market results. The needs of the birds are always met. Do you ever hear birds flying through the air saying, "I wonder if I'll have enough to eat today"? The birds never knew we had a Great Depression. Only people jump out of windows in panic and fear of what's coming.

Flowers are always dressed nice. They don't wait for the new styles, or become concerned that they're wearing last season's clothes. God provides for them and they don't even have a job. Neither birds nor flowers live in our daily world. As Christians, we're in the world but not of it. We don't live in this world either!

To worry about your food is to put yourself below the level of a bird. To worry about clothing is to put yourself below the level of a flower. People are created superior to plants and animals. Jesus watches over nature, but He didn't die for birds or flowers; He went to the cross for people. He loves nature, but He loves us more.

God will supply for us according to His riches in glory. His supply isn't according to Wall Street or First National Bank. Stock averages can go up and down, but the economy of heaven will never fail! (BY)

JUNE 10
FAITH IS THE ANTIDOTE FOR FEAR
MARK 4:35-41

"And he said unto them, Why are ye so fearful? how is it that ye have no faith?" (Mark 4:40).

Many people today accept fear as just a normal part of life. Notice that Jesus rebuked His disciples for being fearful. He didn't accept it as normal. He wouldn't have reproved them for something beyond their control. We can and should overcome fear!

We don't need to be insensitive to those who are experiencing fear. Since fear torments (1 John 4:18), we should have compassion on them. However, in our efforts to comfort, we don't need to embrace and promote fear as normal. That's not what Jesus did. The "normal" Christian today would've said to the disciples, "That's okay, boys, I know just how you're feeling." Jesus didn't respond that way. The average Christian today is living so far below what God intended that they think a victorious Christian life is abnormal. It's not! God wants us to live lives that are free from fear.

In this instance, Jesus mentioned that the disciples didn't have faith. Faith and fear cannot peacefully coexist. They are enemies and opposing forces. If faith is strong, it'll drown out fear. Those who are ruled by fear are not ruled by faith.

It takes faith to overcome our fears. Specifically, it takes faith in the goodness and faithfulness of God (Gal. 5:6). Only when we can abandon ourselves to Him will we be able to overcome the fears that confront us every day. Do you have fear? If so, find a promise that'll give you victory in that area and believe God! (AW)

JUNE 11
OUR FAITH MUST BE IN GOD
MARK 11:20-26

"And Jesus answering saith unto them, Have faith in God" *(Mark 11:22).*

This verse is often used to teach that we must have faith in our faith. It's true that we need to understand and believe that the faith we have is sufficient to accomplish anything we need from the Lord. But this verse specifically teaches that our faith should be in God, not in our faith.

Our faith has to be in someone other than ourselves or we're simply "New Agers." If our faith is in ourselves or circumstances, we are doomed to fail. When our faith is in God, our faith is potent!

Hebrews 12:2 says we are to look ***"unto Jesus the author and finisher of our faith."*** Faith begins and ends with God. Faith is totally dependent on Him. A person whose faith is truly in God will not find it more difficult to believe for big things and easier to believe for minor problems. Everything is small compared to God's ability. He's limitless. If our faith is in God, then our faith should know no limits.

Is your faith in God? It's easy to tell. Can you believe for anything, or are certain things too big? If your faith is limited, then your faith isn't totally in God. You're still basing too much on yourself and others. When your faith is in God alone, nothing's impossible (Mark 9:23, 10:27).

We can limit God (Ps. 78:41). One of the quickest ways to do that is to make your faith dependent on yourself instead of Him. Take the limits off God by putting your faith totally in Him. It's in His power, ability, and holiness that you should have faith, not in your own. (AW)

JUNE 12
WHAT DO YOU HAVE IN YOUR HAND?
EXODUS 12:11

***"And thus shall ye eat it; with your loins girded, your shoes on your feet,
and your staff in your hand"*** *(Ex. 12:11).*

When something is repeated many times in the Bible, it's for a good reason. The principle of looking to what we have and not to what we don't have is taught over and over again in both the Old Testament and the New. The reason is we repeat the same mistake many times.

It's almost human nature to look at how far we still have to go instead of how far we've come. When I speak to couples with marriage problems, I know the first few months will be the most difficult. Discouragement comes easily when you think of two or three years of work. You won't get out of this situation overnight, but you can come out of it faster than you got into it. There must be an attitude of thankfulness each day for every inch of progress. Every journey begins with the first step. God can multiply one seed into a crop.

When Jesus asked the disciples how much food they had to feed the multitude, they responded with a description of the five loaves and two fishes saying, ***"What are they among so many?"*** (John 6:9). Jesus took those same loaves and fishes, blessed them, and multiplied them.

We need to learn from Jesus, to bless what we have even if it looks small. Only by blessing what we have can it ever be multiplied. Instead of blessing the few who come, many ministers complain about the many who didn't. If you keep cursing the empty seats, the full ones will be empty someday too. People don't want to come to a church where they're rebuked week after week for those who didn't attend.

Your small amount of talent, teaching ability, or money can be much when you bless it and give it to the Lord. With one stick, Moses delivered an entire generation. What can you do in yours? (BY)

JUNE 13
DON'T LOOK BACK!
HEBREWS 11:1-15

"And truly, if they had been mindful of that country from whence they came out, they might have had opportunity to have returned" (Heb. 11:15).

If Abraham and Sarah had been mindful of the country they left, they would've been tempted to return. However, since they weren't mindful of that country, they weren't even tempted to return. What a revelation! Their temptation was linked to their thoughts. You can't be tempted with something you don't think about. Therefore, control your thinking and you can control temptation. Any of us could be powerful men or women of God if we could stop being tempted. By controlling our thinking, we can do just that!

Many people have missed this simple truth. They try to control their actions but don't realize that actions are a direct result of the way they think. They allow themselves the luxury of pondering things they shouldn't, and then when temptation comes, they struggle to remain faithful to God. Often, they wonder why they're so tempted. It's because of their thoughts.

God has called all of us to leave things behind. It may not be a country, but a lifestyle or friends. Maybe there are habits or hobbies the Lord has asked you to lay down. The secret to walking away from them is not dwelling on what you've left behind. Thinking *What if. . .* is a faith killer. We don't need to be looking back; we need to look forward at the things God has promised us!

Don't be mindful of what you've left behind. Take a look ahead through faith at what God is calling you to. You'll find that your positive thoughts will bring you hope instead of temptation. (AW)

JUNE 14
THOUGHTS MUST BE REPLACED
HEBREWS 11:1-16

"But now they desire a better country..." (Heb. 11:16).

You can't get rid of negative thoughts by rebuking them. Unwanted thoughts must be replaced with new ones.

Think of an apple. Now quit thinking of an apple. Rebuke thoughts of an apple. Don't think of an apple in Jesus' name. Refuse to think about apples. Are you still thinking about apples? Of course you are. In that method of trying to control your thoughts, you are mentioning and continuing to focus on apples. That's not the way to get rid of thoughts.

Instead, think about strawberries. See a beautiful plump red strawberry. Think how sweet it would taste. Imagine a whole strawberry patch with all the delicious berries just begging to be picked. Or think about bananas. See a whole bunch of them. Imagine going to some tropical island and picking them yourself. Wouldn't that be great?

If you continue that line of thought, in just a short time, you'll have lost the thoughts about apples. You can only get rid of thoughts by replacing them with other thoughts.

Sometimes our efforts to resist negative or sinful thoughts actually strengthen their hold on us. The better way is to replace them with God thoughts. God thoughts come from His Word. As we read God's Word, His thoughts begin to control our thinking, and soon the negative thoughts are gone.

Abraham found something better to think about than what he left behind. Don't you have something better to think about today? (AW)

JUNE 15
HOW TO BE STRONG IN FAITH
ROMANS 4:16-25

"He staggered not at the promise of God through unbelief;
but was strong in faith, giving glory to God" *(Rom. 4:20).*

Abraham's faith was strong because he gave glory to God. Glorifying and praising God is a vital part of faith. We aren't strong in faith if we aren't praising God.

If someone was believing for a million dollars and it finally came to pass, what do you think their reaction would be? It might differ somewhat from person to person, but there would be some action of praise. It's impossible to imagine the full manifestation of answered prayer without praise being present. So when faith is complete, praise is always present. Likewise, when praise is absent, faith is weak.

Satan always fights against our faith because faith is the victory that overcomes the world (1 John 5:4). He uses circumstances that look opposite to what we're believing for to try to discourage us. The way we stay strong until the manifestation comes is through praise. As Paul put it in Colossians 2:7, we abound in faith with thanksgiving.

Praising God for the answer before we see it makes us stay in the realm of faith. It's only through faith that we can praise God for what we're believing before it comes to pass. Therefore, a commitment to praise God at all times (Ps. 34:1), even in the face of adversity, compels us to stay in faith. Praise makes us focus on what God has promised and not on what the situation looks like.

Let faith be strong in you today by praising God in advance for the manifestation of that for which you are believing. (AW)

JUNE 16
FAITH IS OUR TICKET
ROMANS 5:1-10

"By whom also we have access by faith into this grace wherein we stand,
and rejoice in hope of the glory of God" *(Rom. 5:2).*

God's grace is His ability, available to us on an unearned, undeserved basis. The way we gain access to His grace is through faith. It's not our holiness, but faith that opens the door to grace.

The Greek word translated *access* in verse 2, literally means "admission." Just as a ticket grants us admission into a movie, faith grants us admission into God's grace. Without a ticket, there's no admission into a movie. Without faith, there's no access into God's grace.

In other words, grace comes at a price, but the price isn't our holiness. Jesus paid that price. We don't earn God's grace, but we must believe in order to receive it. God's grace has come to everyone (Titus 2:11), but not everyone benefits from it, because not everyone puts faith in the grace of God.

Some refuse to believe in God's free grace because they're in denial. They deny there is a God or that He intervenes in their affairs. Others believe in a God that wants to bless them, but can't let go of the concept that He'll only give them what they deserve. Both attitudes are unbelief, which stops the grace of God from working in our lives.

The faith that grants us admission into God's grace is the faith that we can't do anything to merit His favor. We simply trust that Jesus has totally paid the price for everything we need and rest in His finished work. That's the ticket! Anything more or anything less won't grant us admission. (AW)

JUNE 17
WHAT DOES FAITH SAY?
ROMANS 10:6-13

"But the righteousness which is of faith speaketh on this wise, Say not in thine heart, Who shall ascend into heaven? (that is, to bring Christ down from above)" (Rom. 10:6).

Faith talks. It's impossible to have faith without expressing it through the words we say. *"Out of the abundance of the heart the mouth speaketh"* (Matt. 12:34). Those who say they are believing God but speak things contrary to what they're believing for are deceived. We can tell what we really believe by listening to the words we speak.

Are you negative? Do you say things like, "I know it'll rain if I wash my car," "I never win anything!" "Nothing ever goes right for me"? All these statements are indicative of believing the wrong thing. Instead of believing you are blessed as the Word of God states (Eph. 1:3), you've let the negative circumstances of life convince you that you're cursed. But if you're a born-again Christian, that's not so!

What should you do if you're negative? Do you change the way you talk so your experiences change? Yes and no. It's true that you will have what you say (Mark 11:23), but it's not that simple. You must say the right things AND believe from your heart that they'll come to pass (Rom. 10:10). It's not enough just to change your talk; you must change what you believe in your heart. If you do that, then what you say will automatically change.

The only way to change your beliefs is to choose to make God's Word the absolute authority in your life. God's Word expresses God's beliefs. As you saturate your thinking with God's Word, His faith becomes your faith, and your mouth will reflect that. What are your words telling you? (AW)

JUNE 18
IF IT ISN'T FAITH, IT'S SIN!
ROMANS 14:16-23

"Whatsoever is not of faith is sin" (Rom. 14:23).

Most people think of sin as breaking some commandment. Although that is sin (1 John 3:4), there's much more to it than that. Sin isn't only the things we do that are wrong, but it's also failing to do the right things that we should. In short, *"Whatsoever is not of faith is sin"* (Rom. 14:23).

Our beliefs drive our actions. *"For as he thinketh in his heart, so is he"* (Prov. 23:7). No one can consistently act contrary to what they believe in their heart. When under pressure or in fear, we may act hypocritically for a short time, but overall, our actions follow our hearts. Therefore, the key to controlling our actions is controlling what we believe in our hearts.

This makes holiness very simple. Instead of being conscious of thousands of dos and don'ts, all we really need is to believe right and we'll act right. Those who are acting contrary to God's Word are believing contrary to God's Word in some way. Adultery is not a hormonal problem; it's a result of not having the same values as God. If we believed the way God does, we'd never violate our marriage covenant.

Sin isn't smart—it's emotional. Changing our thinking, our beliefs, will change our actions. Those who try to act right without believing right are destined for a life of frustration and schizophrenia. The Christian life is not behavior modification but a change of heart. Through the new birth, we've been given a new spirit that is perfect. Our heads are the problem. As we renew our minds, our actions will change automatically. Believe God's Word and let the change begin! (AW)

JUNE 19
FAITH ISN'T SIGHT
2 CORINTHIANS 5:1-9

"For we walk by faith, not by sight" *(2 Cor. 5:7).*

Paul contrasted walking by faith to walking by sight. They are not the same thing! Faith is seeing the unseen. Faith is seeing with our spiritual eyes instead of with our physical ones.

There are all kinds of things that we can't see with our physical eyes. We've come to accept that there are microorganisms everywhere, but we can't see them without a microscope. There are radio and television signals around us at this exact moment, but we can't see or hear them unless we have a machine that receives these signals and rebroadcasts them through a medium we can perceive.

Likewise, there is a real spiritual world that exists beyond our physical sensory ability to perceive. That realm does exist, and we can "see" it by faith. Through the renewing of our minds, we can come to trust what we see by faith more than what we see with our natural eyes. It's just a matter of training.

We've been trained to believe only what we can see, taste, hear, smell, or feel. We have to be retrained to believe what God's Word says regardless of our physical senses. True faith doesn't ignore our senses but isn't limited to them either. Once we begin to access the spiritual realities that are ours in Christ, then the physical world around us will bow its knee to the greater truths of the spiritual world.

Faith perceives what's true in the spiritual realm and makes it true in the physical realm. Decide to walk by faith today! (AW)

JUNE 20
EVERY NEED IS MET IN THE PRESENCE OF GOD
PHILIPPIANS 4:19

***"But my God shall supply all your need according
to his riches in glory by Christ Jesus"*** *(Phil. 4:19).*

No matter what need a person has, no matter what emergency occurs, no matter what the problem is—God is the answer! I can't tell you how many times I've been faced with seemingly impossible situations. I'd get out my prayer towel and get down on my face before the Lord. I'd cry out to God—sometimes all night—but when I got up, I knew in my spirit that I had my answer. God doesn't just make a way where there seems to be no way. He makes a way where there is no way! Nothing's impossible with God!

The Bible tells us in Ephesians 1:18, ***"The eyes of your understanding being enlightened; <u>that ye may know</u> what is the hope of his calling, and what <u>the riches of the glory of his inheritance in the saints</u>"*** (emphasis added). Also, Ephesians 3:16 says, ***"That he would grant you, according to <u>the riches of his glory</u>, to be strengthened with might by his Spirit in the inner man"*** (emphasis added). Colossians 1:27 says, ***"To whom God would make known what is <u>the riches of the glory</u> of this mystery among the Gentiles; which is Christ in you, the hope of glory"*** (emphasis added). The glory is the manifest presence of God. He wants us to know that when we enter into His glory, all the riches of heaven are there to meet our needs.

I've seen people who have struggled and struggled with something with seemingly no results. I've seen those same people come, sit in the glory of God, and in five minutes, the Lord took care of what was impossible for years! Oh, child of God, if you have a need, get into His presence. Look up! Keep your eyes focused on Jesus. Worship Him and you'll see that every need is met in the presence of God. (BN)

JUNE 21
PRESSURE EXPOSED THE CRACK
ROMANS 5:3

"We glory in tribulations...knowing that tribulation worketh patience" (Rom. 5:3).

The Greek word for *worketh* in this verse means "something on the inside working itself to the outside." When we trust God, tribulation causes patience, which is already inside us, to be worked to the outside. Tribulation works out patience. This is why we can glory (rejoice) in tribulations. We know that it's more than just receiving an answer to a problem—we're developing godly character. Long before patience is brought forth in us, the pressure of circumstances brings much more to the surface.

A friend of mine told me a story about a summer job he had between years in college. He worked on the offshore oil rigs in Louisiana. Being a newcomer and a temporary employee, he had the jobs not too many others would take. One of them was testing oil pipe before it was put in use. The oil company didn't fully trust the manufacturer and would test each piece of pipe before putting it below the water in the gulf to handle great amounts of oil flow. To test whether the pipe would handle the oil pressure, my friend would pump in water under great pressure to see if any hidden flaws or cracks were overlooked in production.

Often, when the pressure would reach a few hundred pounds per square inch, a small stream of water would shoot from a section of the pipe. My friend would turn down the pressure, weld the crack and file it smooth. One day, when a stream of water shot from a small crack in a pipe, the Lord said to my friend, "The pressure didn't create the crack, it revealed it."

We often blame Satan for our anger, bitterness, and temper flare-ups. The pressure didn't create the character flaw; it revealed what was already in us. We need to fix the crack, repent, receive forgiveness, and then patience will develop. (BY)

JUNE 22
HOW DETERMINED ARE YOU?
MARK 5:25-34

"When she had heard of Jesus, came in the press behind, and touched his garment" (Mark 5:27).

One of the ingredients of faith is *determination*, which is defined as "the power to make choices, set goals, and to act upon them firmly in spite of opposition or difficulty." This woman was determined. She had already spent years and all of her money on doctors. Yet nothing had helped. She was actually worse. Most people would've just given up by then, but this was one determined lady. She heard of Jesus and knew that she would receive her healing through Him. She found Him, but there was another obstacle: A multitude thronged Him.

The Greek word for *throng* that was used in verse 31 means "to compress, i.e. crowd in on all sides." How would this frail, sickly woman ever make it through the crowd? On top of all this, the woman's issue of blood made her unclean. She wasn't supposed to be in public, because she would defile them. If someone recognized her and revealed her uncleanness, Jewish law allowed the crowd to stone her to death. But she would not be deterred.

She crawled her way through the crowd and touched the hem of Jesus' garment. That's the only way she could've done it. You can't just bend over and touch the hem of someone's garment in a throng of people. She was on her hands and knees. This woman would've done anything to get her healing.

Most people wouldn't do what this lady did. They wouldn't go to all that trouble. They wouldn't put their lives in jeopardy by being in a crowd that might stone them. They wouldn't get on their hands and knees and crawl through a throng of people. And they probably wouldn't get healed either! Most people lack her type of determination.

What stands between you and what you need from the Lord? Make sure it's not your lack of determination. (AW)

JUNE 23
THE LAWS OF FAITH
MARK 5:25-34

"And Jesus, immediately knowing in himself that virtue had gone out of him, turned him about in the press, and said, Who touched my clothes?" (Mark 5:30).

Was it possible that Jesus really didn't know who touched Him? Certainly it was! Jesus was God manifest in the flesh, but His physical mind had to grow in wisdom (Luke 2:52). This means that Jesus had limitations to His physical mind just as we do. It was through His Spirit that He was able to draw on the mind of God just as we do. When the woman didn't come forward on her own, Jesus perceived who she was (Luke 8:47), but this happened after she was healed.

The significance of this is that Jesus didn't size this woman up before virtue went out of Him to heal her. That's the way most people feel God does things: They bring their requests before the Lord and He evaluates them on whether they have enough faith or holiness and so forth. If they pass the test, God heals them. If they don't, their requests are denied. That's not accurate.

God's power is governed by laws. He doesn't make a case-by-case determination of who receives what. He's provided all we need. And if we put His laws in motion, then His power flows. That's what this woman did.

She was determined (Luke 11:5-13, 18:1-8). She also spoke her faith by saying, *"If I may touch but his clothes, I shall be whole"* (Mark 5:28, 11:23-24). She acted on her faith and the power of God flowed (James 2:17).

If you grab a live electrical wire, the electric company doesn't send a special jolt of electricity out to shock you. No! There are laws that make electricity flow. It's not personal. Likewise, there are laws that govern the flow of God's power. Learn what they are, and start receiving from God today! (AW)

JUNE 24
FAITH IS A FEAR KILLER
MARK 4:35-41

"And he said unto them, Why are ye so fearful? how is it that ye have no faith?" (Mark 4:40).

The disciples were in a terrible situation. It was life threatening. It's not like they were wimps. As experienced fishermen who had survived many storms on that very lake, they knew they were truly in a life or death situation. This was serious! Yet Jesus asked them, *"Why are ye so fearful?"*

I'm sure they were shocked. What a question! Who in his right mind wouldn't be fearful? Most of us would agree completely, but Jesus didn't see it that way.

Jesus went on to ask why they didn't have any faith. The implication was that if they had faith in what He had told them, they wouldn't have been fearful. Jesus had said, *"Let us pass over unto the other side"* (verse 35). He didn't say, "Let's get in the boat and drown halfway across." They were in unbelief.

The disciples were overwhelmed with the natural situation. They were drawing on everything they'd learned about the laws of sailing, but they weren't thinking about what Jesus had told them. They were looking for a natural solution when they'd been given a supernatural word from the Creator Himself. They failed to take into account that Jesus was onboard. They had forgotten His words.

Our world accepts fear and faithlessness as normal. If we aren't careful, we will too. However, anything but faith is abnormal from God's perspective. Faith kills fear, just as fear kills faith. They're opposing forces. Choose to make faith the norm for your life. (AW)

JUNE 25
IT'S OUR TURN!
MARK 4:35-41

"And he was in the hinder part of the ship, asleep on a pillow: and they awake him, and say unto him, Master, carest thou not that we perish?" (Mark 4:38).

This was not a genuine question on the disciples' part. It was a criticism and a complaint. These disciples were fighting for their lives and Jesus wasn't doing a thing. It's not like He didn't know what was happening. This was a small open boat that was full of water (verse 37). Jesus had to be aware of the situation. Yet, He was doing nothing. They wanted Him to do something—bail water, row, something!

We, too, sometimes think that the Lord isn't doing His part. We're fighting to survive, yet it seems like our prayers go unanswered. Where's God? Does He care? The answer is always yes.

Jesus had already done His part. He'd taught ten parables that very day on how the Word works when we believe. Then He told His disciples, *"Let us pass over unto the other side"* (verse 35). This was like their pop quiz on what He'd been teaching. He said they were going over, not under. Would they believe His Word or be overcome by the circumstances?

Jesus did His part when He gave them the Word that would take them over to the other side. Their part was to believe that Word and put it to work by acting in faith. They should've stilled the storm or commanded the boat to stay afloat. Instead, they blamed Jesus.

Likewise, we often gripe at the Lord when He has already done His part. He's paid the price and given us the promise. Now we must believe and put the Word to work. It's our turn. Believe God's promises and take control of your impossible situations today. (AW)

JUNE 26
FINANCIAL PROSPERITY IS IN CHRIST'S ATONEMENT
2 CORINTHIANS 8:1-15

"For ye know the grace of our Lord Jesus Christ, that, though he was rich, yet for your sakes he became poor, that ye through his poverty might be rich" (2 Cor. 8:9).

This verse couldn't be any clearer. It's a part of Christ's atonement for us to be financially rich. Yet many Christians persist in their belief that God delights in poverty for His children. That's not true!

The way many people have gotten around the obvious truth of this verse is to say that Jesus came to make us rich spiritually, not materially. But the whole context of this verse deals with money. Jesus died to produce financial prosperity for us. He would no more make us poor than He would make us sin. He died to free us from both sin and poverty. We need to get the same attitude toward poverty that we have toward sin.

There is no doubt that many people have learned lessons as the result of their sins. People have been broken and come to the end of themselves because of their own disobedience. But does that mean the Lord led them into sin? Did God want them to commit adultery so they could learn the value of the mate He'd given them? Certainly not!

Likewise, people can learn things through poverty. They can learn the value of things that money can't buy. But poverty itself is a killer. We should seek to overcome poverty the same way we seek to overcome sin. God put poverty in the same category as sin and redeemed us from it. We should do the same. Those who don't take advantage of the prosperity God has provided aren't taking advantage of the atonement of Christ in its entirety. (AW)

JUNE 27
JESUS GAVE US A BLANK CHECK!
JOHN 16:23-24

"And in that day ye shall ask me nothing. Verily, verily, I say unto you,
Whatsoever ye shall ask the Father in my name, he will give it you.
Hitherto have ye asked nothing in my name: ask, and ye
shall receive, that your joy may be full" (John 16:23-24).

Many believers have a poverty mentality. The Bible says, *"For ye know the grace of our Lord Jesus Christ, that, though he was rich, yet for your sakes he became poor, that ye through his poverty might be rich"* (2 Cor. 8:9). Some would say, "Well, I don't think Jesus would wear fancy clothes like that." No? Even Jesus wore clothes that were so nice that the guards wanted them. His coat was the best available at the time because *"the coat was without seam, woven from the top throughout. They said therefore among themselves, Let us not rend it, but cast lots for it, whose it shall be"* (John 19:23-24).

Jesus told us to ask. Now, if what you want is not in line with God's Word, you have no business asking for it. God won't give you something out of selfish motivation or greed. He won't answer a prayer that involves manipulating the will of someone else—that's witchcraft. But, 1 John 5:14-15 says, *"And this is the confidence that we have in him, that, if we ask any thing according to his will, he heareth us: And if we know that he hear us, whatsoever we ask, we know that we have the petitions that we desired of him."* Hallelujah!

Jesus has given us a blank check. All we must do is sign it. I don't have to live on "Poverty Lane" or "Barely Get By Street." When I want something in line with God's Word, I'll sign my blank check on "Abundant Blessing Boulevard" by asking the Father in Jesus' name, in faith believing, and I know that I'll have the petition that I desire of Him! (BN)

JUNE 28
FAITH TAKES HUMILITY
MATTHEW 15:22-28

"Then Jesus answered and said unto her, O woman, great is thy faith:
be it unto thee even as thou wilt. And her daughter was made whole
from that very hour" (Matt. 15:28).

This is an interesting portion of Scripture. We see Jesus speaking to this woman in a way that He didn't speak to anyone else. It appears rude at least and mean at worst. Yet, in the end, He seemingly changes and compliments her on her great faith. What was happening?

Jesus wasn't sent to the Gentiles during His earthly ministry. That would come after His resurrection. During His brief ministry on earth, Jesus was sent to fulfill God's covenant to the Jews. This woman was a foreigner. She wasn't an Israelite, so she wasn't in covenant with God. Therefore, she had no right to receive deliverance for her daughter.

All Jesus was doing was bringing this woman to the place where she realized that the miracle she sought was not deserved. He compared her to a dog. Any proud person would've been offended, but it didn't deter her. She said even dogs are given scraps.

Jesus responded by saying that this woman had great faith. What made her faith so great? For one thing, she wasn't arrogant. She didn't claim any virtue of her own as the reason why God should deliver her daughter. Her faith was 100 percent in the mercy of God and not in any goodness of her own.

Our own goodness often gets in the way. We feel that God owes us something. He doesn't owe us anything. The faith that gets results is a humble faith that only trusts in God's goodness, not God's justice. (AW)

JUNE 29
AN ATTITUDE OF WILLINGNESS
EXODUS 35:29

"The children of Israel brought a willing offering unto the LORD, every man and woman, whose heart made them willing to bring for all manner of work, which the LORD had commanded to be made by the hand of Moses" (Ex. 35:29).

Above the amount that a person gives in an offering, the Lord is looking for the right attitude behind the giving. Willingness is the heart condition God wants. Moses requested that no one bring an offering unless they were willing to do so (Ex. 35:4-5). The offerings were so great for the building of the tabernacle that Moses had to tell the people to stop giving.

God's desire for willingness hasn't changed in the New Testament. Paul told of the willingness of the Macedonian believers to give toward the need of the saints at Jerusalem (2 Cor. 8:3). He told of the same dilemma that Moses faced. So much money came in for the saints' needs that Paul had to constrain the Macedonians not to give any more (2 Cor. 8:4). Imagine a church service today in which the offering is so large that the pastor asks the people to stop giving. More than enough is received, yet the congregation compels the pastor to continue receiving their gifts. This is the power of willingness!

It's not only obedient giving that brings financial prosperity, but the attitude of willingness that backs it. *"If ye be willing and obedient, ye shall eat the good of the land"* (Is. 1:19).

Your heart can be made willing through studying the promises of God, prayer, and an openness to the Holy Spirit. Openness means looking for opportunities to sow. When you go to a church service, seminar, or evangelistic meeting, take your checkbook with you. During the meeting, be open to the Holy Spirit as to what to give. If He doesn't speak to you something specific, purpose in your own heart what you will give, and the Holy Spirit will bless and multiply it (2 Cor. 9:7, 10). (BY)

JUNE 30
PETER'S FAITH DIDN'T FAIL
LUKE 22:31-61

"But I have prayed for thee, that thy faith fail not: and when thou art converted, strengthen thy brethren" (Luke 22:32).

Jesus informed Peter that Satan desired to have him so he could sift him as wheat (verse 31). We know through Scripture that later that night, Peter denied knowing Jesus three times (Luke 22:54-62). It looked like the devil succeeded. However, Jesus said, *"I have prayed for thee, that thy faith fail not."* What's the deal? Did Jesus pray a prayer that wasn't answered? Certainly not!

In this verse, Jesus also spoke of what Peter should do when he was converted. Therefore, Christ foresaw Peter's denial. Yet He prayed that his faith wouldn't fail, and it didn't. It's possible to fail in our actions but not fail in our hearts.

That night, Peter said he would follow Jesus to the death (verse 33), and proved it by trying to defend the Lord against the Roman soldiers who came to arrest Him (Luke 22:50-51). This was a suicide mission. If Jesus had not intervened, Peter would've been killed. Peter's heart was committed to Jesus.

Just like many of us, Peter was unprepared for the spiritual battle he encountered. If the war would have been in the physical realm, with fists and swords, Peter would've fought to the death. But he didn't know how to stand spiritually. Peter failed in his actions, but not in his heart. He proved this by the remorse he experienced after seeing Jesus turn and look at him (Luke 22:61).

Maybe you have failed the Lord some way in your actions. Jesus has prayed for you that your faith would not fail. You can get up again, and if the result is success, then you aren't a failure even though you may have failed. (AW)

JULY 1
WHAT DID THEY DOUBT?
GENESIS 3:1-13

"For God doth know that in the day ye eat thereof, then your eyes shall be opened, and ye shall be as gods, knowing good and evil" (Gen. 3:5).

Adam and Eve's sin was unbelief. Eating the forbidden fruit was just the action that expressed the unbelief that was already present in their hearts. What did they doubt? There were two things that the serpent seduced them into disbelieving.

First, they doubted God's word about what the consequences would be if they ate from the tree of the knowledge of good and evil. God said they would die. Obviously, when they chose to eat of the fruit, they no longer believed that. So they doubted God's word. There would not have been any action of sin if they had refused to doubt what God said.

Even more important, Adam and Eve doubted God's love for them. The devil accused God of not wanting what was best for them. Satan said God was denying them something that would make them better. This was a direct attack on God's love and integrity. The Lord had been wonderful to them. He provided everything for them and even visited with them every day in the cool of the evening. However, Adam and Eve chose to doubt God's love. They took the word of a talking snake over the word of God.

Likewise, it's illogical for us to ever doubt God's love. We now have a revelation of just how far God's love extends that Adam and Eve never had. Yet, we worry about whether our needs will be met and our bodies healed. We try to justify these worries by saying that everyone has them. "They're just normal." They are only normal for people who don't know God's great love. When we receive a full revelation of God's love, our doubts will vanish. (AW)

JULY 2
HOW DO YOU FEEL ABOUT MONEY?
1 TIMOTHY 6:1-11

"For the love of money is the root of all evil: which while some coveted after, they have erred from the faith, and pierced themselves through with many sorrows" (1 Tim. 6:10).

Money isn't the root of all evil. It's the love of money that is. Many people who have very little have a greater love and lust for money than others who have lots. The amount of money one has isn't the issue; it's the attitude one has toward money that Paul is warning against.

If money itself were evil, then we would all be in trouble, because we all need money to exist. Having just enough evil to survive wouldn't be any better than having lots. Money is not evil, and those who have less money aren't any holier than those who are rich. Money is amoral. That is, it's neither good nor bad. It's the person's attitude who has the money that determines how its power is used—either for good or bad. A twenty-dollar bill can be a blessing or a bribe. The money can't determine that. It's the holder of the money that directs its power.

Money is like food. We must eat to exist. But an abnormal desire to eat will kill us. So will an abnormal love for money and what it can produce. But on the other extreme, a hatred for food will also lead to death. It takes a certain amount of food to keep us healthy and alive. It also takes a certain amount of money to keep us going. It takes even more money to allow us to be the blessings God wants us to be. There is a right amount of food for each of us, and a right amount of money also.

Do you have enough money to do all the Lord wants you to do? If not, increase your hope today, and get ready to prosper! (AW)

JULY 3
TRUE PROSPERITY ISN'T SELFISH
2 CORINTHIANS 9:1-15

"And God is able to make all grace abound toward you; that ye, always having all sufficiency in all things, may abound to every good work" (2 Cor. 9:8).

Most Christians who oppose financial prosperity do so because they equate it with greed. There's no doubt that many Christians err in this regard. The love of money is the root of all evil (1 Tim. 6:10), but true prosperity as the Bible teaches it isn't selfish. As this verse says, the Lord prospers us so we can have enough to give to every good work. Those who are unable to give to everything they would like haven't yet reached the level of prosperity that God has provided for them.

Another verse that makes this point is Ephesians 4:28, which says, *"Let him that stole steal no more: but rather let him labour, working with his hands the thing which is good, that he may have to give to him that needeth."* God prospers us so that we can bless others. Therefore, the individual with the biblical concept of prosperity isn't selfish at all. They want to prosper so they can be a blessing to others. And as the money flows through, there's always plenty for you!

The person who says "I have enough. I would never ask God for any more" shows that they think prosperity is for them. With that attitude, it would be selfish to believe for more money. But once you see that prosperity isn't only for you but so you can be a channel of God's supply to others, then this "I have enough" attitude becomes selfish.

What's your reason for wanting to prosper? Is it all for selfish gain, or do you want to be a blessing to others? If God can get it through you, He'll get it to you. (AW)

JULY 4
TITHING IS PUTTING GOD FIRST
DEUTERONOMY 14:22

"Thou shalt truly tithe all the increase of thy seed, that the field bringeth forth year by year" (Deut. 14:22).

Many people read about tithing and use the excuse, "Yeah, but that was Old Testament stuff." Jesus said Himself in Luke 11:42, *"But woe unto you, Pharisees! for ye tithe mint and rue and all manner of herbs, and pass over judgment and the love of God: these ought ye to have done, and not to leave the other undone"* (emphasis added). He wasn't saying that the New Testament was coming and that nobody should tithe anymore. Nothing could be further from the truth. It's a spiritual principle. He specifically said, *"These ought ye to have done."* When we put God first, all of our needs will be met. *"But seek ye first the kingdom of God, and his righteousness; and all these things shall be added unto you"* (Matt. 6:33, emphasis added). No man is really consecrated until his money is dedicated.

The tithe wasn't instituted so that God could get our money or as a payoff to get something out of Him that He didn't want to give us; it was designed as a vehicle to get the blessings of God to us so we could be blessed. When we tithe, we're showing the world, the devil, the Lord, and even ourselves that God is first in our lives—in every aspect. When you are faithful in tithing, it shows that you have victory over greed. It shows that you have understanding of spiritual things.

The tithe is God's. It's holy to Him and belongs to Him. But it's only a starting point. When we can, we should be faithful to give above and beyond that in offerings. But the tithe is the start. If you want your business to be successful, make faithful tithing your business! (BN)

JULY 5
MOTIVATION
1 CORINTHIANS 13:1-3

"And though I bestow all my goods to feed the poor, and though I give my body to be burned, and have not charity, it profiteth me nothing" *(1 Cor. 13:3).*

Man views things on the surface, while God looks at the heart (1 Sam. 16:7). In the Lord's eyes, the motives behind our actions are more important than the actions. Quite possibly, the greatest illustration of this is in the area of giving.

This verse says that if we give 100 percent of our resources to the poor but we aren't motivated by love, it profits us nothing. Then Paul said that if we make the ultimate sacrifice of giving our lives for another but do it with the wrong motive, it's a waste. Giving must be from the heart with a self-less motive to get the desired results.

The proper motivation for giving comes when we understand why God wants us to give. Is it because He needs our money? It's often presented that way, but in reality, God doesn't need our money. However, He does desire us to trust Him in every area of our lives, which includes our money. Giving is the way we express our faith in God as the source of our prosperity.

If God wasn't real and His promise of multiplying back to us what we give to Him wasn't true, then giving away a portion of what we have would be stupid. However, God is real, His Word is true, and giving shows faith that He will fulfill His promise. So, the real reason God wants us to give is so that we can walk in faith with Him concerning our finances.

Anyone who says "I'll give when I can" is saying "I'll give when I don't have to believe God." They've missed the whole point. God wants us to trust Him. Express your absolute faith in God today by being a cheerful giver. (AW)

JULY 6
FAITH WITHOUT LOVE IS NOTHING
1 CORINTHIANS 13:1-13

"And though I have all faith, so that I could remove mountains, and have not charity, I am nothing" *(1 Cor. 13:2).*

Faith is a powerful force. Faith is our victory that overcomes the world (1 John 5:4). Without faith it is impossible to please God (Heb. 11:6). All things are possible to those who believe (Mark 9:23). However, faith is not the greatest distinguishing characteristic of a Christian—love is (1 Cor. 13:13). If we develop our faith to the point that we can move mountains, but don't do it motivated by God's kind of love, we are nothing.

A gun can be a beneficial thing, but it depends on how it's used. Putting a weapon like a gun in the hands of a child is irresponsible. There needs to be maturity and character in the person using it, or the results can be disastrous.

Likewise, faith is dangerous. Misused faith can kill us, or others. Many people have died over arguments of faith. Wars have been fought and terrible atrocities done in the name of faith. God's kind of faith is always tempered with agape love. Galatians 5:6 says that faith works by love. If godly love isn't present, then it's not true biblical faith.

False faith leads to spiritual pride, which in turn is the ONLY source of contention (Prov. 13:10). We must never let our faith become a club to beat others with. Godly faith is for the purpose of experiencing His love and making that love known to others.

Give yourself a checkup from the neck up, and make sure the motive behind your faith is God's kind of love. God's kind of love gives birth to God's kind of faith. (AW)

JULY 7
WRAPPED IN GOD'S LOVE
MATTHEW 24:1-13

"And because iniquity shall abound, the love of many shall wax cold" (Matt. 24:12).

I went through some trying times in Vietnam. Aside from the pressures every soldier experiences in war, I was fighting a war of another kind. I had lived a very sheltered life, and suddenly, I was thrust into the midst of a world full of temptation and sin that I never knew existed. Iniquity truly abounded.

Yet, my love for the Lord was at an all-time high, while my situation was at an all-time low. The abundance of iniquity doesn't have to make our love for the Lord cool off. I was being driven closer to Him because of choices I made.

One night, while on bunker guard, I was shivering because of the cold. I was wet and chilled to the bone. As soon as my watch was over, I went inside the bunker, wrapped up in a blanket and began to feel the warmth come back into my body. It was a wonderful feeling that I still remember.

I also remember praying a prayer. I compared the chill to the sin that was all around me. Without protection anyone would get cold, but if the Lord would wrap me in His love like I was wrapped in that blanket, I knew I could make it.

Iniquity is sending a chill through our society today as never before. Unprotected, anyone's love for the Lord will grow cold, but that doesn't have to happen. You can dress for the weather. A little extra time in the arms of the Lord will warm your heart so that instead of your love growing cold, you'll melt the hardened hearts of those around you. (AW)

JULY 8
LOVE HOLDS EVERYTHING TOGETHER
COLOSSIANS 3:12-17

"And above all these things put on charity, which is the bond of perfectness" (Col. 3:14).

There are many virtues necessary to live a productive Christian life. Colossians 3:12-13 lists some of them such as mercy, kindness, humility, meekness, long-suffering, forbearance, and forgiveness. Others could be added to this list, such as faith, hope, and love.

There's so much change that needs to take place in our lives that sometimes we can get overwhelmed. Is there a way to prioritize these things? Or is there one key that unlocks all these doors? The answer is an emphatic YES! Love is the key. All these virtues are simply an outgrowth of God's kind of love. Make loving God your focus and all these virtues will naturally follow.

This verse says that love is the bond of perfection. The NIV translates this as, *"And over all these virtues put on love, which binds them all together in perfect unity."* Love is like the spiritual glue or mortar that takes all the different elements of the Christian life and cements them together. Held together by God's love, they have strength. Without love, these virtues will crumble like bricks without mortar stacked on a building.

Knowing God's love for you will cause you to express God's love toward others through mercy, kindness, humility, etc. People who lack these traits in their dealings with others, lack understanding of God's love for them. You can't give away what you don't have. Instead of beating yourself up for what you aren't doing, seek a revelation of what God has already done for you. When that comes, so will all these virtues. (AW)

JULY 9
NO FARMER EVER HARVESTED WHAT HE INTENDED TO SOW
ECCLESIASTES 11:4

"He that observeth the wind shall not sow;
and he that regardeth the clouds shall not reap" (Eccl. 11:4).

Excuses. It's often said that the road to hell is paved with good intentions. But good intentions never paid a bill, and they certainly never blessed anyone. No farmer has ever reaped a harvest on seed that he intended to sow. Can you imagine a farmer saying, "Nope, I don't believe I'll go out and plant this corn today. It looks like it might rain a bit and I sure don't want to get my new John Deere wet"? So he tosses the seed in a barn someplace. Come harvest time, what do you think that farmer will find in his fields? Nothing. If you don't plant seed, you can't expect a harvest.

"In the morning sow thy seed, and in the evening withhold not thine hand: for thou knowest not whether shall prosper, either this or that, or whether they both shall be alike good" (Eccl. 11:6). It's our job to sow seed. Whenever you have the opportunity, whenever you can, put some seed in good ground. If you want to prosper, don't just scatter your seed to the wind, and don't hoard it. Sow it in faith, believing. If you sit on your sack of seed, the only thing you'll get is a seed-sack sofa! (BN)

JULY 10
FAITH BRINGS UNDERSTANDING
HEBREWS 11:1-3

"Through faith we understand that the worlds were framed by the word of God, so that things which are seen were not made of things which do appear" (Heb. 11:3).

In the Dark Ages, the church demanded acceptance of all its commandments and beliefs without any explanation or justification. The infallibility of the pope left no room for error. This led to terrible situations both inside and outside the church. Science was despised and many scientists were persecuted.

Then came the Reformation, the Renaissance, and the Age of Enlightenment. The world was found to be round instead of flat. Many things that the church had pronounced as plagues from God were found to be the result of viruses and unsanitary living conditions. Many "God"-imposed limitations were found to be only limitations placed on people due to ignorance.

This caused a total shift in people's thinking, from a blind faith in religion to an age of reasoning where they scoffed at faith. No doubt, this liberated us from many of the misconceptions and errors of false religion, but it also left modern man void of simple faith.

The author of Hebrews says that some things can only be understood through faith. God did not deem it necessary to explain everything to us. He is greater and more complex than we can understand with our peanut brain. It's impossible to figure out Him and His ways completely. We must have faith in God.

In this day of technology, the need for faith is greater than ever before—not a blind faith that leads to superstition, but an educated faith that is schooled in God's Word. Faith is not mindless; it just acknowledges that there is a dimension of spiritual realities that we cannot examine in a test tube. The only way we'll ever truly understand them is to believe God's Word. (AW)

JULY 11
HOPELESSNESS CAUSES DEPRESSION
PSALM 42:1-43:5

"Why art thou cast down, O my soul? and why art thou disquieted within me? hope in God: for I shall yet praise him, who is the health of my countenance, and my God" (Ps. 43:5).

In Psalm 42 and 43, the psalmist asks the question three times, "Why are you cast down, O my soul? And why are you disquieted within me?" That's a really good question. People still ask this question today, but very few come up with the right answer.

Today, people blame depression on circumstances or chemical reactions in the body. That's not what these scriptures say. These verses make it clear that depression is caused by a lack of hope. Our circumstances don't make us depressed unless we allow them to steal away our hope. The chemical reactions in our bodies are the result of depression, not the cause.

Hope and depression are opposites. Where there's hope, depression can't exist. Where there's depression, hope doesn't exist. Therefore, maintaining hope is essential to having positive emotions.

Life constantly wars against hope. Life is a terminal experience. The only way to have true hope is to be more influenced by God than by experiences. Our God is the God of all hope (Rom. 15:13). There's a promise of victory in the Word of God for every negative experience we will ever encounter in life. Hope is available. We just need to take advantage of it.

Hope comes from God through His Word (Rom. 15:4). Therefore, constantly meditating on God's Word is the way to have hope and beat depression. Fire up hope and watch depression melt away! (AW)

JULY 12
NO ONE HAS AN EXCUSE
ROMANS 1:18-20

"For the invisible things of him from the creation of the world are clearly seen, being understood by the things that are made, even his eternal power and Godhead; so that they are without excuse" (Rom. 1:20).

When I was in Vietnam, I often drove past an ancient temple that always caught my attention. The jungle was beginning to overtake it as trees grew out of the bricks in the top and sides of the structure. The thing that intrigued me was that this temple was three separate buildings, yet one. Each building was about three stories high and separated by only a few inches.

I asked around and found out that this was indeed a temple to a deity that was one God but manifest in three personalities. Amazing! And this temple predated the introduction of Christianity to Vietnam by nearly 500 years. This is a vivid illustration of the above scripture.

The Lord put an intuitive knowledge of Himself inside every person who has ever walked on the earth. Even His Godhead is known by His creation. That's what this temple reflected. In the later verses of Romans 1, Paul speaks of how mankind perverted this knowledge and went into idolatry and other perversions. I'm not saying that these people were worshipping the one true God that we know, but it does verify that they had a kernel of truth that could only have come from Him.

Therefore, those who have never heard a clear presentation of the Gospel of Jesus Christ aren't off the hook. Although they won't be held accountable for what they don't know, they have a built-in homing device for God and will have to give an account of what they did with that knowledge. As you minister to others, remember that God has already shown them the truth in their hearts. (AW)

JULY 13
FAITH IS A HEART ISSUE
ROMANS 10:8-17

"For with the heart man believeth unto righteousness" (Rom. 10:10).

I encountered a few people in Vietnam who claimed to be atheists. They argued with me that they had no doubt in their hearts about their stand. They felt no conviction from God. They were sure there was no God. Yet when the bullets started flying, these same men cried out to God at the top of their lungs. Truly, there are no atheists in foxholes.

It's only a mind game that some people get into that embraces the concept of atheism or agnosticism. No one truly believes that in their heart. The Scripture proves this in Romans 1:18-20. Therefore, when witnessing to a professed atheist, there's no need to discuss the existence of God. They know better. Just use the Word, and trust that the Holy Spirit will bear witness to the truth.

You may think, *But they don't believe in God or the Bible.* That doesn't matter. You don't have to believe in a sword to get killed by one. The Word is a sword (Eph. 6:17) and it will work regardless of what they say they believe, if you'll use it in faith. You must count on the Lord to deal with their hearts.

It's with the heart that man believes. Faith is not a head issue, but a heart issue. If we get sidetracked from speaking to a person's heart, we lose the convicting power of the Holy Spirit. The Holy Spirit works on hearts, but that doesn't mean that faith doesn't make sense—it's the ultimate wisdom. However, faith will always be a heart issue. No one will ever be argued into accepting the Lord.

God called us to be witnesses, not judges or the jury. Just tell people what God has done for you, and let the Holy Spirit do His job. He'll draw all men unto Jesus through working on their hearts. (AW)

JULY 14
THE POWER OF EXPERIENCE
JOHN 9:1-38

"He answered and said, Whether he be a sinner or no, I know not: one thing I know, that, whereas I was blind, now I see" (John 9:25).

In Vietnam I held a Bible study with about seven or eight men. Everything was going well until a man who claimed to be an atheist showed up. He was a Princeton intellectual who tore me to shreds. He made me look like a fool for believing in God. The whole group left with him as they laughed at me.

Thirty minutes later, I was still sitting there wondering what I could've done differently, when this same atheist walked back into the chapel and sat down. I prayed and asked the Lord to give me another chance. To my amazement, he came over and gave me the shock of my life.

He told me he wanted what I had. I couldn't believe it! I said, "You out-argued me. You made me look like a fool, yet you want what I have?" He explained that his whole life was based on an argument. If someone would have out-argued him the way he did me, he would've killed himself. He saw that I had something stronger than an argument. I had faith that came from a personal experience with God. He wanted that. I learned firsthand that a man with an experience is never at the mercy of a man with an argument.

The blind man whom Jesus healed didn't have any theological training, yet his experience with Jesus gave him a better understanding of God than the Pharisees had. He didn't know everything, but he couldn't be talked out of what he did know. His assurance convicted all the theologians who were present.

If you've experienced the love of God, you're an expert. Regardless of what arguments others may offer, your experience is a stronger witness. Be bold and show others the way today! (AW)

JULY 15
PROFILE OF AN AMBASSADOR
2 CORINTHIANS 5:20

"Now then we are ambassadors for Christ" *(2 Cor. 5:20).*

First, an ambassador is a high-ranking minister of state, often chosen from a royal family, sent to another country to represent their own nation.

We are all members of the royal family of God. There is no higher family in the universe and no greater royalty than God's family. We are chosen from the best family to represent the Lord Jesus on earth.

Second, an ambassador doesn't become a citizen of the country in which they are living, but remains a citizen of the country they came from. Philippians 3:20 (NIV) says, **"Our citizenship is in heaven."** The moment we were born again, our citizenship was changed from this world to heaven. We are truly in this world, but not of it. When Satan tries to put the sickness, disease, and poverty of this world on us, we can claim diplomatic immunity.

Third, an ambassador's needs are not met by the economy of the country they are in, but by the country they are from. An ambassador doesn't care if the economy of the country they are in collapses, because their needs are supplied from their home country. Our needs are not supplied by Wall Street, or the First National Bank, but by God's riches in glory. Just like God supplies for the birds (Matt. 6:25-26), He supplies for us. Birds aren't concerned about the stock averages. They didn't even know the Depression occurred. They ate just as well. So can we!

Fourth, ambassadors do not live under the laws of the country they are in, but live by the laws of the country they are from. Our laws are written in the Word of God. The only way we can be put under the laws of the world is to be ignorant of God's promises. Satan can only deceive us when we are ignorant of who we are in Christ and what our privileges are. (BY)

JULY 16
WHAT'S IN YOUR HAND?
1 PETER 5:5-11

"Casting all your care upon him; for he careth for you" *(1 Pet. 5:7).*

My youngest son was almost three before he talked. There was nothing wrong with him; he was smarter than the rest of us. Why should he talk when he had three people who got him whatever he wanted with only a point and a grunt? This had to change!

So one day, coming out of a restroom, he tried to open the door, but the spring was too tight for him to do so. He looked at me and grunted, but I told him he would have to talk before I opened the door. He refused and wouldn't let go of the door handle. Others were waiting to get out, and I needed to open the door, but I would've had to squeeze Peter's hand to get the door open. I had to get him to let go of the door before I could open it.

I had no sooner done that, when the Lord spoke to me and said, "That's the way it is with you. You have your problems so tight in your little hands that I can't do anything about them until you let go." Wow! I instantly knew what He was talking about.

I had cares about finances for the ministry. I was thinking day and night about what I could do to turn the situation around. I hadn't cast my care on Him. I was still holding it tight in my little hands. I figuratively opened my hands and said, "Lord, I give this problem to You. You open the door." He did, of course, and our needs were supplied.

Are you keeping the Lord from intervening in your situation because you have such a tight grip on the problem? Let it go by casting all your care upon Him because He cares for you. He can handle your problems better than you can! (AW)

JULY 17
PUT GOD'S NEEDS FIRST!
MATTHEW 6:24-34

**"But seek ye first the kingdom of God, and his righteousness;
and all these things shall be added unto you"** *(Matt. 6:33)*.

The main principle expounded here is that we can't do two things effectively at the same time (verses 24-25). Our true strength lies in being single-minded. But how can we keep from being focused on providing the basics of life for ourselves and our families? Jesus gave us the promise that if we put His kingdom first, then God the Father will provide for our needs. It's that simple!

Because it's so easy to get caught up in a lust for money and what it can provide, the Lord gave us a better system. We should use our jobs and other revenue producing abilities to first and foremost advance the kingdom of God. If we do that, then the Lord will make sure that our needs are met. We can literally live to give instead of living to get and just give occasionally. Giving can be our focus.

How do you know if you're seeking first the kingdom of God with your money? One sure way to tell is in your giving. Do you give a tithe and offerings first, before paying bills and fulfilling personal wants, or do you first take care of your needs and give what's left over? That's not putting first the kingdom of God.

Someone may say, "I don't have any extra." But you do have God's promise. He promises that if you put His kingdom first, He'll provide these other things. You may not be able to see this, but that's why we call it faith. If you honor the Lord first with your money from a true heart, God will make miracles and blessings come your way. You won't be without. That's His promise. (AW)

JULY 18
HOW DOES FAITH INCREASE?
LUKE 17:5-10

"And the apostles said unto the Lord, Increase our faith" *(Luke 17:5)*.

In the above verse, the apostles requested the same thing from Jesus that millions of Christians ask for today. They wanted more faith. Jesus stunned them with His answer, just as the truth about faith stuns people today.

We don't need more faith! The faith every Christian has is sufficient to uproot a tree and cast it into the ocean if they would just use it. The solution isn't getting more faith, but simply using what we have (verse 6).

Jesus went on to counter a wrong attitude that most people have about faith. Faith must be viewed as a slave. Slaves do what they are told. Masters don't request slaves to work; they make them work. That's the way we should view faith. Faith is something we can command; it's our slave. We don't have to passively hope or request faith to work. We take control and command it!

The reason the disciples didn't see their faith work harder for them was because they hadn't demanded more from their faith. They thought believing for miracles was so hard, it took more faith than what they had. That's not true for them or us. We've underestimated our slave. We've thought we needed many slaves when the truth is this slave (faith) is so powerful, it can accomplish whatever we demand of it.

Our world doesn't understand the power of faith, and sadly, neither do many Christians. We know our faith works, but we've incorrectly thought that our needs are larger than our faith. Put your faith to work, and don't let it rest until it gets the job done. You'll be blessed by what it can do. (AW)

JULY 19
YOUR "LITTLE BIT" CAN FEED A MULTITUDE!
MARK 6:41-44

"And they did all eat, and were filled" *(Mark 6:42).*

Most people are familiar with this account in the life of Jesus. In John 6:9, we found out that it was a little boy's sack lunch that fed the multitudes: ***"There is a lad here, which hath five barley loaves, and two small fishes: but what are they among so many?"*** Jesus was out teaching a multitude of people—five thousand men, not including women and children (Matt. 14:21). It had been a long time since anyone had eaten. The disciples wanted Jesus to send the people away so they could go try to find some food. But that wasn't what He had in mind. Jesus had compassion on the multitude. ***"But Jesus said unto them, They need not depart; give ye them to eat"*** (Matt. 14:16). He took what the little boy offered out of love and multiplied it to feed a huge crowd. ***"And they took up twelve baskets full of the fragments, and of the fishes"*** (Mark 6:43). They had enough to go around and more to spare. Our God is able to do exceeding abundantly above all that we ask or think, according to His power that works in us (Eph. 3:20). Don't look at your insufficiency—look to God's all-sufficiency!

This isn't the only time we see Jesus feeding a multitude in Scripture. Again, in Matthew 15, thousands crowded around Jesus to hear the Word of the Lord. Those people were so hungry for God that in three days time, they didn't budge, not even to eat. (Many Sunday morning churchgoers could take a lesson from that!) Again, the disciples looked at their lack and wanted to send the people on their way to fend for themselves. And, once again, Jesus having compassion on these people said, ***"They continue with me now three days, and have nothing to eat: and I will not send them away fasting, lest they faint in the way"*** (Matt. 15:32). He took the little bit they had and multiplied it so all four thousand men (plus women and children) were completely satisfied. They even had seven baskets extra. God is the God of more than enough!

We can learn a powerful lesson in giving if we'll just keep our hearts like the heart of that little boy with the little lunch. I've purposed in my own heart that I will give my "little bit" to Jesus so He can multiply it to meet needs abundantly. (BN)

JULY 20
YOUR GIVING DETERMINES YOUR HARVEST
2 CORINTHIANS 9:1-15

"He which soweth sparingly shall reap also sparingly; and he
which soweth bountifully shall reap also bountifully" *(2 Cor. 9:6).*

This verse is saying that there's a direct relationship between the seed we sow and the harvest we reap. Another way of saying this is: You can determine your harvest by the amount of seed you sow.

In the natural realm this is an indisputable fact. No one would argue that a farmer harvests proportional to his sowing. We would consider a farmer crazy if he sowed very little seed but expected a big harvest. Yet in the spiritual realm, people do this all the time. Many people give very little money, if any at all, to the Lord and then wonder why He doesn't supply their needs. That's crazy! Big harvests demand big sowings.

A farmer doesn't just plant seed from what he has available. He predicts what his needs will be and then sows enough seed to meet those needs. He borrows money if he has to, but he sows enough seed to meet his projected needs.

What are your needs? Is the money you're giving to the Lord's work enough to reap the harvest you want? If it isn't, then you need to increase the money you're sowing into God's kingdom.

Try this: Instead of just giving a tithe on what you have, move up to the next level. What income do you need? Start tithing on that figure, and watch the money come in. Your giving determines your harvest! (AW)

JULY 21
AUTHORITY OVER SATAN'S POWER
LUKE 10:19

"Behold, I give unto you power to tread on serpents and scorpions,
and over all the power of the enemy: and nothing shall by any means hurt you"
(Luke 10:19).

Jesus didn't give us power over Satan, but authority over his power. To be truthful, authority is greater than power. That's a radical statement today. With all of the fitness magazines and karate movies, we are led to believe that we'll have confidence in life when we have large muscles and great physical strength. This whole idea puts the emphasis in the wrong place.

Satan may be more powerful than us, but we have control over him. One demon was stronger than the seven sons of Sceva. Before the seven could reach the front door of the house, one demon-ized man overcame them, wounded them, and tore off all their clothes (Acts 19:16). Jesus has given us authority through His name over all the strength of Satan and his kingdom.

A policeman standing in an intersection simply raises his hand and traffic comes to a halt. He doesn't have to be a big, muscular man. The cars, buses, and trucks are more powerful than the police officer and could easily run over him. Yet, the drivers of these powerful vehicles recognize the officer's authority. They stop at a simple hand signal and go when he allows them to go. They know if they resist his authority, they'll face the power. The police officer simply calls the station and the police department will bring more officers, guns, and dogs if necessary to stop the lawbreaker. Power backs authority.

When we as believers use the name of Jesus, all hell comes to a halt. We may not be big or physi-cally strong, but Satan must stop. He knows if he runs over us, he'll have to face the power—AGAIN. He faced it once, at the cross, and lost. Jesus has given us authority over all the power of Satan! (BY)

JULY 22
FAITH PRODUCED THE MIRACLE
ACTS 3:1-16

"And his name through faith in his name hath made this man strong,
whom ye see and know: yea, the faith which is by him hath given him
this perfect soundness in the presence of you all" *(Acts 3:16).*

Many people mistakenly think that miracles happen because of some special gift on an individ-ual's life. This has led them to believe that miracles don't happen today, because all the apostles are dead. However, there are still apostles alive today. Ephesians 4:11-13 says that apostles and prophets are given to the church until we become perfect and measure up to the fullness of Christ's stature. That certainly hasn't happened yet, so apostles must still be in the church today.

Miracles never took place just because of a call on someone's life. In the instance above, Peter says very plainly that it was the faith in the name of Jesus, which this paralyzed man had, that pro-duced his healing. We certainly still have faith today, because you can't please God without it (Heb. 11:6). We still have the name of Jesus with all its privileges and benefits. You can't be saved without it (Acts 4:12).

Therefore, faith in the name of Jesus is what produces results. People with special gifts only aid a person's faith; they aren't a substitute for faith. If this wasn't so, then everyone would be healed through those who have the gifts of healing and miracles. That's not the way it happens. The indi-vidual receiving the healing must believe too.

Don't let Satan deceive you, that because you don't have any special anointings or callings, you can't receive your miracle from God. If you have Jesus, and faith in what He can do, you have all you need to receive anything from God. Exercise your faith in Jesus today! (AW)

JULY 23
WHY DOES GOD WANT YOUR MONEY?
PSALM 50

"If I were hungry, I would not tell thee: for the world is mine, and the fulness thereof" (Ps. 50:12).

Have you ever wondered why the Lord told us to give to Him? It's not because He needs it. This is what He says in Psalm 50. He tells the people that He isn't going to eat their sacrifices. He owns all the cattle on a thousand hills. What did He need their sacrifices for? If God was hungry, would He look to us to satisfy Him? Certainly not! Then why did He ask for the sacrifices? Why does He ask us to give if He's not in need?

God doesn't want Sunday-only Christians who give Him only an hour or two per week. He loves us and wants to be involved in every part of our lives. We spend a majority of our time earning a living. How does He get involved in that part of our lives? He asks us to give Him ten percent.

If there is no God and if what we give is not multiplied back to us, then giving away ten percent of what we have is foolish. It's moving away from our goal instead of toward it. That's just the point. It takes faith in God and in His Word to give away a portion of what we have. That's the reason He asks us to do it. It's so we can move into faith in the financial part of our lives.

Therefore, the person who wants to give and plans on giving when they have some extra cash is missing the main purpose of giving. It's to thrust us into a realm of faith. If you wait to give until it takes no faith to trust that God will multiply it back to you, then you've missed the point.

Give in faith to the Lord today. It's your faith that He really wants. (AW)

JULY 24
NEWS OR PROPHECY?
EPHESIANS 1:13

"In whom ye also trusted, after that ye heard the word of truth, the gospel of your salvation: in whom also after that ye believed, ye were sealed with that holy Spirit of promise" (Eph. 1:13).

The word *Gospel* literally means "good news." It's important that you understand that news is always something that's already taken place. The dictionary defines *news* as "recent events or happenings." If it hasn't already occurred, it isn't news.

The reason it was so easy to believe the Lord for the born-again experience was because our salvation was presented as news. If we would have been told that Jesus might come and die for our sins, no one would've been born again. Even if we could've been persuaded that Jesus was willing to die for our sins, the devil would try to convince us that salvation certainly couldn't be for us. When we hear that God has already provided salvation through the death of His Son, it's easy to believe and receive. There's no reason to doubt something that's already happened.

This is a key to receiving every benefit of our salvation. Anything that God has promised us has already been provided through the atonement of Christ. That's where all the work of salvation was accomplished. Jesus only died once. He's now seated at the Father's right hand (Heb. 10:12). His atonement is complete. Everything is already a done deal. The Lord isn't going to heal us; it's already been done (1 Pet. 2:24). Joy isn't something we need to ask for; it's something we already have in our spirits. It just needs to be released.

If you haven't already done so, start viewing the Gospel as good NEWS. Believe that whatever you need is already yours in Christ, and experience the difference that believing the Gospel makes. (AW)

JULY 25
HAS GOD BEATEN YOU?
HEBREWS 4:12-16

"Let us therefore come boldly unto the throne of grace, that we may obtain mercy, and find grace to help in time of need" (Heb. 4:16).

I once had a dog that was three-fourths German shepherd and one-fourth chow. I got her to be a watchdog for my mother while I was away in Vietnam. She looked ferocious, but was afraid of everyone—including me.

She'd come running toward me, stop, roll over on her side, and then whimper as she inched the rest of her way up to me. This dog had been beaten with a trace chain as a puppy and had never gotten over it. Her behavior infuriated me. Although I wasn't the one who had beaten her, I was often accused of mistreating her by people who saw how she acted.

One day the Lord told me that I was just like my dog. I didn't approach Him with the boldness He desired. I drew near to Him like He was going to beat me. I often told my dog, "I wish you would just once come and jump up in my lap like a normal dog would!" God told me the same thing. He said, "I wish you would come to Me like I was your Savior who loves you and died for you instead of someone who's going to hit you."

Do you come boldly before the throne of grace the way this verse instructs us, or do you come before the Lord in fear of judgment for some wrong that you've done? God loves you and has removed your sins from you as far as the east is from the west (Ps. 103:12). It would give the Lord great pleasure for you to boldly come to Him today and call Him "Abba Father" (Gal. 4:6).

We should exercise as much sense as a normal dog and trust the mercy of our Master. He's never given us reason to approach Him with anything but boldness. (AW)

JULY 26
THE MIGHTY PALM TREE
PSALM 92:12

"The righteous shall flourish like the palm tree: he shall grow like a cedar in Lebanon" (Ps. 92:12).

This is a strange thought. Why would God compare the righteous believer to a palm tree? How can you put a cedar and a palm in the same verse? What is majestic or beautiful about a palm tree? Very few palms are good for fruit and they give little shade.

You must consider the context of this verse. David was watching the seeming prosperity of his enemies. He felt small among the mighty nations on the earth in his day, yet he knew they would eventually fall and Israel would endure forever. He also knew those kings who rose up against him would come to destruction, yet his kingdom would never end (verses 9-10). David had God's word on it. His attitude was that he wouldn't only just survive but FLOURISH!

Can you name a tree that not only exists in harsh conditions, but flourishes? The palm tree. Palm trees grow in deserts. Where there seems to be little or no water, you'll find palm trees. Where the heat is unbearable for humans, let alone for vegetation, you'll find palm trees. They not only survive, but they grow and grow tall! You can see them from some distance away.

The secret of the palm tree is its system of nourishment. A palm tree is different than any other type of tree. All other trees receive water and minerals through the bark. If you cut the bark completely around the tree (ring it) you'll kill it. Yet with the palm, you can not only cut the bark but weave it or even remove it and the tree lives. Why? A palm tree pulls its life through the inside of the trunk, not through the bark.

A strong believer will not only survive in terrible circumstances and in the midst of their enemies, but will flourish like the palm. This follower of God doesn't live by their flesh, their outward man, but draws their strength from their spirit, their inward man, which is filled with the Holy Spirit and God's promises. (BY)

JULY 27
DON'T FAINT!
PSALM 27:1-14

*"I had fainted, unless I had believed to see the goodness
of the LORD in the land of the living"* (Ps. 27:13).

Without faith, life is depressing. The joy that this world offers is only temporary and ultimately ends up in sorrow. Everything around us that's new and shiny today will one day be old and dull. Every relationship will experience difficulties sooner or later, and some of them won't survive. Life itself is a terminal condition. If all one sees is the physical world and its temporal truths, then there's reason to give up and faint.

The good news is that Christians aren't limited to what they see. There is a spiritual kingdom that every believer is a part of. Its rewards and privileges far outweigh any hardship we'll ever encounter. This kingdom and its King are awesome beyond description. Christ's kingdom is infinitely greater in power and pleasures than anything in the world. Yet, it takes faith to see and experience this.

Anyone who's feeling faint from the problems this world brings is not believing that Christ's kingdom will be on earth as it is in heaven (Matt. 6:10). Somehow, the Enemy has removed our attention from the wonderful things of God and focused it on the temporary problems of this life. But we don't have to stay that way!

Believing that God will bring you through will put joy back in your heart. The joy of the Lord is your strength (Neh. 8:10), and instead of fainting, your strength will be renewed like the eagle's. You will run and not be weary. You'll walk and not faint (Is. 40:30-31). See by faith today, and let your heart be encouraged! (AW)

JULY 28
RENEW YOUR STRENGTH
ISAIAH 40:28-31

"Even the youths shall faint and be weary, and the young men shall utterly fall: But they that wait upon the LORD shall renew their strength; they shall mount up with wings as eagles; they shall run, and not be weary; and they shall walk, and not faint" (Is. 40:30-31).

No one can stand alone against all the pressures of this life. God didn't make us to function independently of Him. We are created to be God-dependent (Jer. 10:23). Therefore, every human endeavor that's not ordered and empowered by Him is doomed to fail (Ps. 127:1). The good news is that we can live a life wholly dependent on God and soar above every problem the devil throws our way. This isn't only possible—it's the way He wants us to live! This is the normal Christian life.

How can this happen? The key lies in waiting on the Lord. The Hebrew word translated *wait* means "to bind together, i.e. collect, or (figuratively) to expect." It's this figurative meaning that's being employed in this verse. Isaiah was speaking of looking to the Lord in expectation of good. That's what we call "faith."

Only through faith can we renew our strength, run without growing weary, and walk without fainting. Faith is spiritual energy. With it, we are strong. Without it, we are weak. Faith comes from God through His Word (Rom. 10:17). Therefore, to have faith we must seek God through meditating on His Word.

Jeremiah said, *"The LORD is good unto them that wait for him, to the soul that seeketh him"* (Lam. 3:25). God promised, *"Seek ye me, and ye shall live"* (Amos 5:4). Jesus declared, *"Seek, and ye shall find"* (Matt. 7:7). Seek the Lord with all your heart today (Jer. 29:13) and be energized! (AW)

JULY 29
WAIT ON THE LORD
PSALM 27

"Wait on the LORD: be of good courage, and he shall strengthen thine heart:
wait, I say, on the LORD" (Ps. 27:14).

Waiting on the Lord means looking unto Him. It means seeking the Lord with anticipation that He will reward you. It means having faith in God.

When a good waiter waits on his customer, he pays attention to them. He may be out of sight, but he's always watching. When their glass needs to be filled, he fills it. He serves his customer as a servant serves his master. We've all been frustrated by waiters and waitresses who've ignored us. Those aren't the ones we give big tips.

To wait on God means to be attentive to Him—to seek Him continually and always listen to His voice. Just as a waiter gives better service if he only has one customer, we wait on the Lord better if He's our only focus. We can't serve two masters (Matt. 6:24). Our hearts must be focused on God alone.

If a waiter gives his undivided attention to his customer, he receives a reward. The better the job, the better the tip. If we wait on the Lord, He'll encourage us and strengthen our hearts. What a reward!

Are you in need of more courage? Could your heart stand to be strengthened? The way to obtain these things is to wait on the Lord. The more you wait, the more you're encouraged and strengthened. Wait, I say, on the Lord! (AW)

JULY 30
WITH ALL YOUR HEART
JEREMIAH 29:11-14

"And ye shall seek me, and find me, when ye shall search for me
with all your heart" (Jer. 29:13).

I've talked to many people who knew they needed God in their lives, yet they felt like it was so hard to connect with Him. They said, "I've prayed, but the Lord never answered." Jesus told us, **"For every one that asketh receiveth; and he that seeketh findeth; and to him that knocketh it shall be opened"** (Matt. 7:8). God never fails us. So, what's the answer?

The answer is revealed in this verse. The Lord said we will seek Him and find Him when we search with ALL our hearts. Failure to connect with God is not because of any lack of faithfulness on His part but a lack of seeking with ALL our hearts on our part. Therefore, the key is in our hearts. Focusing all our attention on the Lord unlocks the door to a relationship with Him and everything it produces.

The Lord loves us and desires to help us through our troubles, but He doesn't want us to come to Him only when we're having problems. So many people are in the desperate situations they're in because they've totally ignored the leading of the Lord in their everyday lives. They want Him to miraculously bail them out of the pit they dug for themselves. Then they go right back to doing the same things that got them in trouble in the first place. They weren't seeking God with all their hearts, they just wanted out of trouble!

Sometimes it's best for a parent to deny their child's request to teach them a greater truth. Likewise, the Lord knows our hearts and only reveals Himself to those who seek Him wholeheartedly. Get serious with the Lord today and you'll find Him! (AW)

JULY 31
GOD'S NO CHEAPSKATE!
1 KINGS 5, 6

"So Solomon built the house, and finished it" (*1 Kin. 6:14*).

God's not a cheapskate or stingy. He's not mediocre and certainly isn't poverty-minded. When God does something, He does it with excellence. And He expects His children to do the same! That means we use what we can to obtain the best resources available in whatever we do. Don't get me wrong—more expensive isn't always better. The key is excellence!

The Illinois Society of Architects did a study in 1925 to determine the cost value of Solomon's temple. Those figures were adjusted into 1997 inflation dollars. Vallapardus states that the talents of gold, silver, and brass used for construction were valued at well over 315 billion dollars ($315,439,838,700), with the jewels close to the same figure! WOW!

When looking at the records of ancient historian Flavius Josephus, the vessels of gold were valued at what today would be seventeen billion dollars ($17,207,335,492.55) and the vessels of silver almost thirty billion dollars ($29,772,422,400). If you want to nitpick about the type of suits ministers wear, consider the priests' vestment and the singers' robes—ninety-two million dollars ($92,158,500)! Those would be some choir robes, wouldn't they? The trumpets alone would've been nine million dollars ($9,170,000) by today's currency rates.

Now, add into the mix the expense of the building materials, labor, and so forth. It took 10,000 men hewing cedars; 70,000 bearers of burden; 80,000 hewers of stone; 3,850 overseers (managers/supervisors); all of which were employed for more than seven years. Besides wages, Solomon gave them $308,752,845.45 in bonuses! That comes to $1,884.36 per person in bonuses alone!

Solomon took care of his workers. The cost of their daily food for the seven and a half years it took to complete the temple has been estimated at $3,158,014,484.80. Materials other than gold, silver, jewels, and so forth cost $116,703,701.45.

If you add all of the estimates of everything pertaining to Solomon's temple, it cost close to 800 billion dollars ($797,790,000,000)! Astounding! No wonder the temple was the wonder of olden times!

God wants His people to prosper and be blessed so they can be a blessing. There's no lack in heaven and there shouldn't be lack in the life of a believer. The key is to know your Source. God is our Source. Meditate on 2 Corinthians 9:8: *"And God is able to make all grace abound toward you; that ye, always having all sufficiency in all things, may abound to every good work."* (BN)

AUGUST 1
YOU CAN STOP GOD
DEUTERONOMY 7:12-21

"If thou shalt say in thine heart, These nations are more than I; how can I dispossess them?" (*Deut. 7:17*).

The Lord had just told the Jews that He would deliver all the inhabitants of the land into their hands and they would conquer them. But then He added, "If you doubt, I can't expel them." What a statement! The Lord was saying that He has to work through His people to accomplish His purposes.

This same truth is verified many other places in Scripture. Psalm 78:41 says, *"Yea, they turned back and tempted God, and limited the Holy One of Israel."* Satan can't limit God. Jesus and the devil already fought face to face, and Jesus is the undisputed champion. The only tool Satan has left is us. He tempts us and if we get into unbelief, we limit God.

Ephesians 3:20 makes the same point saying, *"Now unto him that is able to do exceeding abundantly above all that we ask or think, according to the power that worketh in us."* The Lord only does more than we ask or think ACCORDING TO the power that's at work in us. The words *according to* mean, "to the degree of; in proportion to." If there's no power of faith working in us, there will be no positive answer from God.

It's amazing how many people miss this simple truth. They ask the Lord to help them but become upset with Him if they don't see the desired results. They are the ones at fault, not God! It takes faith to receive from Him. Because of the Lord's great love for us, He has bestowed so much authority upon us that He cannot—because He will not—move independently of us. God has bound His operation in our lives according to our faith and cooperation. Let the power of faith work in you today, and watch what God can do! (AW)

AUGUST 2
LITTLE BY LITTLE
DEUTERONOMY 7:12-26

"And the LORD thy God will put out those nations before
thee by little and little: thou mayest not consume them at once,
lest the beasts of the field increase upon thee" (Deut. 7:22).

The Lord promised His people total and complete victory, not only over people who were their enemies but also over sickness, barrenness, crop failure, and problems with their animals. He made provision for every area of their lives. God is a good God, and He receives pleasure from our prosperity (Ps. 35:27). Yet this verse makes a startling statement. The Lord wouldn't grant them these victories all at once.

Most of us would ask, "Why not? If it's God's will for us to succeed in these areas, why doesn't He just do it all at once?" The Lord's answer is that we aren't able to handle success all at once. In the case of these Israelites, if the Lord had driven their enemies out of Palestine all at once, the beasts of the field would've taken over the land before the people could have possessed it. The houses would've fallen into decay. The crops would have been overtaken with weeds. It would've ceased to be a land flowing with milk and honey, and the curse would have dominated it.

Likewise, the Lord won't grant us victories faster than we can possess them. Success without the character to properly manage it would lead to our own destruction. Letting a child drive before they're ready could kill them and someone else. Our heavenly Father loves us much more than to do something like that. God wants us to prosper (3 John 2), but our maturity dictates the timing.

Make maturing in the Lord your focus and you'll find that your Father will grant you the things you need as soon as you're able to handle them. (AW)

AUGUST 3
TIMING IS EVERYTHING
GENESIS 15:13-16 EXODUS 12:40-42

"Now the sojourning of the children of Israel, who dwelt in Egypt,
was four hundred and thirty years" (Ex. 12:40).

In Genesis 15:13, God told Abraham that his descendants would be in a foreign land for 400 years. In Exodus 12:40, we find that they were actually there for 430 years. Why the extra thirty years of bondage?

If we subtract the forty years that Moses spent in the wilderness (Acts 7:30) from the total 430 years of bondage, we discover that Moses killed the Egyptian (Ex. 2:11-12) in the 390th year of captivity—ten years before their time was up. In Acts 7:24-25, we find that Moses *"supposed his brethren would have understood how that God by his hand would deliver them: but they understood not."* This means that Moses knew God's will for his life and was trying to set the Jews free when he killed the Egyptian, but he totally missed the timing. In fact, he was ten years premature.

We can't speed up God's timing, but we can delay it. In our impatience, we often want to microwave our miracle or ministry. But all that our impatience does is delay the whole process. The Lord gives us our answers as we are able to receive them. If it seems like things aren't coming as fast as we want, we need to check what's wrong with us—not try to speed up God.

The Lord uses us as much as we are usable. Instead of praying "O God, use me!" we need to pray "O God, make me usable!" The Lord wants to use us and answer our prayers more than we want to be used or for our prayers to be answered. It takes time to become a usable tool. Our impatience might cost us forty years in the wilderness and others thirty extra years of bondage. Don't make Moses' mistake. It's not enough to know God's will—we need to know His timing too! (AW)

AUGUST 4
THE MAN WITH THE WATER POT
MARK 14:13

"And he sendeth forth two of his disciples, and saith unto them, Go ye into the city,
and there shall meet you a man bearing a pitcher of water: follow him" (Mark 14:13).

Jesus was about to celebrate the Last Supper with His disciples and needed an upper room to hold the feast. It would take a big room to accommodate Jesus and the twelve disciples. When the disciples had exhausted their list of available rooms, they asked the Lord where to look. He told them they'd find the upper room by following a man with a water pot. What timing God has! Think of the divine arrangement He had to make in order for the disciples to arrive at a particular intersection at the same time as the man with the pot of water. This man would be a sign and a guide from God!

How many of us can look back on our lives and give God the glory for the men with water pots that have been there at the right time for us? Finances, healing, and divine wisdom are only a few of the needs we've had when a servant of God met us and helped steer us in the right direction. Thank God for His many supernatural appointments!

Is there anything better than meeting a man with a water pot? Yes—being the man with the water pot! There was probably a day when this fellow had need of a helper with a water pot to guide him. After that wonderful encounter, he probably told God, "If I can ever carry a water pot and lead others, please allow me to repay the debt of gratitude I owe." Since that day, the Holy Spirit had used him on more than one occasion to lead others into the will of God, including the disciples of Messiah.

God helps us so we can help others. *"Who comforteth us in all our tribulation, that we may be able to comfort them which are in any trouble, by the comfort wherewith we ourselves are comforted of God"* (2 Cor. 1:4). Get your water pot and hit the streets! (BY)

AUGUST 5
WHAT'S YOUR TEMPERATURE?
PSALM 146

"Happy is he that hath the God of Jacob for his help,
whose hope is in the LORD his God" (Ps. 146:5).

Hope excites the heart. Where there is hope, there's rejoicing!

Think back to a time in your life when there was great anticipation of good. Perhaps, this could be childhood when you were awaiting the opening of presents at Christmas or a birthday party. Maybe you were so excited over a family vacation or the arrival of a family member, so much that you couldn't sleep. There was excitement and joy. That's the way it is when there's hope!

Psalm 146:5 makes it clear that those who hope in the Lord are happy. It's impossible to have true hope without some degree of joy. We can distinguish true hope from mere desire by the joy that accompanies it. If we aren't rejoicing over the desired outcome, then we aren't truly hoping. Just as we can tell if we're sick by taking our temperature, we can tell if we have hope by examining our joy.

If you have a fever, you don't just shake the thermometer down; you seek to remove the sickness, and then your temperature will return to normal. If you lack joy, don't just force yourself to rejoice. Work on your hope, and rejoicing will naturally follow. Lack of hope is a sickness that'll make your discontentment rise. You should check your spiritual temperature often by checking your joy. If it's low, you could be suffering from lack of hope.

Hope comes from the promises of God's Word (Rom. 15:4). Get in the Word, and let hope come. Your hope will be reflected in your joy! (AW)

AUGUST 6
THE POWER OF PARTNERSHIP
LUKE 5:1-7

"And they beckoned unto their partners, which were in the other ship,
that they should come and help them. And they came, and filled both the ships,
so that they began to sink" (Luke 5:7).

Partnership is powerful! A partner is someone who helps you do what God has called you to do. It's people coming together, working together, believing together, giving together, and pooling resources together for kingdom purposes. I can't accomplish alone what I'm able to do with partners linked together with me in faith. When you sow into the finances of your church, you're partnering with them. You become a partner with Jesus. You become a part of everything your church does. And you reap the reward for every life touched!

Jesus needed to get God's Word out, and He needed someone to help Him do it. There were no radios, televisions, CDs, DVDs, or internet back then. He needed partners to help Him reach out—and so do we. The disciples needed help too! They were fishermen who fished all night and caught nothing. They had bills to pay. The sailors wanted their paychecks. The insurance companies didn't understand that they didn't catch any fish the night before. They still wanted their premiums. The payment on their boats was coming due. The disciples needed some fish. They needed some money. So Jesus and the disciples came together in partnership. It was a divine connection, a divine appointment. Together they would prosper more than they would individually. We need faith partners in our lives. If you don't have faith in an area, find someone who does and partner with them!

Matthew 18:19 says, *"If two of you shall agree on earth as touching any thing that they shall ask, it shall be done for them of my Father which is in heaven."* Ask God to send you Holy Ghost faith partners, and watch the power that's released into your life to prosper! (BN)

AUGUST 7
CAN JESUS BORROW YOUR BOAT?
LUKE 5:1-7

"And he entered into one of the ships, which was Simon's,
and prayed him that he would thrust out a little from the land.
And he sat down, and taught the people out of the ship" (Luke 5:3).

Today, Jesus is still looking for partners and saying, "Can I borrow your boat? I want to partner with you." What if Jesus walked up to you and said, "I'd like to go out to eat with you. Would you buy My lunch?" Why, you'd beg, borrow, and do anything you had to in order get enough money to take Jesus out to lunch. And you wouldn't take Him to some low-budget, fast food place either. You'd take Him somewhere a little nicer, wouldn't you? Please, realize that Jesus is saying today, "I want to partner with you. I want to partner with your bank account. I want to partner with your time. I want to partner with your business, your family, your talent."

Some people see Malachi 3 as negative. It's not negative! The same Lord who said to bring all the tithe into the storehouse also said that He'd rebuke the devourer. "Bring all your tithe and I will help you. I'll take care of the insects, and I'll take care of anything negative. You do your part, and watch Me go to work on your behalf. Watch Me multiply your little loaves and fishes. Watch Me help you do what you're not able to do on your own!" When you're obedient to bring your tithes and offerings, or anything else the Lord asks of you, you aren't throwing it away. You're sowing it. It's not waste! Some people look at big beautiful churches and say, "This is a big church. They don't need my money." They miss the whole point. Tithing is God's way to get it back to you—multiplied. It's not a get-rich scheme—it's a divine partnership arrangement!

Jesus is appealing for partners today. I want to be in partnership with the Lord Jesus Christ! Let's pray, "Lord, I'll be Your partner today. You can use my boat. You can use my talent. You can use whatever You want to use. Sign me up!" God blesses people who enter into faith covenant partnership with Him. (BN)

AUGUST 8
PARTNERS CATCH MORE FISH!
LUKE 5:1-7

"And they beckoned unto their partners, which were in the other ship,
that they should come and help them. And they came, and filled both the ships,
so that they began to sink" (Luke 5:7).

Idle nets produce nothing; only the net that is cast into the water catches fish. The more nets, the more fish. Why partner? So we don't lose the harvest that God has given us! When Peter obeyed the Lord in casting his net once again, he didn't realize the blessing that was going to come. It was a net-breaking, boat-sinking load! There were so many fish that he had to call out to his partners to help bring in the haul. Partners catch more fish. If it were only Peter in his boat, they would've lost all those other fish. How many fish would they have caught if they had more partners?

It's like the lady who is retired and at home. Physically, she may not be able to go out on the street. Physically, she may not be able to visit prisons or do some of the things you can because of certain limitations she has. But when she sends her tithe in to her local church, she instantly becomes a partner with the Lord Jesus Christ. She makes it possible to bring in a bigger haul of fish. She can't go, but she's sending someone who can. She's partnering with Jesus!

There is no shortage of fish, because there's no shortage of sinners. If you reach one pastor, you're reaching hundreds, even thousands of lives. Peter allowed Jesus to use his boat so He could get the Word to the people. God always pays for His order. Fishing was Peter's livelihood. Jesus more than paid for the use of that boat by the haul of fish Peter and his partners brought in. By partnering with the Lord to get the Gospel out to people, you will prosper. Remember, partners catch more fish! (BN)

AUGUST 9
GOD WANTS YOU TO DO WHAT YOU CAN'T
LUKE 5:1-7

"And they beckoned unto their partners, which were in the other ship,
that they should come and help them. And they came, and filled both the ships,
so that they began to sink" (Luke 5:7).

The just really shall live by faith! If the devil can get you away from faith in God, you'll go down. I often say that I'm out there so far now, I can't make it without faith! You can't play conservative, run-of-the-mill church games, walk in fear, and have God's best. There comes a time when you just have to cut the cord and go for it. At some point, you must launch out into the deep!

While visiting the Holy Land, a minister asked some fisherman about their nets. They explained that there were different kinds of nets. They were using shallow water nets—the kind they don't use out in the deep. The Galilee is deep, and when Jesus said "Launch out your nets into the deep," He was saying "Do what you can't do." Those nets weren't made to catch all kinds of fish. But He said, "Do what you can't do." You'll never know faith until you do what you cannot do. You'll never really experience the wonderful blessing faith is until you do what you cannot do!

As long as I do what I have the ability to do, it's just me—my strength. I don't need God so much in the things He's naturally gifted me to do. But when I get out there and it's beyond me— that's when it becomes supernatural! That's when God can get tremendous glory.

When the disciples did what Jesus told them to do, they caught a whole bunch of fish. In fact, they caught so many they had to call for partners. That's why we need partners nowadays. We're out there in the deep water catching some big fish. You can stay in the shallow water and catch minnows the rest of your life, or you can launch out there where the big fish are. The choice is yours. Do what you can't! (BN)

AUGUST 10
GOD WILL NEVER GO BANKRUPT!
2 CORINTHIANS 1:20

**"For all the promises of God in him are yea, and in him Amen,
unto the glory of God by us"** *(2 Cor. 1:20).*

Godly partnership is an investment that—when we enter into it in faith—is a sure investment. Have you ever heard one of those "great opportunities" on the radio? They pull the same thing when they tell you about super car deals. After the wonderful ad, another little voice comes in and rapidly mumbles a bunch of things. You ask, "What did they say?" It's a disclaimer, because nobody can promise, and guarantee without failure, a return on your money. They may look good and have a good track record—and there are certain signposts you can look for—but no one on the face of this earth has a guaranteed return, except for God Almighty.

When you give to the kingdom of God, your partnership is guaranteed. Partnership with Jesus always pays, because He's a debtor to no man. Anything Jesus wants—let Him have it! Give Him your time, your talents, your ability, your finances. Then you'll experience the joy of reaping the harvest together. Doing things God's way—partnering with Him—guarantees a return in your life and in the lives of those around you. He's kept every promise He ever made. Everything God ever said, He's either done it, in the process of doing it, or—rest assured—He will do it. It shall come to pass!

Jesus Christ is the same yesterday, today, and forever (Heb. 13:8). God has never gone bankrupt and He never will. Invest in His kingdom and you'll have capital gain here on earth and a crown of glory in the world to come! (BN)

AUGUST 11
THE GREATEST LOVE
ROMANS 5:1-8

**"But God commendeth his love toward us, in that,
while we were yet sinners, Christ died for us"** *(Rom. 5:8).*

Jesus said, **"Greater love hath no man than this, that a man lay down his life for his friends"** (John 15:13). These verses take that thought a step further. It's conceivable that a man would die for someone he loves. That's happened before. There are even some people who would dare to put their lives on the line for the sake of principle. But God sent His only Son to die for us while we were still sinners!

The Lord didn't just die for those who were godly. The truth is we've all **"sinned, and come short of the glory of God"** (Rom. 3:23). There were no "godly" people from His perspective. And the Lord didn't limit His sacrificial death only to those He knew would accept it either. He died for the sins of the whole world, not just those who believe on Him (1 John 2:2). Jesus is **"the Saviour of all men, specially of those that believe"** (1 Tim. 4:10).

Christ died for us before we accepted His love. He died for the sins of the world knowing that most would reject His act of love. This goes beyond any love that we can find outside of God. God's love is totally independent of any worth on our part.

Understanding this, is a major ingredient for enjoying a healthy relationship with the Lord. If we feel we must be worthy of His love and goodness, we'll never accept it. God loves us because He is love, not because we're lovable. (AW)

AUGUST 12
DO YOU HAVE AN ALTAR?
1 KINGS 18:17-38

"And with the stones he built an altar in the name of the LORD: and he made a trench about the altar, as great as would contain two measures of seed" (1 Kin. 18:32).

This is a miraculous story of how Elijah called the fire of God down from heaven. At the time, the nation of Israel was in apostasy. The king was very wicked and the queen had forsaken the worship of God to serve Baal instead. She fed 450 prophets of Baal and 400 prophets of the groves each day from her own treasury. It was a dark time in the history of God's people.

But God had a man named Elijah who made a difference. He told King Ahab to call all the people and the prophets of Baal together for a test. They would both build altars and place sacrifices on them, but they would call on God to light the fire. The God who answered by fire would be the true God. Of course, our God won, because He is the only true God. There never really was much of a contest!

Many people would like to do what Elijah did. They want to see the fire of God fall in a miraculous way so people will fall on their faces and worship Him. But they haven't done what Elijah did. He built an altar and put a sacrifice on it. God's fire doesn't fall on just anything. An altar is where we worship God and a sacrifice is what we offer to Him. Elijah made preparation as well as petition. Then he released his faith.

Our faith isn't a substitute for relationship with God. It's just the finishing touch. I'm speaking of commitment, not perfection. We need to place ourselves on the altar and let the fire of God consume us first (Rom. 12:1). If you'll catch on fire, the world will come and watch you burn! (AW)

AUGUST 13
THE REASON FOR YOUR HOPELESSNESS
1 KINGS 19:4

"But he himself went a day's journey into the wilderness, and came and sat down under a juniper tree: and he requested for himself that he might die; and said, It is enough; now, O LORD, take away my life; for I am not better than my fathers" (1 Kin. 19:4).

Elijah was a great man of God. Yet he became so depressed that he asked God to kill him. He had successfully stood against the king and the whole nation, but the threat of the queen sent Elijah running for his life.

When he was a safe distance away, he sat down and reflected on what he'd done. He became so depressed that he asked God to take his life. Imagine, a man who knew God to such a degree that he had caused a great revival in the land became so discouraged that he wanted to die. What does this tell us?

For one thing, none of us are immune to discouragement or depression. It's not limited to certain personality types or to people with chemical imbalances. Depression comes to anyone who takes their eyes off Jesus.

It's not unusual to experience great discouragement after great victory. In the midst of battle, we turn to God with all our hearts and His power flows. Our adrenaline flows too, and we often think that much of the victory was due to some virtue of our own. That decreases our dependency on God, and we become more self-sufficient. This is a recipe for disaster.

Elijah thought that he could do anything and began to live out of his own abilities just long enough for Satan to strike fear in his heart. We must never put our faith in ourselves. Our total dependency must always be on God alone. It doesn't matter who you are or what you've done, without Jesus you're nothing! (AW)

AUGUST 14
DO YOU THINK YOU'RE BETTER THAN OTHERS?
1 KINGS 19:4

"But he himself went a day's journey into the wilderness, and came and sat down under a juniper tree: and he requested for himself that he might die; and said, It is enough; now, O LORD, take away my life; for I am not better than my fathers" (1 Kin. 19:4).

Elijah had taken his eyes off God. Verse 3 says he SAW Queen Jezebel's threat. It became a reality to him. Yet, just hours before, he was walking in the Spirit with his eyes fixed on the Lord. What happened? This verse gives us a clear insight.

For one thing, he thought he was better than his fathers. Elijah had experienced a string of unbroken successes. He'd been fed supernaturally by ravens. Then God multiplied the widow's food for three years to sustain him, the widow, and her son. Then Elijah raised the widow's son from the dead. There was no precedent for that! He called fire down from heaven, which caused a great revival in Israel. Then he prayed so earnestly that a three-year drought was broken. This so excited him that he outran a chariot (1 Kin. 18). Elijah thought he could do anything!

But then he failed. He'd withstood the king and 850 prophets of Baal, but one woman sent him fleeing in fear. There's no doubt that Elijah started out in the power of the Lord, but he confused God's anointing on his life with some virtue of his own. That's when he failed. At one time, Elijah thought he was better than his fathers because of how God had used him, but it was only a matter of time until disaster struck.

The truth is, God has never had anyone qualified working for Him yet. And we aren't going to be the first either! So let's stay humble and recognize that God loves us and uses us because He is love, not because we are lovable. (AW)

AUGUST 15
A SERVANT CALLED MONEY
MATTHEW 6:24

"No man can serve two masters: for either he will hate the one, and love the other; or else he will hold to the one, and despise the other. Ye cannot serve God and mammon" (Matt. 6:24).

We don't really own the money in our pockets. We don't really own our homes, cars, clothes, or jewelry. Who owned them before you were here, and who will own them after you're gone? *"For we brought nothing into this world, and it is certain we can carry nothing out"* (1 Tim. 6:7).

God calls us stewards of this world's goods, not owners. He's the real owner of everything (Ps. 50:10, Hag. 2:8). A steward is hired by the owner to distribute the goods as the owner sees fit. A steward is responsible for the goods and servants of his or her master. God is the Master, money is the servant—and we stand in between. We are servants of God and money is our servant. Money is a terrible master, but a good servant. God is the true and wonderful Master.

Money's a great servant! A servant takes orders and accepts no credit. The servant gives all credit to the one who sent them. A servant is like another set of hands and feet for their master. They can go where the master cannot and do what the master cannot. Yet the master receives the credit.

The Great Commission tells us to go into all the world (Matt. 28:19-20, Mark 16:15). We know there are those who are called to go to other countries, but some must stay "by the stuff" and work at jobs to support those who go. When we send our finances into the uttermost parts of the earth to support a prophet, evangelist, or teacher, our money allows more people to receive Jesus, be filled with the Holy Spirit, get discipled, and receive healing. It's as if we went ourselves! We're rewarded equally with those who went to battle. The money doesn't receive the credit for all the changed lives; we receive the credit and God receives the glory! (BY)

AUGUST 16
BEGGAR OR BELIEVER?
MARK 10:46-52

*"And they came to Jericho: and as he went out of Jericho with his disciples
and a great number of people, blind Bartimaeus, the son of Timaeus,
sat by the highway side begging"* (Mark 10:46).

Prior to this time, Bartimaeus had no option but to be a beggar. Man had no cure for his blindness. But that day, there was one passing by that wasn't only a man. Others had told Bartimaeus about how Jesus healed blindness. His plea to the Son of David showed that Bartimaeus recognized Jesus as his Messiah. This was his day. God was passing by. Nothing else mattered!

Bartimaeus could have made a different choice. A multitude was passing by. He could have made more money begging that day than he would've received in months. This was the break of a lifetime! Beggars think that way.

But Bartimaeus became a believer that day. He wasn't thinking about an opportunity to continue his beggarly existence for another month or two. He was thinking of a brand-new life—a life free from begging, an independent life where he could make it on his own, a life where he could help someone else.

What choices are you making? Are you so occupied with continuing the status quo that you're missing your opportunity to change your life? Are you so busy making a living that you don't take time to study or pray? Are you unable to go to church because of the demands of your business? That would be like Bartimaeus not calling out for his healing because of his great opportunity to beg.

Today, don't let the demands of everyday life cause you to miss Jesus as He passes by. Don't be a beggar, be a believer! (AW)

AUGUST 17
HOW DESPERATE ARE YOU?
MARK 10:46-52

*"And many charged him that he should hold his peace: but he cried the more
a great deal, Thou Son of David, have mercy on me"* (Mark 10:48).

It's amazing how much influence other people have on us. There is an intense desire for each of us to conform to those around us. We want to be part of the group. We don't like to stand out from the crowd. We want to be accepted. But the crowd is never going to go all the way with God. Those who receive God's best always have to buck the crowd. Therefore, a herd mentality is a tremendous detriment to serving God.

Bartimaeus was compelled to conform to what others expected of him. Others could choose where they wanted to live or what they wanted to do for a living. A blind man had no choice but to beg. I'm sure Bartimaeus hated the way his life was headed. But what choice did he have? Man had no cure for his problem.

However, Bartimaeus had heard about someone who was more than just a man. He'd made other blind men see. Maybe He could do the same for Bartimaeus? Inside that blind beggar's body was the heart of a believer. Bartimaeus was longing for the day when Jesus would pass his way.

When that day came, he wasn't going to let anyone stop him from receiving his miracle. Others were embarrassed at his outburst, but he'd spent a life in embarrassment and shame, and wasn't about to continue it. If he didn't do something different, things would never change. It was now or never!

There's something powerful about desperation. Are you desperate enough to do whatever it takes to change? Don't let others stop you from receiving God's best! (AW)

AUGUST 18
PREPARE FOR SUCCESS
MARK 10:46-52

"And he, casting away his garment, rose, and came to Jesus" (Mark 10:50).

In Bartimaeus' day, beggars wore clothing that distinguished them as beggars. Therefore, for Bartimaeus to cast away his garment was significant. He wasn't planning on going back to begging. He was believing God for a miracle and acted accordingly.

Bartimaeus was blind, so of course he couldn't see the clothing he wore. But others could, and he was obligated by the society he lived in to wear the clothes appropriate to his place in life. Beggars weren't like everyone else. They weren't productive members of society. They might be tolerated or pitied, but they weren't admired. They definitely weren't allowed the same privileges as those who were normal. Bartimaeus must have hated the differences that his blindness imposed on him.

No doubt, he dreamed about what it would be like to have his sight. And since he'd heard of Jesus healing the blind, he probably became very specific in what he would do if Jesus ever passed his way. One thing he knew for sure: If Jesus came by his place, he would let nothing and no one stop him from receiving his healing; he'd never go back to begging. Bartimaeus knew he'd be healed and would never need his beggar's clothes again.

How convinced are you that God will answer your prayer? Have you held on to your "old clothes" just in case nothing happens so you can go back to your old beggarly existence? That's not faith. Meditate on God's promises until you see yourself receiving whatever you need. Then make no plans to go back to where you were before. (AW)

AUGUST 19
SUPERNATURAL PROTECTION
MALACHI 3:11

"And I will rebuke the devourer for your sakes, and he shall not destroy the fruits of your ground; neither shall your vine cast her fruit before the time in the field, saith the LORD of hosts" (Mal. 3:11).

We are entering the days when it will take more than a home security system to protect us. We need the hand of God Almighty on our lives. Here is the testimony of Alexander H. Kerr, founder of the Kerr Glass Manufacturing Company, a company still known for its quality fruit jars. Mr. Kerr was born again in the meetings of Dwight L. Moody. After his conversion, Kerr earnestly desired to see if tithing was still applicable in modern times. He covenanted with God to set aside ten percent of his income for the kingdom of God. At the time, he was deep in debt. But Kerr knew that if it was a principle of God, putting it into practice would honor the Lord and bless him. Almost immediately, Mr. Kerr started to reap the harvest on his seed sown.

It was during that first year of tithing that he started the fruit jar company. The company was located in San Francisco and was in operation at the time of the famous San Francisco Earthquake. One of the tragic results of the earthquake was terrible fires that destroyed almost everything in their path. The Kerr Glass Manufacturing Company was right in the heart of where the fires were. And, his company was probably the most flammable building in the area. People told Kerr that he'd be totally devastated. He responded by saying that if that were true, then God's Word was a lie. He stood on Malachi 3:11 knowing that God promised to rebuke the devourer and believing that He'd be true to His Word.

Mr. Kerr received a telegram telling him that his business was "somehow" miraculously saved. He went to investigate and found that while it was true that the surrounding area was completely destroyed, not one item of his company was touched—not even the wooden fence that surrounded his property. The flames burned everything around them, and even leaped over his property, but his business was untouched. After this, Mr. Kerr went on to publish several tracts (the first one was titled *God's Cure for Poverty*) and distributed them in every case of jars he shipped. By the time he went on to be with the Lord, over five million of these tracts were circulated. What a testimony!

Mr. Kerr's testimony is not an isolated case. The same principles that protected him and brought him from poverty to being a millionaire (for the glory of God) will work for you and me today. God is faithful to His promises. When we're faithful to tithe, He'll be faithful to rebuke the devourer for our sakes! (BN)

AUGUST 20
FIRST GIVE YOURSELF
2 CORINTHIANS 8:5

"And this they did, not as we hoped, but first gave their own selves to the Lord, and unto us by the will of God" *(2 Cor. 8:5).*

How many times during an offering have you thought, *This church just wants my money?* Even worse, have you ever thought that's all God wants from you? With so much teaching in the Old and New Testaments on giving, you might just think that!

God has chosen the giving of money throughout history to fund the preaching of the Gospel. He could send angels to do this work, but He'd rather use redeemed people. He could raise up many rich folks, give them gold and silver mines, and relieve us of the responsibility of giving tithes and offerings. But He hasn't.

Why offerings and why everyone? Every time we give into spreading the Gospel, it's a test of our love for God. Far beyond the act of giving is the attitude behind it. Finances are a very important part of our life—one of our highest priorities. Jesus told us, *"Where your treasure is, there will your heart be also"* (Matt. 6:21). If you want to find someone's love—their highest priority—find out where they spend their money.

GOD DOESN'T WANT OUR MONEY FIRST—HE WANTS US! If God has us, He has our money. If He has our hearts, He has everything we own. This is why God wants willing givers. He wants us to present our *"bodies a living sacrifice"* unto Him (Rom. 12:1).

Many Christians give to get God off their backs. They give money to relieve themselves of the guilt of not serving Him. In other words, they buy God off. They bribe Him. But God can't be bought. He doesn't want money without our hearts. He'd rather we not give if our hearts aren't right with Him (Matt. 5:23-24). *"Every man according as he purposeth in his heart, so let him give; not grudgingly, or of necessity: for God loveth a cheerful giver"* (2 Cor. 9:7). (BY)

AUGUST 21
WHO DO YOU THINK YOU ARE?
JUDGES 6:11-24

"And the angel of the LORD appeared unto him, and said unto him, The LORD is with thee, thou mighty man of valour" *(Judg. 6:12).*

Gideon was a man mightily used of God. He took 300 men and defeated an army that numbered in the millions. It was one of the greatest military victories of all time. Yet, Gideon didn't start out in confidence.

The angel of the Lord greeted him with, *"The Lord is with thee, thou mighty man of valour."* But Gideon responded saying, "Why then can't I see it?" He didn't see himself as a mighty man of valor at all. He was hiding his threshing of wheat from the Midianites so they wouldn't steal his meager harvest. Gideon didn't see himself the way God saw him.

The rest of his story is a succession of tests that Gideon gave God to convince himself that the Lord was really with him and that He would do what He said He would. But the truth is that Gideon was a mighty man of valor the moment God said he was. It just took him awhile to recognize it. God knew who Gideon really was before he did.

Likewise, God knows who we are and what our capabilities are. He's the one who created us. Furthermore, this isn't just limited to our personal talents and abilities. Every Christian has the promise that they can do the same works that Jesus did. Each one of us has unlimited potential in Christ, but it doesn't matter what our potential is. The determining factor is who WE believe we are.

Gideon was finally persuaded that what God said about him was true. When we become convinced that what God says about us is true, then we'll see victory too! (AW)

AUGUST 22
DON'T BYPASS THE ALTAR!
JUDGES 6:25-32

"And build an altar unto the LORD thy God upon the top of this rock,
in the ordered place, and take the second bullock, and offer a burnt sacrifice with the wood of the
grove which thou shalt cut down" (Judg. 6:26).

The same day the Lord first appeared to Gideon, He gave him instructions to tear down the altar, which his father had made. He told him to make a new altar to the Lord. People often skip over this and go straight to Gideon's great victory over the Midianites, but this is a very important detail.

An altar is where we worship. This symbolized Gideon forsaking all other forms of worship and committing himself to God alone. This was no small deal! The townspeople wanted to kill Gideon for what he did. Gideon knew that, which is why he accomplished this deed at night. He knew the risk he was taking, and his actions showed a total commitment to the Lord. Gideon was willing to follow God, even unto death.

Our victories come out of relationship with the Lord. Failure to maintain intimacy with Him is the biggest reason for defeat in battle. Before God could really use Gideon, He needed him to be committed and focused on Him.

Notice that God didn't have Gideon tear down the altar before calling him. God's gifts and callings are independent of our performance. The Lord has never called anyone because they were worthy. But once the call comes, we'll never succeed apart from an intimate relationship with our heavenly Father.

Are you trying to bypass the altar and go straight to the battle? That's not God's plan. Remove anything that takes away your devotion from the Lord, and then you'll be ready for battle. (AW)

AUGUST 23
DO YOU HAVE TOO MUCH?
JUDGES 6:33-7:8

"And the LORD said unto Gideon, The people that are with thee are too many for me to give the
Midianites into their hands, lest Israel vaunt themselves against me, saying,
Mine own hand hath saved me" (Judg. 7:2).

Gideon had been struggling with unbelief. That's why he put a fleece out before the Lord. Now God told him he had too many people. Although they were already grossly outnumbered, the Lord instructed him to thin the ranks.

So Gideon told all who were afraid to leave the battle. Twenty-two thousand men went home. That left 10,000, but there were still too many. The Lord directed Gideon to separate the men according to how they drank from the brook. God chose the 300 who knelt down on one knee to drink by cupping their hands and bringing the water up to their mouths. It wasn't the way they drank that impressed Him; He just chose the smaller group.

God didn't want anyone else to take credit for the victory. He wanted the number of men to be so small that there would be no doubt in anyone's mind that the victory was a miracle. He specifically put them in an impossible situation so His people would come to know just how awesome He was.

Now don't misunderstand. The Lord didn't bring the Midianites against His people. He didn't cause the problem. But once the problem was there, the Lord specifically led Gideon in such a way that it would take a great miracle to see the deliverance.

It's the same today. The Lord may lead you to do things that look crazy to the natural mind just so He can reveal Himself to you in a miraculous way. The Lord often spurns conventional wisdom so you'll know your deliverance is totally from Him. (AW)

AUGUST 24
LITTLE IS MUCH WHEN GOD IS IN IT
1 SAMUEL 14:1-23

"And Jonathan said to the young man that bare his armour, Come, and let us go over unto the garrison of these uncircumcised: it may be that the LORD will work for us: for there is no restraint to the LORD to save by many or by few" (1 Sam. 14:6).

The nation of Israel was in a bad situation. The Philistines had come against it with 30,000 chariots; 6,000 horsemen; and soldiers as numerous as the sands of the seashore (1 Sam. 13:5). Israel's soldiers were so frightened that they hid themselves in caves, thickets, and pits—anywhere they thought would be safe. Only 600 of Saul's army stayed with him.

But Jonathan, Saul's son, wasn't afraid. He took his armor bearer and went over to challenge the Philistines. There were only two of them against hundreds of thousands, but they didn't care. They were willing to risk their lives to fight the Lord's battle.

They only slew about twenty men, but that was enough. The Lord used that to put fear in the hearts of the Philistines so that they started killing each other. The NIV says, *"Then panic struck the whole army—those in the camp and field, and those in the outposts and raiding parties—and the ground shook. It was a panic sent by God"* (1 Sam. 14:15).

Jonathan didn't have to destroy the whole army. All he did was defeat twenty soldiers. Then God took that and multiplied it into a great victory. Sometimes we let the hugeness of a task overwhelm us. We don't have to accomplish the whole thing at once. Sometimes all we have to do is take that first step of faith and God will multiply our efforts. Take a step toward what God has called you to do, and watch Him increase it! (AW)

AUGUST 25
EVERYTHING AFTER ITS OWN KIND
JOHN 3:6

"That which is born of the flesh is flesh; and that which is born of the Spirit is spirit" (John 3:6).

There's a spiritual law found from the very beginning of the Bible: Everything produces after its own kind (Gen. 1:12). This is true with plants, animals, fish, birds, and man. It's true in the spiritual kingdom as well as in the natural. It's also true with God!

Love produces love and hate produces hate. Green beans produce green beans, turnips produce turnips, cats produce cats, dogs produce dogs, and people produce people. God produces spirits.

Every living thing passes on attributes. Turnips smell, taste, and look like turnips. Cats have whiskers, dogs have tails, and people have hands and feet. I received all of man's attributes when I was born. I have the same feet and hands I was born with. I didn't go to the doctor when I was two years old to have my original hands removed and two-year-old hands attached. My original hands had the ability to grow to their present size. I simply learned to use what was given to me at birth. These hands, which at one time couldn't even hold a bottle, can now drive a car.

When you were born of God you received all of His attributes. You have the same love, joy, and patience you were given when you received Jesus as your Savior. You also have the same measure of faith. You don't have to trade your faith in for more. One of the most unscriptural prayers you can pray is, "God, give me more faith!" That's like saying, "God, give me more hands!" Just like the hands on your natural body, you need to learn to use the faith you were given at the new birth. Your faith, which at one time couldn't trust God for a pair of socks, can believe Him today for the house payment, divine healing, and souls to be won. Like developing a natural muscle, your faith needs to be fed and used. It will grow! (BY)

AUGUST 26
OUR COVENANT GIVES US THE ADVANTAGE
1 SAMUEL 17:17-51

"And David spake to the men that stood by him, saying, What shall be done to the man that killeth this Philistine, and taketh away the reproach from Israel? for who is this uncircumcised Philistine, that he should defy the armies of the living God?" (1 Sam. 17:26).

David saw Goliath differently than all the other Israelites. They looked on his height, which was between nine and a half and eleven and a half feet, while David looked at him in the light of his covenant with God. That's what David was referring to when he called Goliath *"this uncircumcised Philistine."*

Circumcision was the sign of the covenant God had with the Jews. That covenant wasn't only about Jehovah being their God, but it promised them victory over their enemies. God was on their side. Goliath didn't have that covenant. He was the one God had promised the Jews He'd utterly destroy before them. Therefore, David's mention of Goliath being uncircumcised was really David declaring, "I'm the one with God on my side!" God plus anyone or anything is superior to anyone or anything without Him!

It was David's confidence in God—as expressed in the covenant He made with His people—that was the basis of David's faith. It's the same for us. God's Word and promises, which are recorded therein, must be the foundation of our faith. Those who aren't controlled by God's Word will be controlled by what they see. As believers, every one of us faces giants, but we also have a covenant that places God on our side. It's just a matter of what we focus our attention on.

Where is your focus? Are you looking at the bigness of your problems or at the awesomeness of your God? The choice is yours, and the victory is the Lord's! (AW)

AUGUST 27
EXPERIENCE PRODUCES HOPE
1 SAMUEL 17:17-51

"Thy servant slew both the lion and the bear: and this uncircumcised Philistine shall be as one of them, seeing he hath defied the armies of the living God" (1 Sam. 17:36).

Most Christians have heard the story of David killing the giant, Goliath. Who hasn't dreamed of doing some heroic act like that themselves? In reality, most of us can't really see ourselves taking that type of risk. A situation like that is just too big and too dangerous. How did David do it?

Verse 36 gives us the answer. David had already faced a lion and a bear, which tried to kill one of his sheep. He'd defeated them with his bare hands. That gave him confidence that he could defeat Goliath. David had experienced God's delivering power before, and that gave him boldness. It's just like Romans 5:4 says, *"Experience [produces]...hope"* (brackets mine).

Many of us don't put God to the test in our everyday lives, and we miss out on these confidence building experiences. We're waiting for the big conflict where we can slay Goliath in front of the multitude. But if we aren't faithful with the small responsibilities on the backside of the desert when no one is watching, we won't have the hope and faith to win the giant tests of life.

No one would've blamed David for sacrificing one of his sheep to save his life. Certainly, his father would rather have his son than a sheep. Likewise, there are many problems in life that we can survive without putting God's power to the test. Most people won't notice. They'd do the same thing themselves. But then, most people can't slay giants either.

Walk in God's best today, even in the smallest matters. It'll give you experience, which in turn will give you hope when the real trials of life come. (AW)

AUGUST 28
TRUST WHAT GOD HAS GIVEN YOU
1 SAMUEL 17:17-51

"And David girded his sword upon his armour, and he assayed to go; for he had not proved it. And David said unto Saul, I cannot go with these; for I have not proved them. And David put them off him" (1 Sam. 17:39).

David was the only one willing to fight Goliath. Everyone else was afraid, even King Saul. Yet when David was on his way to the battle, everyone wanted to give him advice on what he needed to do. What advice could they have given? They were the ones who'd been hiding in caves because of fear. If David would have taken their advice, he never would've fought Goliath!

King Saul's advice was for David to wear his armor. That sounded logical. Goliath was wearing armor, so why shouldn't David? But what good would Saul's armor do David? It hadn't done Saul any good. He was shaking in his armor just like everyone else!

David had enough sense to recognize that God was his Source. He decided not to depend on anything else that could hinder him. Saul was the tallest man in Israel (1 Sam. 10:23) and David was just a young boy. There's no doubt that Saul's armor didn't fit David. It just would've gotten in his way. David's trust was in the Lord, not in Saul's armor.

Other people might mean well with their advice, but we need to have our own weapons. We especially don't need to take advice from those who are doing nothing. Don't let the person who says it can't be done interfere with the one who's doing it!

What has God done for you? What's worked in the past? Stir up those gifts and callings and they will work again! (AW)

AUGUST 29
STEWARDS MUST BE FAITHFUL
1 CORINTHIANS 4:2

"Moreover it is required in stewards, that a man be found faithful" (1 Cor. 4:2).

As a new pastor, I desired to open a bookstore in our church. This would enable us to place Bibles, good teaching tapes, and books in the hands of our congregation. I tried to think of every qualified person among our people to open and maintain a bookshop. I talked with many who had handled money or worked in retail shops before, but no one wanted the position.

A young girl worked in our audio department as a faithful and dedicated volunteer. On a few occasions, I thought of her to take the position in our bookstore. She was faithful, but not qualified—so I forgot her.

One Saturday I was walking through our empty auditorium praying for the Sunday service and I caught her out of the corner of my eye. She was faithfully volunteering on Saturday to set up the microphones and the audiotape and speaker levels for the Sunday service. When I looked at her, this scripture came out of my heart, *"Moreover it is required in stewards, that a man* [person] *be found faithful"* [brackets mine]. The *Amplified Bible* says *"[essentially] required."* Faithfulness isn't requested; it's required! God told me in that moment, "You've been looking for qualifications; I look for faithfulness. You can teach a person qualifications, but you can't teach them faithfulness." Let's let faithfulness be our highest priority in ourselves and others!

Paul told Timothy to take the Word and *"the same commit thou to faithful men, who shall be able to teach others also"* (2 Tim. 2:2). When Timothy found them, they were only faithful. But one day they would learn—be able—to teach.

Although Paul was a qualified man when God saved and called him, the Lord placed him in the ministry for his faithfulness: *"He counted me faithful, putting me into the ministry"* (1 Tim. 1:12).

When we stand before the Lord, He won't say to us, "Well done, thou good and <u>qualified</u> servant." God will reward us for our faithfulness! (Matt. 25:21). (BY)

AUGUST 30
WHAT'S YOUR SECRET?
JUDGES 16:4-20

"Entice him, and see wherein his great strength lieth" *(Judy. 16:5).*

Samson is renowned for his great strength. He killed a lion with his bare hands. He defeated thousands of enemy troops with only the jawbone of an ass. Anything the people could bind him with was broken in two like flax touched by a flame. He took the gates of the city, including the side posts, and carried them to the top of a nearby hill. He also pulled an entire theater down, killing thousands of people who were seated there.

Most pictures of Samson portray him as a man with massive muscles. If that were accurate, why then would everyone be trying to find out the secret of his great strength? If he was muscle-bound, they'd know why he was so strong. However, the truth is that Samson didn't look like a weightlifter. Thinking he did causes us to miss the real miracle of this story.

Samson's strength was not natural; he wasn't a strong man in himself. It was when the Spirit of the Lord came upon him that Samson manifested supernatural strength. Samson probably looked like an average man. It was God's supernatural ability, based on a covenant He'd made with Samson's parents, that Samson believed in and followed, that gave him his strength.

Likewise, it's not our own strength that produces victory in our lives. Thinking that we must have some superior power in ourselves and we just need to trust God for a little extra help is the very reason why most Christians fail. God's power is manifested perfectly when we realize our complete weakness (2 Cor. 12:9-10). Our critics should be astounded like Samson's enemies were, wondering what the secret is of our great power. Unlike Samson, we can tell them, "The strength of my life is faith in Christ!" (AW)

AUGUST 31
IT'S NOT OVER YET!
JUDGES 16:21-30

"Howbeit the hair of his head began to grow again after he was shaven" *(Judges 16:22).*

This story from Samson's life is both tragic and encouraging. It's tragic that a man who was so richly endowed by God didn't develop the character necessary to realize the full potential of his gift. Samson experienced tremendous personal loss because of his unfaithfulness to the Lord. But his hair began to grow again.

The source of Samson's great strength was his covenant with God. One of the terms of that covenant was that Samson's hair should never be cut. Samson violated that agreement. He didn't do it directly, but he laid his head in the lap of the Enemy, which always leads to disaster. Delilah shaved his head while he slept and his strength left him. The Philistines captured him, put out both his eyes, and made him grind corn like an ox.

In the midst of total failure, which came through no one's fault but his own, Samson's hair began to grow again. Praise God He made us so our hair can grow back!

Regardless of how you may have failed or what you may have lost, it's not over yet! Our God is a good God, full of mercy. There's always another chance. Spiritually speaking, there's no limit to how many times our hair can grow back. Samson had to call on God again—in faith with all his might—but his strength was renewed. His last act was his greatest accomplishment. Likewise, we too can come back from failure. Through faith in God, the best is yet to come! (AW)

SEPTEMBER 1
WHOSE LIFE ARE YOU TOUCHING?
ACTS 9:1-22

"And there was a certain disciple at Damascus, named Ananias; and to him said the Lord in a vision, Ananias. And he said, Behold, I am here, Lord" (Acts 9:10).

Everyone knows about Saul who later became known as the Apostle Paul. God used him to write half the New Testament. But do you know the person who brought sight back to Paul, ministered to him the baptism of the Holy Spirit, and gave him the prophecy he based his entire ministry on?

We often forget the Anne Sullivans who reach the Helen Kellers of this world. But without these people who aren't as famous as their disciples, we wouldn't have people like the Apostle Paul.

After this verse, Ananias isn't mentioned ever again in Scripture. As far as we know from the biblical account, Ananias never did any other great exploits. Certainly, he never did anything as earthshaking as his ministry to Paul. Yet, Ananias was a vital link in the chain of events that brought us one of God's greatest men.

In our modern day of distorted values, we've lost sight of the Ananiases of this world. We measure success by cold statistics that often overlook factors like loving parents who sacrificed so their children could succeed, or teachers who took a little extra time to make the difference in one pupil's life. We often fail to realize the potential of our own small acts.

Anyone can count the seeds in an apple, but only God can count the apples in a seed. Likewise, the potential of our deeds of love and faith to others are beyond human comprehension. Don't pass up an opportunity to bless someone else today. You could be ministering to the next Apostle Paul! (AW)

SEPTEMBER 2
WHERE ARE YOU?
ACTS 9:10-22

"And there was a certain disciple at Damascus, named Ananias; and to him said the Lord in a vision, Ananias. And he said, Behold, I am here, Lord" (Acts 9:10).

God called Ananias' name and he answered, *"Behold, I am here Lord."* What would've happened if Ananias wasn't there? What if he was doing something else and wasn't listening to God? The Lord might have found somebody else to do His will, but we don't know for sure. We can say this: Ananias would've missed the greatest opportunity of his life! How many people get to lead someone to the Lord who impacts the world like the Apostle Paul did?

There is great significance in the fact that Ananias was there. He was in a place of communion with the Lord. He was listening and attentive to Him. This doesn't come overnight. Certainly Ananias had spent much time in God's presence. How many days, weeks, or years had Ananias spent seeking the Lord before this time? As far as we know, God hadn't done anything before in his life that was as spectacular as what He was leading him to do at this time. However, Ananias remained faithful. He was there when the big opportunity came.

We often fail to recognize that we aren't normally going to see angels or have visions during our times of fellowship with the Lord. We won't always have goose bumps running up and down our spines. There is just the gentle peace and assurance of faith that God is with us. The spectacular comes only on occasion, but we must constantly practice waiting on the Lord.

Do you think God has ever called you and you weren't there? Don't let that happen today. Make sure your antenna is up and your faith is switched on so when the Lord calls your name, you'll hear Him! (AW)

SEPTEMBER 3
A GOOD RULE FOR REAPING
PROVERBS 6:6-8

"Go to the ant, thou sluggard; consider her ways, and be wise:
Which having no guide, overseer, or ruler, Provideth her meat
in the summer, and gathereth her food in the harvest" (*Prov. 6:6-8*).

The ant is a great example to us of God's plan to prosper His children. Ants are diligent workers. You've never seen a lazy ant, have you? God does not prosper believers who will not work.

God told Adam to be fruitful, multiply, and replenish the earth. But before He gave Adam a wife and family, He gave him a job. Adam had to tend and guard the Garden of Eden. Having a job isn't part of the curse. Even in paradise, man had to work. Adam was to provide an income and a home before he met Eve.

I heard a testimony of a man who prayed for prosperity, and all he received were job offers. Prosperity begins with a job, faith, and love: **"Let him labour, working with his hands the thing which is good, that he may have to give to him that needeth"** (Eph. 4:28). We should look to our job to give us seed to begin giving to others.

But how should we work? The lesson of the ant is: If you can work without supervision, you'll have more than enough. Paul warned the Ephesians not to work **"with eyeservice, as menpleasers"** (Eph. 6:6). This means we are not to work when the boss is looking and quit working when the boss is gone. We are to work as unto the Lord, because Jesus is with us all the time. We should work because Christ is watching over us, not because the supervisor is present.

Christians should be the best workers at the factory or office. As God's representatives, we should be there early and leave late. Believers shouldn't spend longer on lunch than needed and should put forth maximum effort at everything they do. We should set the standard for excellence! (BY)

SEPTEMBER 4
RECONCILED
2 CORINTHIANS 5:17-21

"And all things are of God, who hath reconciled us to himself by Jesus Christ,
and hath given to us the ministry of reconciliation" (*2 Cor. 5:18*).

Have you ever slaved over your checkbook trying to reconcile it with your bank statement? Sometimes it seems impossible. You think there must be a mistake. But through perseverance, the error is usually found and the two records agree. They are reconciled.

Reconciled simply means "to bring into agreement, or to make the same." When Jesus reconciled us to God, He brought us into agreement with, and made us just like, God. Some people think this is blasphemy, but that's what this word means.

Our born-again spirits have been made completely new and are reconciled to God. Our spirits are identical. The English word *reconciled* was translated from the Greek word *katallage*, which means "to change mutually." The word *mutually* means "possessed in common; as mutual interests." Since God never changes, it was our spirits that were changed to be just like His.

Some people can't accept this, because they know themselves only from a carnal point of view. They look in the mirror, search their thoughts, and find obvious things that aren't like Jesus. But in your spirit—if you're born again—you've been reconciled to God. Whatever God's Spirit is like is what your born-again spirit is like. Praise the Lord!

God's Word functions like our bank statement, with one major difference: It's never wrong. It's a perfect account of what has taken place in our born-again spirits. Our spirits have been reconciled to God. Now we must reconcile our minds to what the Word says about our born-again spirits! (AW)

SEPTEMBER 5
YOU ARE THE ELIJAH OF GOD!
1 KINGS 17:1-7

"And Elijah the Tishbite, who was of the inhabitants of Gilead, said unto Ahab,
As the LORD God of Israel liveth, before whom I stand, there shall not be dew nor rain these
years, but according to my word" (1 Kin. 17:1).

There's no background given on Elijah other than where he was from. No credentials were cited. His ancestry wasn't a factor. He didn't come from a long line of prophets. His looks and charisma weren't what thrust him to the forefront of everyone's attention. What set Elijah apart from everyone else was that he had the Word of God!

The same is true of every born-again believer. If you're saved, you have the word of the Lord on salvation. If you've ever been healed, you have a word from the Lord that's already been proven through healing manifesting in your body. If the Lord has delivered you emotionally or has shown you truths from His Word, then you too have a word from God. The only difference is that Elijah knew and believed what he had.

We don't properly value the revelation God has given us. Your revelation of salvation is better than any lost person's. You just need to be bold and proclaim it! If you know God wants you well, then you know something that the majority of the people you meet don't know. You must realize that it's God's truth, which has been revealed to you, that gives you authority and equips you to release His power to others.

Elijah put faith in the word God had given him and boldly proclaimed it. We would never have heard of Elijah if he had kept that word to himself. You too are an Elijah of God. You've received a word from the Lord. Now be bold and proclaim it! (AW)

SEPTEMBER 6
ARE YOU THERE?
1 KINGS 17:1-7

"And it shall be, that thou shalt drink of the brook; and I have
commanded the ravens to feed thee there" (1 Kin. 17:4).

This drought in the nation of Israel wasn't only a judgment on the ungodly, but it affected Elijah too. However, the Lord made supernatural provision for him. God commanded the ravens to provide bread and flesh for Elijah to eat every morning and evening. What a great miracle!

But notice in verse 4 that the Lord commanded the ravens to take Elijah's food to the brook Cherith. If Elijah hadn't obeyed God's command and gone there, he would've missed this miraculous provision. God's supply wasn't where Elijah was at the time that the word of the Lord came to him; it was THERE, at the brook.

God always makes provision for our needs, but we only receive it when we're where He wants us to be. The Lord always makes provision for whatever He calls us to do, but He sends it to where we're supposed to be, not necessarily where we are. Those who are waiting for the power of God to manifest before they go and do what God has said will never see it. It's not because He didn't supply it but because they were in the wrong place.

Your provision is where God sends you. If He has told you to boldly witness to others, you won't experience His power until you go and do it. If He's told you to lay hands on the sick and see them recover, His anointing will only be evident once you take the step of faith and do what He's told you to do.

If you can't see God's provision, maybe you aren't THERE yet! (AW)

SEPTEMBER 7
GO & DO
1 KINGS 17:1-7

***"So he went and did according unto the word of the LORD: for he went
and dwelt by the brook Cherith, that is before Jordan"*** *(1 Kin. 17:5).*

Elijah had the Word of God, which set him apart from the other people of his day. This put him in charge, and things happened according to his word. Therefore, the Lord made miraculous provision for his needs. All he had to do was be obedient to go and do what the Lord had spoken. He obeyed and God came through.

What would have happened if Elijah had not gone and done what the Lord told him to do? He could have starved, and all the great miracles that God worked through him later wouldn't have happened. The fire of God wouldn't have fallen from heaven and the nation of Israel wouldn't have experienced a revival. A widow would have died of starvation and her son would never have been raised from the dead.

We are always keeping statistics on what our labors for the Lord accomplish. But how do we qualify what would've happened if only someone would have been obedient to the Lord? Who knows what God wanted to do, but someone didn't go and do what the Lord told them to.

God has created each one of us with something unique, and only as we go and do will we release our God-given gifts to others. We are carrying around someone else's miracle inside of us. If we don't go and do, that person won't receive what the Lord has for them.

Make sure you release what God has put inside you today by going and doing what He tells you to. Other people are counting on you! (AW)

SEPTEMBER 8
JESUS WATCHES YOUR ATTITUDE IN GIVING
MARK 12:41

***"And Jesus sat over against the treasury, and beheld how
the people cast money into the treasury"*** *(Mark 12:41).*

This verse introduces the story of Jesus and the disciples observing the Pharisees who gave large sums of money and the widow who gave her mites. The point of this story isn't how much each gave, but the attitude behind their giving. Notice, Jesus watched *how* the people gave. The Lord was more interested in the heart behind the giving than the actual amount. The woman's amount of money was smaller, but her gift was larger. Jesus said she out-gave them all!

God weighs the quality of our giving more than the quantity. ***"For the love of money is the root of all evil: which while some coveted after, they have erred from the faith, and pierced themselves through with many sorrows"*** (1 Tim. 6:10). The Lord wants us to be in love with Him and to give from that motive.

God gives to us from a motive of love and wants us to imitate Him. ***"For God so loved the world, that he gave"*** (John 3:16). Love motivated God to give His best—His Son. Love should motivate us to give our best to the Lord—our firstfruits. This type of giving honors Him. ***"Honour the LORD with thy substance, and with the firstfruits of all thine increase"*** (Prov. 3:9).

The Pharisees gave out of self-interest, not love for God and compassion toward people. This motive caused them to give large amounts to impress people or to remove a feeling of guilt for not truly obeying God's Word.

Make your giving count! Let every penny you give come from your love for God and His people. Your gifts will advance the kingdom, and you'll receive a reward for being a cheerful giver. (BY)

SEPTEMBER 9
GOD ALWAYS HAS A PLAN!
1 SAMUEL 3:1-10

"And ere the lamp of God went out in the temple of the LORD, where the ark of God was, and Samuel was laid down to sleep" *(1 Sam. 3:3).*

Eli was the high priest of the nation of Israel for forty years (1 Sam. 4:18). He feared God and served Him faithfully, but his sons did not. Although they were carrying out the duties of the priesthood, they were wicked. They took more than the portion God had allowed them (1 Sam. 2:14) and they committed fornication with the women who came to the temple of the Lord (1 Sam. 2:22).

Eli was now an old man in his late nineties. He'd be gone soon, and his sons certainly weren't able to lead the nation in a godly direction. So the Lord chose Samuel to fill the void of spiritual leadership. This phrase, **"ere the lamp of God went out in the temple,"** was talking about more than just the extinguishing of the physical lamp. It was speaking of the spiritual leadership God had invested in Eli.

Before Eli died, the Lord raised up Samuel as a prophet in the land. Sometimes true godly leaders have been in short supply, but they're always there. Any time we start feeling that all the godly people are gone, we've succumbed to the Elijah syndrome (1 Kin. 19:10) and it's always wrong (1 Kin. 19:18). Samuel was brought to Eli as a young boy of two or three and was probably a teenager at this time. The Lord had been working on Eli's replacement for quite awhile. God always has our provision before we even have the need!

At times it may look like things are out of control and there's very little hope, but God always has His person. The world desperately needs godly leaders today. Be still, listen for His call, and then respond as Samuel did by saying, "Speak, Lord, for your servant is listening." (AW)

SEPTEMBER 10
PERSONAL LIABILITY
1 SAMUEL 3:11-18

"For I have told him that I will judge his house for ever for the iniquity which he knoweth; because his sons made themselves vile, and he restrained them not" *(1 Sam. 3:13).*

Eli's sons—Hophni and Phinehas—were very wicked. They perverted the priest's office by despising the Lord's sacrifices and lording it over God's people (1 Sam. 2:12-17). They also committed fornication with the women who came to the tabernacle (1 Sam. 2:22). It's understandable why God judged them, but why did Eli come under judgment?

Some would say it was because he was their father and, therefore, was responsible for their actions. But that's not what the Lord said! In this verse, God declared He was judging Eli because he knew what his sons were doing and restrained them not. Eli wasn't judged for what his sons did. He was judged because he didn't use his authority to restrain them.

Eli did rebuke his sons. In 1 Samuel 2:22-25, he told them that what they were doing was wrong and that they'd be judged by God. However, Eli didn't go on to restrain them from doing these things. He was the high priest. He could've removed them from the priesthood, but he didn't. He preferred his own sons over God (1 Sam. 2:29). Talk isn't enough. Consequences must be attached to wrong actions. Eli didn't act.

Satan often condemns us over the actions of others, especially our children. But God holds us accountable for our own actions, not theirs. God believes in and practices personal liability. Apply this truth in your own life and business today. You're the only one you have absolute authority over and responsibility for. (AW)

SEPTEMBER 11
THE POWER OF GOD'S WORD
1 SAMUEL 5:1-12

"Dagon was fallen upon his face to the ground before the ark of the LORD; and the head of Dagon and both the palms of his hands were cut off upon the threshold; only the stump of Dagon was left to him" (1 Sam. 5:4).

The Ark of the Covenant contained the two tables of stone with the Ten Commandments written on them that the Lord had given to Moses (Deut. 10:2-5). It also contained all the writings of Moses, also known as the first five books of the Bible (Deut. 31:24-26). So the ark contained God's Word.

Israel had been defeated in battle (1 Sam. 4), and the ark had been captured by the Philistines. They brought the ark as a trophy into the temple of their fish God, Dagon. But the next morning, they found the image of Dagon laying face down, prostrate before the Ark of the Covenant. Hoping this was a mere coincidence, they set the statue back up in its place. However, the same thing happened the next morning—except this time Dagon's head and both hands were cut off and placed on the threshold of the temple.

This graphically illustrates the power of God's Word. Neither Satan, nor any of his demons, can stand before it. Only the stump of what the devil was is left to remind us of our vanquished foe. He's already been conquered!

Jesus used God's Word to defeat the devil (Matt. 4 and Luke 4). Anything Christ said would've been Scripture, since He is God. Yet He quoted the same written Word that we have, because He couldn't come up with anything more powerful. God's Word is powerful! The written Word of God that we have is infinitely more powerful than most of us realize. We have that same power that made Dagon fall prostrate before the ark. Put God's Word inside you today, and watch your problems bow down! (AW)

SEPTEMBER 12
THINGS TO COME
1 SAMUEL 9:15-10:13

"And it was so, that when he had turned his back to go from Samuel, God gave him another heart: and all those signs came to pass that day" (1 Sam. 10:9).

Contemplate for a moment how miraculous Samuel's words of knowledge were. The Lord told him he would meet the king-to-be the next day. When Samuel saw Saul, God spoke that this was the one. In Samuel's comments to Saul, he told him that the asses he'd lost three days before had been found. Saul hadn't even mentioned that to Samuel. This was a powerful word of knowledge!

In 1 Samuel 10:2-6, Samuel told Saul that he would meet two men at Rachel's tomb who would tell him the asses had been found. He went on to prophesy that three men would meet Saul in a specific location and told him exactly what they'd be carrying. Then Samuel said they would give him two loaves of bread. How specific can you get? He also prophesied that at the hill of God, a company of prophets would meet him and Saul would join in and prophesy with them. Every one of these things came to pass that same day. This is one of the most awesome displays of the word of knowledge in all the Word of God!

Jesus said that when the Holy Spirit came, He would show us things to come (John 16:13). The New Testament also reveals that what we have in Christ is much better than anything the Old Testament saints had. There's simply no comparison (2 Cor. 3:6-11). God's Word says that the Old Testament saints longed for what we have now (1 Pet. 1:10-12). The very least saint in the kingdom of God has a greater salvation than what Samuel had (Matt. 11:11). Yet, look at how God used him!

It suffices to say that none of us have realized our full potential. Let the Lord challenge you to flow in His supernatural ability today more than ever before. (AW)

SEPTEMBER 13
COMMITMENT, NOT CONVENIENCE
1 SAMUEL 13:1-14

"And Samuel said to Saul, Thou hast done foolishly: thou hast not kept the commandment of the LORD thy God, which he commanded thee: for now would the LORD have established thy kingdom upon Israel for ever" (1 Sam. 13:13).

Many people think that whatever the Lord wills to happen occurs regardless of what we do. This verse proves that wrong. The Lord had plans to establish Saul's kingdom over Israel forever. If Saul would have obeyed, then we'd be talking about the sure mercies of Saul instead of the sure mercies of David (Is. 55:3 and Acts 13:34). David wasn't God's first choice—Saul was. Yet, he didn't accomplish all of God's plans for him because of his disobedience.

Saul's disobedience wasn't hatred for God. Saul had an arrangement with Samuel to wait seven days for him to come and offer a sacrifice before he engaged in battle with the Philistines. Samuel didn't show in the allotted time, so Saul offered the sacrifice himself.

Saul wasn't eager to disobey the Lord. He waited the amount of time Samuel had said. But circumstances "forced" him to disobey God, or so Saul reasoned. The truth is that those who obey the Lord only when it's convenient will never have God entrust true leadership to them.

The kingdom of God is going uphill, while Satan's kingdom is headed downhill. In other words, following God is never the easy thing to do. Those who don't commit themselves to obeying Him at all costs will always find a reason to do otherwise. Obedience is based in commitment, not convenience.

God has great plans for your life (Jer. 29:11). But you need to cooperate by following Him at all costs. Commitment is the key. (AW)

SEPTEMBER 14
MONEY IS NECESSARY FOR SPREADING THE GOSPEL
ROMANS 10:15

"And how shall they preach, except they be sent?" (Rom. 10:15).

God isn't the only one who sends people to preach—people also send people. With the call of God comes a call on many others to prayerfully and financially support those being sent. When God sends, He supports. When people send, they also support.

People never stand alone. An individual called to pastor must have many others called to support them. Ushers, Sunday school teachers, and youth directors are only a few who sense the call of God on their lives to hold up the hands of the one called by God. Behind one calling is the calling of many!

Like God, churches send people to preach. *"Now when the apostles which were at Jerusalem heard that Samaria had received the word of God, they sent unto them Peter and John"* (Acts 8:14). I'm sure the Holy Spirit must have spoken to the hearts of Peter and John to go, but the church also sent them. *"Then tidings of these things came unto the ears of the church which was in Jerusalem: and they sent forth Barnabas, that he should go as far as Antioch"* (Acts 11:22). Throughout the book of Acts, churches cooperated with the call of God and confirmed it by sending out a person or group. This was done by the laying on of hands. *"And when they had fasted and prayed, and laid their hands on them, they sent them away"* (Acts 13:3).

This sending forth must have been done with the giving of finances also. When Paul ran out of money in Corinth, the call of God came to the saints of Macedonia to give and assist him. They sent out ministers to bring the money to Paul and free him from his tent-making occupation to preach the Gospel again without financial restraints.

Every time you send money to a minister of God, you're assisting the call of God on their life. God has sent you to hold up the hands of many who are called and sent into the fields of harvest! (BY)

SEPTEMBER 15
WHO HAVE YOU TOLD?
2 KINGS 5:1-14

"And she said unto her mistress, Would God my lord were with the prophet that is in Samaria! for he would recover him of his leprosy" (2 Kin. 5:3).

This is a wonderful account of Naaman being healed of leprosy. God used Elisha to effect one of the most miraculous healings in the Bible. Thousands have been healed because of this one miracle, and millions of others have been inspired to believe God for His best through the story. None of it would have happened if this slave girl had not spoken to Naaman about the power of God.

This girl was an Israelite who'd been captured by the Syrians and made a slave. She could have been bitter and wished the death of her master. She could have been feeling so sorry for herself that she wasn't thinking about anyone else. But instead, she showed compassion and told her master about the prophet in Israel who could make him whole. Without her witness, Naaman wouldn't have been healed. Her testimony was as much a part of this miracle as Elisha's faith!

Too often we forget those who are responsible for bringing people in need to the ones who can help them. There were four men who let the paralytic down through the roof to be healed by Jesus. The Scriptures say that Jesus saw THEIR faith (Mark 2:5). Andrew brought his brother to the Lord. Although Peter went on to become the more renowned of the two, he wouldn't have been introduced to Jesus without Andrew.

You may not feel equipped to meet all the needs of those around you, but you do know where to send them. Jesus is the answer to every need of those we encounter daily. But how can they believe if we don't tell them? Lord, we pray that You'll help us get beyond ourselves and reach out to others in need with the good news of Your love for them. Amen! (AW)

SEPTEMBER 16
DON'T FORGET THE SMALL STUFF!
2 KINGS 5:1-14

"And his servants came near, and spake unto him, and said, My father, if the prophet had bid thee do some great thing, wouldest thou not have done it? how much rather then, when he saith to thee, Wash, and be clean?" (2 Kin. 5:13).

Naaman came to Israel expecting a miracle. However, he had preconceptions about how it would be done. He was looking for a spectacular miracle. Although he anticipated some mystical exhibition from Elisha, he didn't get it.

Likewise, many people today miss God in their everyday lives because they don't understand that He delights in using the ordinary. Dipping in the Jordan River seven times is nothing special. Countless people had done that before with no miraculous results. But they hadn't done it in response to a command from God. It wasn't the dipping that released God's power, but the obedient faith.

Many people are willing to do some great thing in order to receive a manifestation of God's power. They'll make great sacrifices and travel to the ends of the earth, but very few are willing to do the simple, ordinary, everyday things that are key to unlocking the true power of God.

Are we spending time alone with the Lord? Do we read His Word? Do we listen for His voice to give us guidance? Do we follow His leading to speak to our neighbors, co-workers, and relatives? If we aren't doing these things, then we're like Naaman—wanting results without doing the simple things we've been commanded to do.

If you are truly willing to do the great things which demand more time and effort, then shouldn't you be willing to be obedient in the simple, everyday things that God has commanded you to do? (AW)

SEPTEMBER 17
HOW MANY TIMES HAVE YOU DIPPED?
2 KINGS 5:1-14

"Then went he down, and dipped himself seven times in Jordan,
according to the saying of the man of God: and his flesh came again
like unto the flesh of a little child, and he was clean" (2 Kin. 5:14).

Naaman wasn't told to dip in the Jordan River; he was told to dip seven times in the Jordan River. There's a big difference!

We don't know all the details, but it would appear that this miracle didn't happen gradually. Naaman didn't get a little better with every dip. It's probable that there was absolutely no change in his condition until after he came up out of the water the seventh time. This sounds just like the Lord!

Faith is what pleases God (Heb. 11:6). He loves it when we act in faith. Yet most of us hate acting in faith. We love sight. We prefer to do what we can see, taste, hear, smell, and feel working. If our senses don't perceive anything, we usually quit doing it. That's precisely why we often miss our miracle!

What if Naaman had thought *This isn't doing any good at all!* and quit after the sixth dip? He wouldn't have seen the healing of his leprosy. What if the disciples had not cast their nets in just one more time? They wouldn't have received the miraculous catch (Luke 5:4-7).

What if you don't keep doing what the Lord has told you to do? You may wonder, *Well, what has it produced?* Have you dipped all seven times yet? In the spiritual realm, maybe you're only on the third, fourth, or fifth time. You need to keep doing what the Lord has told you to do—in faith—believing that your labor is not in vain (1 Cor. 15:58). Rejoice—your time is coming! (AW)

SEPTEMBER 18
A BIGGER CUP
PSALM 23:5

"My cup runneth over" (Ps. 23:5).

When the manna fell in the wilderness for the Israelites to eat, we're told that everyone gathered and ate *"according to his eating"* (Ex.16:16).

This meant every person gathered and ate according to their capacity. Skinny people gathered and ate a little and heavy people gathered and ate much. They collected what they could eat. Anyone who gathered too much saw the heavenly bread spoil.

This Old Testament story is used as an example of New Testament financial prosperity. *"As it is written, He that had gathered much had nothing over; and he that had gathered little had no lack"* (2 Cor. 8:15). The meaning is simple. If you want to be able to handle more prosperity, you must increase your capacity. God gives more to those who can handle it. If your cup is running over and you're losing what God is giving, build a bigger cup.

You may think that's easier said than done, but really it's simple. Your cup is your understanding of God's Word. Knowledge and application of the Word is the key to handling more of God's divine provision. The Lord wants us to *"prosper and be in health, even as thy soul prospereth"* (3 John 2).

A line from a popular movie says, "If you build it, they will come." God tells us if we'll build a bigger cup, the prosperity will come. It's not up to us to find more prosperity. That's God's job. Our responsibility is to enlarge our capacity to handle His blessings. Once this is accomplished, the additional prosperity will come.

You don't give a child $1,000. You may give that child an allowance of just a few dollars, but maturity is needed to receive more. With more money comes a greater degree of responsibility. Building a bigger cup—enlarging your capacity to handle prosperity—is just another term for growing up spiritually. (BY)

SEPTEMBER 19
TITHING IS GOD COMING AFTER YOUR POVERTY!
MALACHI 3:10-12

"Bring ye all the tithes into the storehouse, that there may be meat in mine house, and prove me now herewith, saith the LORD of hosts, if I will not open you the windows of heaven, and pour you out a blessing, that there shall not be room enough to receive it" *(Mal. 3:10).*

I recently read a testimony of a man named Oswald J. Smith who pastored a church in Toronto, Canada, during the Great Depression. As you can imagine, there were many, many people who were destitute during that time who would come to the church for assistance. That's where people should be able to go—to church. Through the tithes and gifts of believers, the church should be able to provide for the needs of people. That's exactly how the early church did things. Pastor Smith was responsible for sowing hundreds of dollars into the lives of needy people who had nowhere else to turn except to God. During that time, he observed something very interesting. He asked each person or family that he helped a question: "Are you tithing?" The response every single time was no. Not one person had been faithful to tithe. It was confirmation to him that if God's people would be faithful to tithe, He would be faithful to supply their needs.

Tithing isn't God coming after your money; it's God coming after your poverty. The Lord can't supply a harvest to you unless you plant the seed. If you don't sow anything, He has nothing to increase. If you'd like to see abundance in your life, do it God's way. Tithe, and give offerings above your tithe. Poverty can't stay when God is being glorified by your giving! (BN)

SEPTEMBER 20
HOW DO YOU SEE?
2 CORINTHIANS 5:1-7

"For we walk by faith, not by sight" *(2 Cor. 5:7).*

Imagine for a moment that you're blind, deaf, and trying to cross a busy highway during rush hour traffic. That's not an appealing thought, is it? We rely so heavily on our senses to function in this world that it's hard to think of how life would be without them. We'd have to compensate somehow, or just stop doing many of the things we do.

Faith is in the kingdom of God what our senses are in the natural world. Through faith we see, hear, feel, and experience spiritual reality. Without faith, we're as helpless in the spiritual world as a blind and deaf person is in the physical world. Those who don't operate in faith are missing out on the goodness of God at best and being run over by the devil at worst.

We face unseen spiritual dangers daily. Just as a person cannot go walking with their eyes closed without paying a price, anyone without faith will also be injured in some way. The good news is that every born-again Christian already has faith. It's not just a weak faith, but the faith of God (Eph. 2:8, Rom. 12:3, Gal. 2:20). It's not a matter of being without; it's a matter of not using what we have.

God created us with physical eyes, and He recreated every true Christian with faith. However, it is possible to walk through life with our eyes closed, and it's possible for a Christian to not use their faith. The way we open our spiritual eyes (faith) is through God's Word. God's Word is the window through which we see into the spiritual world. Those who aren't living by the Word are walking by sight and not by faith. Open your spiritual eyes today! Trust what God's Word says more than what your physical senses tell you. (AW)

SEPTEMBER 21
GOD IS SPEAKING
JOHN 10:1-5

"To him the porter openeth; and the sheep hear his voice: and he calleth his own sheep by name, and leadeth them out" (John 10:3).

This verse clearly states that God's sheep hear His voice. In the next verse, Jesus says His sheep know His voice. Finally, verse 5 says His sheep do not know the voice of strangers.

These statements made by Jesus are totally opposite what most Christians experience. The vast majority of believers hear Satan speak to them frequently, but have a hard time hearing the Lord. That's not normal Christianity. Jesus paints a picture showing that His sheep are sensitive to His voice and hard of hearing when it comes to anyone else. That should be the typical Christian experience!

What's happening? Why does our experience seem to be so opposite what Jesus said it should be? We can be assured that the problem is in our hearing, not in God's speaking. The Lord speaks to us continually in many different ways, but we often miss it.

Psalm 19:1-4 declares that God speaks to us through creation. Each day has something new to say to us. However, most people are too busy to notice. God speaks loud and clear through His Word, but few of us can find the time to really listen. Yet, it seems we make the time for just about everything else. Radio, television, newspapers, internet, videos, movies, work, and a multitude of other things all vie for our attention. Quality time with God is often the casualty.

Jesus said that He is speaking and has equipped us to hear. We just need to tune in! (AW)

SEPTEMBER 22
ARE YOU WHERE YOU'RE SUPPOSED TO BE?
2 SAMUEL 11:1-27

"And it came to pass, after the year was expired, at the time when kings go forth to battle, that David sent Joab, and his servants with him, and all Israel; and they destroyed the children of Ammon, and besieged Rabbah.
But David tarried still at Jerusalem" (2 Sam. 11:1).

David was the king and it was the time when kings went to battle. But David tarried in Jerusalem and just sent his troops on ahead. That wasn't the way he did it before. In the next chapter, David's commanding general pleaded with him to return to the battle. If David had done what he was called to do, it's probable that he wouldn't have had this encounter with Bathsheba.

Of course, David had deeper problems than just not being in the right place and doing what he was anointed to do. His relationship with the Lord must have been in decline for some time. Failure to be in touch with God causes restlessness, which often propels us into the wrong place at the wrong time.

Successful people often abandon the very things that brought them to the top. When Saul was little in his own eyes, the Lord promoted him (1 Sam. 15:17). In his success, he abandoned dependency on God. Solomon did the same thing. He started out in great humility and sought only to be faithful to God, but his success corrupted him. This is also what happened to David.

David had reached a point of success where he no longer HAD to seek God. He no longer HAD to fight his own battles. He had others who would do it for him. This left him free to wander, which is exactly what he did.

Hard times aren't the true test of what's inside a person. Everyone seeks the Lord when their backs are against the wall. Life's greatest test is success. Make fellowship with the Lord your first priority—in both good times and bad! (AW)

SEPTEMBER 23
YOU GIVE WHAT YOU HAVE
2 SAMUEL 12:1-6

"And David's anger was greatly kindled against the man; and he said to Nathan, As the LORD liveth, the man that hath done this thing shall surely die" (2 Sam. 12:5).

Have you ever noticed that the guilty are usually the most vocal opponents of the very things they're doing? As Shakespeare said, "Me thinks thou protest too loudly." The hatred we have for our own sin manifests itself in our treatment of others.

There have been many times that I've told a woman who was battered by her husband that this treatment wasn't personal. He can only give what he has. And since he's miserable inside, that's why he mistreats his wife. This has caused wives to look at the situation differently and actually have compassion instead of judgment toward their mates. That key often unlocks the door to the other's heart and starts the healing process.

Are you short-tempered with others? Do you constantly find fault with everything? It's possible that the problem really isn't with others, but with you. Are you upset with yourself? Are you never satisfied with your own performance? Have you not found true forgiveness in the grace of God?

We can't control what others around us do, but we can control ourselves. As we appropriate the love of God that's available to us personally, we'll be able to extend that love to others. If we are void of God's love, it'll show in our treatment of others.

David was miserable inside, and his hatred for his own sin came out in his judgment of others. Don't make that same mistake. Receive God's love and forgiveness today! (AW)

SEPTEMBER 24
YOU GET WHAT YOU GIVE
2 SAMUEL 12:1-14

"And David's anger was greatly kindled against the man; and he said to Nathan, As the LORD liveth, the man that hath done this thing shall surely die" (2 Sam. 12:5).

This parable isn't really about a rich man taking a poor man's sheep; it's about David taking another man's wife and then killing him. Why the pretense? It appears that the Lord was letting David dictate his own punishment. Matthew 7:2 says, *"For with what judgment ye judge, ye shall be judged: and with what measure ye mete, it shall be measured to you again."* This is what happened to David. He received what he gave.

David demanded the death penalty and much more. This man not only had to pay with his life, but was made to make a fourfold restitution. This is what happened to David. David's son had to die, and the sword would never stop pursuing him. More than that, God raised up evil out of David's own house to afflict him. David's wives were taken from him, as he had taken Uriah's wife. Although David committed his sin privately, God would execute His judgment publicly.

Praise the Lord for our superior covenant! God will not judge us the way He judged David. Jesus bore that judgment for us. However, there is still the principle of reaping our own judgment. People treat us the way we treat them. If we're harsh and unforgiving, then people will treat us that way. Those who show mercy receive mercy (James 2:13).

We don't have to learn everything the hard way; we can learn through other people's mistakes. David should be a negative example to us all. We need to remember that the way we judge others is the way we'll be judged. Do you want that? If not, now would be a good time to start sowing mercy. (AW)

SEPTEMBER 25
THE SEED THAT LEAVES YOUR HAND
NEVER LEAVES YOUR FUTURE!
2 KINGS 8:1-6

"And when the king asked the woman, she told him. So the king appointed unto her a certain officer, saying, Restore all that was hers, and all the fruits of the field since the day that she left the land, even until now" (2 Kin. 8:6).

Many of us are familiar with the passage of the Bible where Isaac reaped even in famine (Gen. 26:1,12), but that's not the only example. Do you remember the Shunammite woman in 2 Kings 4:1-37? She and her husband built a prophet's chamber to house Elisha when he was in their area. They planted a seed. They sowed into Elisha's life. Then, when their son died, Elisha prayed and the boy was raised from the dead.

But, as if that wasn't enough, her reaping didn't stop there. *"Then spake Elisha unto the woman, whose son he had restored to life, saying, Arise, and go thou and thine household, and sojourn wheresoever thou canst sojourn: for the LORD hath called for a famine; and it shall also come upon the land seven years. And the woman arose, and did after the saying of the man of God: and she went with her household, and sojourned in the land of the Philistines seven years"* (2 Kin. 8:1-2). God warned her about the famine ahead of time. When it was over, she returned to beg the king to give her back the land that she had deserted for seven years.

Just look how God set it all up: divine connections and divine appointments. It "just so happened" that the king was talking with Gehazi, Elisha's servant, wanting to know about the great things Elisha had done. And, it "just so happened" that Gehazi told him about the Shunammite woman and how her son was raised from the dead. While Gehazi was telling the king about this miracle, in walks the very woman. Coincidence? Not at all! God set it up. The king was obviously hungry to hear about the things of God. He was stirred. The woman told the king of her situation, and not only did he restore her land but also everything that it produced while she was gone. Did you catch that? *Her land was still producing fruit even in famine!* Oh, when we serve God and follow His way of doing things, He'll provide for us! He is faithful! We will reap even in famine! The seed that leaves your hand will never leave your future! (BN)

SEPTEMBER 26
GOD IS OUR FATHER
MATTHEW 7:7-11

"If ye then, being evil, know how to give good gifts unto your children, how much more shall your Father which is in heaven give good things to them that ask him?" (Matt. 7:11).

Did you hear about the little child who went around confessing that his father wouldn't drop him? He had to confess that his father would feed and clothe him too. If it wasn't for his constant badgering, none of his needs would've been met. Of course, you didn't hear that! It didn't happen. Even the worst fathers treat their children better than that!

We often expect more from our earthly fathers than we do from our heavenly Father. This is the point Jesus was making: If we put faith in human relationships, how much more should we be 100 percent confident of God's love and care for us? The best father in the world is evil in comparison to God. Therefore, we should trust Him more than any child trusts their father. Sadly, most Christians haven't entered into the Abba-Father relationship with the Lord yet.

A good parent would never let their child starve. Yet infants cry when they are hungry as if they're starving to death. This is tolerable from an infant, because they don't know any better. But something would be seriously wrong if a teenager still cried each time they wanted their parent to meet a need. Children need to grow up!

Likewise, the Lord provides for our every need. However, very few people have matured beyond the infant stage. We still cry and plead for our needs to be met instead of trusting a loving heavenly Father who has never failed us. Faith pleases God (Heb. 11:6). Show a little faith in your Father today, and praise Him in advance for His provision! (AW)

SEPTEMBER 27
OUR EXPECTATIONS DICTATE OUR EXPERIENCES
JOHN 20:11-17

*"And when she had thus said, she turned herself back, and saw Jesus standing,
and knew not that it was Jesus" (John 20:14).*

Mary didn't recognize Jesus. This is amazing! She was one of the women who followed the Lord and ministered to Him throughout His earthly ministry (Luke 8:2-3). She knew Him well and had heard His voice thousands of times. Jesus honored Mary by choosing her to be the first person He appeared to after His resurrection. Yet, she supposed He was the gardener.

Certainly, one of the principle reasons why Mary didn't recognize Jesus is that she wasn't expecting to see Him alive. The thought that Jesus could be alive hadn't yet entered her mind. Our expectations dictate our experiences!

God is who He is, regardless of what we think about Him. As far as our experience goes, we will only experience Him the way we think He is. For instance, those who believe that God doesn't heal today won't be healed until they begin to believe differently. Those who don't believe in the baptism of the Holy Spirit won't receive it. Those who don't believe Jesus rose from the dead will not recognize the risen Christ, even if He stood before them.

What do you believe about God? If you think He's angry with you, you won't experience His pleasure, even though Scripture says you're accepted in the beloved (Eph. 1:6). If you believe He's forsaken you, you won't recognize His presence, even though He never leaves nor forsakes you (Heb. 13:5).

Mary recognized Jesus when He called her name. It was the personal relationship between them that finally opened her eyes. Listen for Jesus to call you by name today, and see Him as He really is. (AW)

SEPTEMBER 28
WHAT'S YOUR PROBLEM?
PSALM 51

*"Against thee, thee only, have I sinned, and done this evil in thy sight: that thou mightest be
justified when thou speakest, and be clear when thou judgest" (Ps. 51:4).*

As a youth, David faced a lion and a bear with his bare hands and prevailed. This young boy boldly fought the giant Goliath when no one else would. David was fearless in countless battles and never faced a foe he didn't defeat—except himself. David was his own worst enemy. Wild animals couldn't kill him. Countless numbers of enemy troops couldn't destroy him. But his own lust slew him and caused untold grief.

This is the case with us all. The enemies without are nothing compared to the enemy within— our selves. You must kill yourself or it'll kill you. This doesn't mean the end of us, because through Jesus we have a new self—a new identity. We've been born again. We are new creatures in Christ Jesus (2 Cor. 5:17). When the old man dies, the new man lives.

One of the greatest plagues of our world today is a lack of recognizing ourselves as the enemy. People blame their problems on everything and everyone but themselves. The truth is, outside pressures are only influences, not the determining cause of our actions. We're the ones who choose our actions and reactions. Other people aren't our problem. We are our problem. Only in Jesus can we experience freedom from ourselves.

David humbled himself and acknowledged his sin. He blamed no one but himself. He turned from self to God and found forgiveness. We need to do the same. (AW)

SEPTEMBER 29
WHOM DOES GOD PROSPER?
PSALM 35:27

**"Let them shout for joy, and be glad, that favour my righteous cause:
yea, let them say continually, Let the LORD be magnified, which hath
pleasure in the prosperity of his servant"** (Ps. 35:27).

This verse should give you a reason to shout. God delights and has great pleasure when you prosper. I think this verse is trying to wake up most Christians. God is more anxious for you to prosper than you are! Instead of feeling guilty about prospering, you can actually sense God's pleasure over you.

But whom does God delight in prospering? Those who favor His righteous cause. What is God's righteous cause? Souls! When winning the lost is your highest priority, you share God's highest priority. As you give into His work, sowing tithes and offerings to Him, imagine His delight as He searches for ways to bring social, family, business, and financial prosperity to you. His rejoicing then becomes your rejoicing. His joy becomes yours. This verse says you can shout for joy and be glad.

The rejoicing of the Lord then comes through your own mouth. Your lips begin to continually bless the Lord. What should your continual confession be? "Let the Lord be magnified, which hath pleasure in my prosperity." When you put God's desires above your own, His promise to you is, **"Wealth and riches shall be in his house: and his righteousness endureth for ever"** (Ps. 112:3). Your rejoicing can also be continual, because God gives the joy of the Holy Spirit with His prosperity. **"The blessing of the LORD, it maketh rich, and he addeth no sorrow with it"** (Prov. 10:22).

Finally, your prosperity and joy become a witness to the lost. Prosperity is promised to those who will follow after the commandments of the Lord. One result is, **"And all people of the earth shall see that thou art called by the name of the LORD; and they shall be afraid of thee"** (Deut. 28:10). Your prosperity is a witness even when your mouth is silent. (BY)

SEPTEMBER 30
WHERE IS THE FOURTH MAN?
DANIEL 3:1-30

"He answered and said, Lo, I see four men loose, walking in the midst of the fire, and they have no hurt; and the form of the fourth is like the Son of God" (Dan. 3:25).

Most of us see things differently than we should. We look at a situation like the one these three Hebrew children were in and we think that being thrown into the fiery furnace should be avoided at all cost. That's why most people would compromise their beliefs in circumstances like these. However, the safest place to be is where the fourth man is.

This fourth person was none other than the Son of God. In His presence was more than enough power to protect them from the fire. Wherever Jesus is, is where we should want to be. It's far better to be thrown into the furnace with Jesus than to be outside the furnace without Him.

Not everyone sees it that way, because the truth is that not everyone's total security is in Him. We trust in many things other than the Lord. Therefore, it's hard to let go of our natural defenses and place ourselves totally in His hand. However, that's where our true protection is.

Where is Jesus leading you? What has He called you to do? That's where you'll find Him and all His provision. Regardless of what it looks like it may cost you to follow Him, everything you need and desire is where Jesus is. If you're walking closely with Him, you won't be burned.

All of us long to have Jesus walk and commune with us, but are we willing to go through the fire if that's where He is? It's worth it! Jesus is where He's told us to go. There is where we'll find Him and all His supply! (AW)

OCTOBER 1
GIVE THE LORD YOUR BEST & MOST COSTLY
2 SAMUEL 24:24

"And the king said unto Araunah, Nay; but I will surely buy it of thee at a price: neither will I offer burnt offerings unto the LORD my God of that which doth cost me nothing. So David bought the threshingfloor" (2 Sam. 24:24).

David the king looked at every circumstance as an opportunity to sow seed. He also wanted to sow quality seed. David gave generously and blessed the person he was dealing with. In this story, he purchased the threshing floor, which would become the altar for the Ark of the Covenant to rest beside and the future altar of the temple of God.

God gave His best for us. He didn't give an angel to die for us, but His only Son. Jesus is God's finest—His first-fruits.

Another title for our gift to God is first-fruits. It's not called this just because it is given off the top but because it's the best of the crop. The choicest of the crop produces the best when planted. Any farmer knows to look for the best of the seed to plant. You don't eat the best, but sow it. Poor quality seed produces a poor quality harvest. An excellent harvest comes from excellent seed.

I've seen many Christians give poor quality gifts to the Lord. Cars have been given that needed repair, clothing that was old and torn, and appliances that didn't work. Why give someone else your headaches? Mountains are to be removed into the sea, not into someone else's backyard. Would you like someone else's problems? Why then would they want yours?

What you sow, you reap. How would you like a hundredfold return on the junk you've sown? Wouldn't it be better to receive a great harvest of good quality merchandise back into your life? Repair what you're about to give, and make it a gift of quality. Bring it up to a standard that would bless you if someone gave it into your life. It's good to give what you would just as soon keep. It can then be a blessing in the life of the one you're giving it to, just as it would be in yours. (BY)

OCTOBER 2
YOU'RE AN AXE HANDLE
2 KINGS 6:1-7

"But as one was felling a beam, the axe head fell into the water: and he cried, and said, Alas, master! for it was borrowed" (2 Kin. 6:5).

There are many similarities between an axe and us. The axe handle is made of wood, which is the same substance that the axe is designed to cut. But wood can't cut wood. It's the axe head, which is made of iron that does the cutting. However, the axe head is unproductive without the axe handle.

We are like the axe handle. In our humanity, we're incapable of felling the problems in our lives. It takes something much stronger than us to topple our challenges. The anointing of God is the axe head. It's the power that cuts through the difficulties of life. The power of the axe head is dependent on the axe handle. Without the handle, the axe head does nothing. And without the axe head, the handle is powerless.

It's not just God's "sovereignty" that determines what happens in our lives. Although, it certainly isn't our efforts, independent of God, that bring victory. We must have God's ability joined to our availability to strike the blow that defeats the devil.

An axe handle attaches to the head through a hole in which it slips through. Then the handle has to be split by putting a wedge in the top of it. This fixes the handle in place through pressure against the sides of the axe head.

Likewise, the only way we can hold on to the power of God in our lives is to have a clear split between our confidence in ourselves and our confidence in God. The greater the distinction between these two, the more secure the axe head. (AW)

OCTOBER 3
SECURE YOUR HEAD!
2 KINGS 6:1-7

"But as one was felling a beam, the axe head fell into the water: and he cried, and said, Alas, master! for it was borrowed" (2 Kin. 6:5).

Have you ever lost an axe head? I have. It doesn't happen all at once. The head begins to slip, little by little, before it actually comes off. The person using the axe is aware of the slippage, but typically doesn't want to take the time and effort to fix the problem. Consequently, they just keep swinging until the head comes off. I did this once and lost the axe head in thick brush. I didn't find it until the next year. That brought chopping wood to a complete halt. It would've been more to my advantage to take care of the problem right away, but I was too busy.

In the same way, the power of God doesn't just depart from us in an instant. We'll see warning signs if we're paying attention. The Holy Spirit will convict us about spending more time with the Lord. There will be emotional red flags that warn us that something's not right. Typically, we are too busy to take the time to fix the problem.

Once we lose our axe head, we're often too proud to ask for help getting it back. This man had to humble himself, come to Elisha, and ask for help retrieving the axe head. As I testified, the head never comes off with just one swing. This man was foolish in his actions and didn't fix the problem when it started. He just kept swinging until the head came off. It's embarrassing to admit. I know—I've been there and done that!

Where are you? Is your axe head slipping, or have you already lost it? Are you prudent enough to do what it takes to secure the head, or will you humble yourself and admit you've lost it? You're useless without it. Do whatever it takes to get your axe head back! (AW)

OCTOBER 4
WHERE'S YOUR HEAD?
2 KINGS 6:1-7

"And the man of God said, Where fell it? And he shewed him the place. And he cut down a stick, and cast it in thither; and the iron did swim" (2 Kin. 6:6).

The iron of the axe head is the power in the axe. Without it, the handle is useless. This fellow lost his axe head and asked the man of God for help to retrieve it. Many of us have lost the power of God in our lives, and we need help retrieving it.

The first thing Elisha wanted to know was where the man lost the head. To regain the power of God in your life, you need to know where you lost it. Everyone who has walked away from the power of God had a specific point where the separation occurred. With some, there was a dramatic turn from the Lord that's easy to detect. With others, the departure may have been more gradual. But there's always a location where the split took place. The first step to recovery is to go back to the place where you lost your power.

This may be a place where you let bitterness or unforgiveness into your heart. It may be a place where you felt God failed you and you've never reconciled the issue. For many, it's a place where they stopped seeking the Lord with all their hearts and became occupied with other things. Wherever that place is for you is where you'll find your axe head.

If your offense involves another person, you'll need to make things right by asking for forgiveness or making restitution. If that's impossible, you'll just have to go to Jesus and receive your forgiveness. It takes a miracle from the Lord to make your axe head swim, but first you have to throw the stick in the place where you lost your head. (AW)

OCTOBER 5
YOU & GOD ARE A MAJORITY
1 SAMUEL 14:1-23

"And Jonathan said to the young man that bare his armour, Come, and let us go over unto the garrison of these uncircumcised: it may be that the LORD will work for us: for there is no restraint to the LORD to save by many or by few" *(1 Sam. 14:6).*

The Israelites were at war. The Philistines had 30,000 chariots, 6,000 horsemen, and soldiers as numerous as the sand on the seashore (1 Sam. 13:5). The Israelites had a total of 600 men (1 Sam. 14:2). The situation looked so hopeless that the 600 Israelites were all hiding wherever they could. But God had a man!

Jonathan, the son of Saul, had faith in God. He made a tremendous statement that God wasn't limited. He could save by many or by few. And Jonathan was willing to back his faith up with actions. If it didn't work, he'd be dead.

Jonathan went over to the Philistines with his armor bearer and started fighting. He only killed about twenty men in the space of half an acre, but it was enough. God caused fear to come on the Philistines so much that their trembling caused an earthquake (1 Sam. 14:15). The multitude didn't flee because of two men with a sword; they fled because of the fear that God put in their hearts. But it all started with one man who believed that the Lord could do anything.

You may say, "Well that was war. It's different than my situation." I'm sure that Jonathan would've been glad to swap his situation for yours. Nothing is impossible with God! The only thing limiting Him is the lack of people who will take that step of faith.

Jonathan didn't have to defeat the whole army. He only beat twenty men. You don't have to do it all. Just do what you can, and let God do the rest! (AW)

OCTOBER 6
THE PROCESS OF PROSPERITY
MARK 4:26-29

"And should sleep, and rise night and day, and the seed should spring and grow up, he knoweth not how" *(Mark 4:27).*

You go where you sow because where you sow your seed is where you put your emphasis. We must target our seed! There is a process to reaping a harvest from seed we've sown. It's a process of time. It's a process of planting your seed faithfully and consistently—planting in faith believing. We sow seeds in our tithes and offerings, but we also sow seeds by our lives. We sow seeds of kindness and mercy. You need to sow mercy wherever and whenever you can, because you never know when you'll need to reap mercy.

One of the greatest deceptions for people is this: Have it all and have it now. There is a process of time. We've seen people with tremendous anointings, people doing great things for God, and we desire the same. The devil tries to tempt young ministers to take shortcuts—shortcuts in character or shortcuts in the way they receive offerings by using manipulation. Some yield to the temptation to take a little shortcut to get to where someone else is or to have what they see someone else has. Let's not succumb to that. It's a process of time. Just keep sowing seed, and let God bring the harvest. Keep doing what's right because it's right.

Oftentimes our gifts can take us to where our character can't keep us. What you compromise to obtain, you'll ultimately lose. We may not understand how, we may not understand when, but God is responsible. If you'll sow seed in faith, He'll take you to the place you need to be. There is a process to prosperity! (BN)

OCTOBER 7
WATCH YOUR WORDS
MATTHEW 12:31-37

"But I say unto you, That every idle word that men shall speak, they shall give account thereof in the day of judgment" (Matt. 12:36).

My wife and I were trying to go to sleep in a Denver hotel room when a couple checked in to the room next to us. The walls were so thin, you could have heard them talking in sign language! The wife came in the door griping and calling her husband every name you could imagine. He seldom said anything. She wouldn't let him. This went on for nearly an hour until they fell asleep. When they woke up in the morning, she picked up where she left off. The first words out of her mouth were poison. This continued until the man just left the room.

I couldn't restrain myself. I knocked on their door and the woman came to answer. I told her I didn't mean to listen, but I couldn't help it. We had heard every word she'd said. I told her I'd been praying for her and just wanted her to know that Jesus loved her and could take her anger away. She started crying and told me she was already a Christian. She didn't know why she was acting that way. She said she needed help.

I had to go because I was appearing on a Denver television station, but I told her to watch the show, and I'd share with her how to overcome strife. On the air, I told her story without using her name and explained how to stop the hatred. I never heard from her, but I've often wondered what happened. One thing's for sure: That woman learned that her words weren't as private as she thought!

Imagine what it'll be like on judgment day when every idle word will have to be accounted for. It's to our advantage to watch our words now, knowing that someday, they will all be made public. Since we'll have to eat our words, we might as well make them sweet. (AW)

OCTOBER 8
WHAT RANK ARE YOU?
1 SAMUEL 15:1-29

"And Samuel said, Hath the LORD as great delight in burnt offerings and sacrifices, as in obeying the voice of the LORD? Behold, to obey is better than sacrifice, and to hearken than the fat of rams" (1 Sam. 15:22).

God commanded Saul to make war with the Amalekites. His instructions were to kill every living thing—man and beast. Saul didn't do it. As Samuel came to the battle, Saul greeted him with the statement that he had fulfilled God's command. That's when Samuel asked him why all the animals were still alive which should've been killed. Saul reasoned that he had saved the best to sacrifice to the Lord. Then Samuel gave the tremendous truth that obedience is better than sacrifice.

My experience in the military was of the old school. We had no rights. We were GIs (government issues). In basic training, much of what we experienced was designed to break us of our individuality. We were taught to obey, not to think.

I once asked why they did this, and a drill sergeant, in a rare moment of candor, explained it to me. In battle, a commander doesn't have time to explain his orders. The commander has access to information that the normal troops don't. The lives of his troops depend on them trusting him and immediately following his orders without question. The individual soldier doesn't see the big picture. Logistics demand that some people command and others follow.

God is our Commander-in-Chief. When He gives orders, we aren't supposed to interpret or change them. There is a reason for His commands, and He shouldn't have to explain Himself. It all comes down to a matter of rank. Subordinates obey their superiors. By his actions, Saul ranked himself higher than God. I pray that we won't make the same mistake. (AW)

OCTOBER 9
HOW DO YOU SEE YOURSELF?
NUMBERS 13:1-33

"And there we saw the giants, the sons of Anak, which come of the giants: and we were in our own sight as grasshoppers, and so we were in their sight" (Num. 13:33).

I often deal with people who are bothered by what others think about them. I can understand this to a degree. The Lord didn't create us to be rejected. Therefore, no one likes it. We all want to be accepted, but what someone else thinks about you shouldn't determine what you think about yourself!

These leaders of the Israeli nation let the opinion of the people in the land of Canaan influence their thinking. They saw themselves as grasshoppers compared to the giants of the land. In reality, it was like the old cliché, "The bigger they are, the harder they fall!" It didn't matter how big these people were. God could handle them! The Israelites would have nice big houses to dwell in after they'd conquered them.

What other people think about us is not the important thing; it's what we think about ourselves that controls us. These people saw themselves as grasshoppers. A grasshopper isn't going to fight a giant. Contrast this with the way David viewed himself against the giant Goliath (1 Sam. 17). David referred to the fact that Goliath was uncircumcised, which meant that he didn't have the covenant with God that David did. David saw himself as the one with the advantage, and that's the way it turned out.

Each of us face giants and there are always plenty of people (like these spies) to tell you that you can't win. However, it doesn't matter how *they* see you. The question is: How do *you* see yourself? (AW)

OCTOBER 10
RESURRECTION
PHILIPPIANS 3:10

"That I may know him, and the power of his resurrection" (Phil. 3:10).

It seems like we've made Christianity into a religion centered around the cross where Jesus died. We have crosses on our churches and pulpits. We even dangle them on our wrists and necks as bracelets and necklaces. I'm glad our crosses are empty, because Jesus is no longer there. But is the empty cross what the New Testament believers centered their lives around? No, it's not.

The cross was where our problems—sin, sickness, and poverty—were removed. The Old Covenant—the Law—was crucified with Jesus, nailed to His cross, and removed once and for all. It's wonderful for our problems to be removed, but more necessary and exciting for the answers to be given!

It was the empty cross that solved our problems, but the empty tomb brought our answers. Death was conquered at the cross, but life was given at the resurrection. Sickness was destroyed at the cross, but healing came through the resurrection. Jesus became our poverty on the cross, but our prosperity came through resurrection power.

The focal point of Christianity is the empty tomb—not the empty cross. For three days while the cross was empty, Jesus was still dead.

This would make us no different from any other religion on earth. All their founders are dead. But Jesus came back from the dead!

We don't confess the cross in order to be born again, but the truth that Jesus was raised from the dead by the power of God the Father. Our daily prayer, like Paul's, should be to know Jesus in the power of His resurrection.

Perhaps the emblem of Christianity shouldn't be an empty cross around our neck, but a rock with a hole in it. Jesus is no longer in the grave—He's risen from the dead! (BY)

OCTOBER 11
ARE YOU LOOKING BACK?
HEBREWS 11:8-19

"And truly, if they had been mindful of that country from whence they came out, they might have had opportunity to have returned" (Heb. 11:15).

God told Abraham to leave his old country and head for a new land that the Lord would give him. There was no physical manifestation of this promise during the next 100 years of Abraham's life. So how did he stay in faith?

This verse tells us that Abraham and Sarah didn't think about the country they left behind. If they had, they would've had the opportunity to return. This means that temptation to disbelieve was linked to what they thought on. One could say, "Since they didn't think on the country they left, they weren't even tempted to return." You and I can be great men and women of God if we aren't tempted to do anything else!

Few Christians feel any responsibility to limit their thoughts about things contrary to what God has promised them. The religious system as a whole ridicules those who are so fanatical that they only think on God's Word. It's considered wise to gather as much information as possible about the problem we're facing. In the process, we usually become more mindful of the problem than the promise. We open wide the door to temptation through considering all the possible negatives and then wonder why it's so hard to believe God. This is not the way Abraham succeeded in faith.

Abraham didn't consider anything except what God spoke to him. Paul said, *"This one thing I do"* (Phil. 3:13). What do you say? What do you consider? If all you think upon is God's Word, then all you can be tempted with is faith in God. Today, set your heart and mind on God alone! (AW)

OCTOBER 12
WHAT ARE YOU CONSIDERING?
ROMANS 4:13-25

"And being not weak in faith, he considered not his own body now dead, when he was about an hundred years old, neither yet the deadness of Sara's womb" (Rom. 4:19).

Abraham's faith wasn't stronger than ours—it was purer. This verse tells us that when God promised Abraham a child in his old age, he didn't consider his own body or the deadness of Sarah's womb. What a statement! *Consider* means "to deliberate on, examine; to think or deem." Abraham didn't think on anything contrary to what God promised him.

Most of us would've gone to the doctor and asked, "Is this really possible?" We would have had Sarah tested to see if she was capable of conceiving. We would've tried to remember if anyone we knew had ever had a child when they were 100 years old. Only after considering every negative thing would we have gone back to God's promise and tried to muster up the faith to believe what He said.

Our believing or doubting is inextricably linked to what we think on. We cannot be tempted with something we don't think. Therefore, refusing to think on negative things means we can't believe negative things. The real strength of Abraham's faith was in what he considered and what he failed to consider. Unbelief had no inroad into Abraham's life because he refused to think on things contrary to God's Word.

What do you consider? Do you listen to all the unbelief of this world and then try to overcome it with a little time with God each day? You can't let the sewage of this world flow through you without it hindering your faith! Strong faith like Abraham's is faith that only focuses on what God says. (AW)

OCTOBER 13
HOW DO YOU SEE?
GENESIS 22:1-14

"And Abraham said unto his young men, Abide ye here with the ass; and I and the lad will go yonder and worship, and come again to you" (Gen. 22:5).

This account of Abraham's obedience to God is one of the most inspiring stories in the entire Bible. Any parent knows that love for their own flesh and blood would forbid such a sacrifice. Not only that, but Isaac was Abraham's promised seed that he waited twenty-seven years to receive. All his hopes rested in this boy. The magnitude of Abraham's love and commitment to God goes beyond inspiring to nearly condemning. How could he have done this? What enabled him to pass this test?

Verse 5 gives us the key to Abraham's obedience. He told his servants that he and Isaac would go, worship, and come back again. He didn't say, "We'll go worship and I'll come back." He told them that *they* would both worship and come back again. Abraham knew Isaac would return with him alive!

This is verified in Hebrews 11:17-19. This passage says that Abraham was *"accounting that God was able to raise him up, even from the dead"* (Heb. 11:19). The Greek word translated *accounting* means "to estimate." It was also translated *counted* four times. Abraham counted on God to raise Isaac from the dead, if necessary. He knew that Isaac was God's promised seed. Therefore, he had to live for God to fulfill His word. Abraham never saw Isaac dead.

The reason why many of us would fail a test like this is because we would see our son dead. We'd think about what it would be like to kill our only son and then imagine life without him. We'd also meditate on the guilt of knowing we were the murderers. After considering all the negatives, we'd try to believe God. But it doesn't work that way. The key to having strong faith is having weak doubts. We can starve our doubts by only thinking on God's Word. (AW)

OCTOBER 14
FILL YOUR HORN & GO!
1 SAMUEL 16:1-13

"Fill thine horn with oil, and go" (1 Sam. 16:1).

Samuel was the one who anointed Saul to be king over Israel. He'd seen him mature from the frightened boy who hid at his inauguration to a warrior king (1 Sam. 10:22). He also saw Saul reject the Lord and the Lord reject Saul. Samuel, as God's representative, had refused to see Saul, but still mourned for him (1 Sam. 15:35). This must have hurt him deeply.

In the first verse of chapter 16, God was saying to Samuel, "Get over it! Quit looking back and look forward! My 'Plan B' will be better than My 'Plan A.'" God wasn't mourning or sulking. Why should Samuel? God told him to fill his horn with oil (symbolic of the Holy Spirit) and go anoint a new and better king.

People often become captives of the past and what might have been. If we aren't careful, that attitude will cause us to miss what God is doing now. The Lord is never at a loss. Regardless of what men do, God has another way to accomplish His purposes.

You may have sorrow because of personal failures. You may be mourning because of loved ones' failures. Regardless of how you arrived where you are, God has somewhere better for you. The world has never seen anyone manifest all God had for them, except Jesus. There's more for each of us!

But we must fill ourselves with the Holy Spirit and go on with what God has called us to do. The only way any of us can fail is if we fail to fill ourselves and go! (AW)

OCTOBER 15
HOW'S YOUR HEART?
1 SAMUEL 16:1-13

"But the LORD said unto Samuel, Look not on his countenance, or on the height of his stature; because I have refused him: for the LORD seeth not as man seeth; for man looketh on the outward appearance, but the LORD looketh on the heart" (1 Sam. 16:7).

Samuel came to Jesse's home to anoint one of his sons to be king. The first king of Israel, Saul, was a head and shoulder taller than anyone else in the nation (1 Sam. 9:2). He was the choicest of all the men in the land. Samuel supposed that the next king would be similar. As he looked on Jesse's oldest son, Eliab, he thought this was the one. Eliab must have been an impressive looking man!

But the Lord had someone else in mind. David, the youngest of Jesse's sons, *"had a healthy reddish complexion and beautiful eyes, and was fine-looking"* (1 Sam. 16:12, AMP). David wasn't what you'd consider "king material." He kept sheep, played the harp, sang, and wrote music. But God sees us differently than others see us—and even how we see ourselves!

Our modern society has put a premium on the outward appearance. People abuse their bodies to achieve the perfect shape. Some people actually kill others to have the right standard of living and be in the proper social group. All of that is vanity. All of that will fade with age, if nothing else. In the Lord's sight, it's the qualities of the heart that are valued.

How's your heart? How is the heart of the person you work with or live with? Due to their earth-suit, you might be passing another "King David" by. The real person is living inside! (AW)

OCTOBER 16
GOD ONLY ASKS YOU TO GIVE
WHAT HE WANTS YOU TO HAVE MORE OF!
MATTHEW 25:15-30

"And so he that had received five talents came and brought other five talents, saying, Lord, thou deliveredst unto me five talents: behold, I have gained beside them five talents more. His lord said unto him, Well done, thou good and faithful servant: thou hast been faithful over a few things, I will make thee ruler over many things: enter thou into the joy of thy lord" (Matt. 25:20-21).

There was a couple in our church who were faithful in serving and giving. They were big on sowing. They asked me to come over to dedicate their new house. I don't get to do things like that very often anymore, but this time I was able to go. When I arrived, I saw that it was a very beautiful home. With grins from ear to ear, they told me, "God gave us this house." I thought, *God gave it to them? They probably mean that He worked out the financing or gave them a super deal on the home.* They reiterated, "No, Pastor. You don't understand. God gave us this house!" It was theirs—free and clear.

I know of a young man in our church who was believing God for the money to pay his tuition to go to school. As he was sitting in the service, he felt the Lord prompting him to give the twenty-dollar bill he had in his wallet. At first he thought, *Lord, You know I can't give that twenty. I need it to go toward my tuition!* Within a brief amount of time, the young man obeyed God and put the money into the offering. After the service, a businessman in the church walked up to the young man and said, "Son, the Lord put it on my heart to give you this." It was a large sum of money—just the thing the young man needed. It makes me think of what would've happened had the young man not been obedient to give that twenty? It can never be stressed too much: God only asks you to give what He wants you to have more of. (BN)

OCTOBER 17
LASTING FRUIT
JOHN 15:1-16

"Ye have not chosen me, but I have chosen you, and ordained you, that ye should go and bring forth fruit, and that your fruit should remain: that whatsoever ye shall ask of the Father in my name, he may give it you" (John 15:16).

The Lord didn't instruct us to just bear fruit; He ordained us to bear fruit that remains. There's a difference!

In our world of statistics today, there is tremendous emphasis on evangelizing the world for Christ. The predominant way the church goes about trying to accomplish this goal isn't the way Jesus instructed. He clearly told us to go into all the world and make disciples, not just converts (Matt. 28:19). Disciples are converts who have matured in their relationship with the Lord to the point that they're stable and can share their faith with others. Disciples are lasting fruit.

It's shortsighted to push for converts more than disciples. It's easier to make converts than disciples, but the kingdom of God isn't really built that way. Today, we have millions of people who prayed the sinner's prayer to escape hell, but they aren't committed to God and aren't a good testimony for the kingdom. Since we're so big on statistics, someone should count the number of people who have been forever turned off to the Lord because of the example of some hypocritical converts.

Jesus sees the end from the beginning. Therefore, He doesn't rejoice with us over some of the inflated numbers we proclaim. He wants lasting fruit. Make sure you're in that group today, and then help others bring forth fruit that remains. (AW)

OCTOBER 18
ONE MORE TIME
JOHN 21:1-6

"And he said unto them, Cast the net on the right side of the ship, and ye shall find. They cast therefore, and now they were not able to draw it for the multitude of fishes" (John 21:6).

Often, the difference between acting on God's Word and doing our own thing isn't in the action itself, but in our heart attitude. Jesus didn't tell these disciples to do anything they hadn't already done. They'd been casting their nets all night and hadn't caught any fish.

This wasn't the first time Jesus performed this miracle. When He first called these disciples to follow Him, he did the same thing. They'd been fishing all night and had no fish. There was no logical reason why casting the net one more time on either side of the boat would make any difference. But in obedience, they did it anyway. On both occasions they caught a multitude of fish!

There are many parallels between the miraculous catch of fish and our lives. Most people basically do the same things. They try to be productive and raise good families, but there's a world of difference between doing it in our own strength and doing it in the Word of the Lord.

These disciples were in the same place, using the same net, but the difference was the interjection of God's Word, and faith and obedience to it. You may have done everything you know to do without receiving the results you desire, but have you stepped out in obedience to God's Word? What does the Lord have to say to you about your situation? Find out. Then obey it, and expect miraculous results! (AW)

OCTOBER 19
THE MOST IMPORTANT QUESTION
JOHN 21:15-17

"When they had dined, Jesus saith to Simon Peter, Simon, son of Jonas, lovest thou me more than these? He saith unto him, Yea, Lord; thou knowest that I love thee. He saith unto him, Feed my lambs" (John 21:15).

This was one of the very last times Jesus was with His disciples before He ascended back to the Father. The whole plan of God was just hours away from being committed into the hands of these men. Everything Jesus had accomplished, and was yet to accomplish, would soon be committed into their trust. What a profound moment!

What would the Lord deem the most important thing to say to these disciples? What last-minute instructions would you give if you were in this situation? Surprisingly to many, the Lord questioned Peter about his love. Three times Peter denied that he knew Christ. Now, three times, Jesus asked Peter if he loved Him.

The most important issue for all of us is our love for the Lord. Everything else revolves around this issue. It's easy to get so busy serving the Lord that we don't have any time to fellowship with Him. Ultimately, this leads to emptiness, frustration, and ineffectiveness.

Prior to his denial, Peter loved Jesus enough to be willing to fight to the death for Him (Luke 22:33 and John 18:10). But it's easier to fight than it is to suffer. Peter didn't love the Lord more than himself. That's why He not only asked Peter if he loved Him but if he loved Him more than these.

Do you love Jesus more than anything or anyone? That's the most important question! (AW)

OCTOBER 20
MIND YOUR OWN BUSINESS!
JOHN 21:18-24

"Jesus saith unto him, If I will that he tarry till I come, what is that to thee? follow thou me" (John 21:22).

In verse 18, Jesus told Peter that he would glorify Him in his death as a martyr. It's impossible to know the exact effect this had on Peter. No doubt, it was profound. But one thing is obvious—it caused Peter to wonder what would happen to John.

One of the critical mistakes we often make is to examine what God has called us to do in the light of what others are called to do. This isn't wise. Jesus wisely told Peter to mind his own business. What would happen to John shouldn't affect Peter.

Early church tradition says that John was boiled in oil but miraculously didn't die. He was then banished to the isle of Patmos where he wrote the book of Revelation and eventually died a natural death. How would this knowledge have affected Peter? Would it have made him bitter? Would he have thought it unfair for him to die a martyr's death, while John escaped the same? Who knows?

Comparing ourselves with others isn't smart (2 Cor. 10:12). Like water, we tend to seek the lowest level. Comparing ourselves with others often makes us compromise God's best for us or feel condemned because we haven't reached someone else's stature. We don't need those comparisons!

Your life shouldn't be a race with others. True happiness and a sense of fulfillment are found in focusing on what God has called you to do and doing it with all your heart! (AW)

OCTOBER 21
CAN YOU PASS THE TEST?
MARK 4:35

"And the same day, when the even was come, he saith unto them,
Let us pass over unto the other side" (Mark 4:35).

What "same day" was this verse referring to when Jesus told His disciples to sail to the other side of the Sea of Galilee? It was the same day Jesus had taught the multitudes and the disciples the parable of the good and bad ground, the sower and the seed. Why is this important to know? When Jesus finished teaching this parable, He asked His disciples if they understood. They answered, "Yes."

Jesus knew what was coming. He knew they would go to the other side of the Sea of Galilee and minister to a man possessed with a legion of demons. He also knew that Satan would try to take their lives on the way across the water. The teaching they had just received would be used within a few hours after hearing it.

The parable teaches about a sower, seed, good ground, bad ground, and an enemy who tries to steal the Word through persecution and affliction. Jesus would now put the disciples to the test.

Jesus (the Sower) told them, *"Let us pass over unto the other side"* (the seed was sown). He didn't say, "Let's try to go over." Neither did He say, "Let's go halfway and sink." The promise was given—telling them they would make it. Halfway across the water, a storm erupted (persecution and affliction from Satan) to take the word from their hearts. Jesus was so assured they'd make it, He went to sleep and rested on His own promise. The disciples panicked and blamed the Lord for not caring. Jesus woke up, calmed the storm, and then rebuked His disciples for their lack of faith. They proved they hadn't yet understood the parable. They also proved they were hard ground. Jesus took them safely over, but they failed the test of faith.

Between you and the will of God is a Sea of Trouble. Take hold of a promise and rest in it. The promise will sustain you, and you will make it to the other side! (BY)

OCTOBER 22
HOW BIG ARE YOU?
1 SAMUEL 17:1-11

"And there went out a champion out of the camp of the Philistines, named
Goliath, of Gath, whose height was six cubits and a span" (1 Sam. 17:4).

When I was a teenager, I went to a Golden Gloves boxing match where there were thousands of people. I noticed a baldheaded man way down close to the ring who looked like he was standing through the entire match. Then he stood up. This man was a giant! I found out he was called the Corn King Giant and was nine feet six inches tall. I ran down to see if I could get up next to him. My eyes were level with his belt buckle. It was quite an experience!

Goliath was about that size. But David was even smaller than me. Goliath was twice as tall as David. David probably weighed no more than the coat of mail that Goliath wore. But David was bigger on the inside than Goliath was. David was God's anointed king.

We too often evaluate things only in physical terms. Physically, Goliath was a giant. But in trusting God, he was a dwarf. David was the giant in that category, and that's the most important thing. Anyone who's strong in believing God is a giant in the spiritual realm and able to do great exploits.

We overestimate and overemphasize the physical problems that confront us. The spiritual realm is where the real power to live life comes from. Everyone born of God is a spiritual giant with powers far greater than anything the physical realm can ever confront us with.

Ask God to open your eyes to who you are in the spirit. You'll find that you're a giant who's been intimidated by dwarfs. (AW)

OCTOBER 23
YOU'RE THE ONE WITH THE COVENANT
1 SAMUEL 17:12-30

"And David spake to the men that stood by him, saying, What shall be done to the man that killeth this Philistine, and taketh away the reproach from Israel? for who is this uncircumcised Philistine, that he should defy the armies of the living God?" (1 Sam. 17:26).

There were a number of keys to David's faith that enabled him to kill Goliath. One of those keys was David's knowledge of and faith in God's covenant with the nation of Israel. The Lord had said that no man would be able to stand before His people (Deut. 11:25). Goliath was just a man—and an uncircumcised man at that! This meant he didn't have a covenant with God. David placed his faith completely in God.

Every one of the Israelite soldiers had that same covenant, but the covenant is of no effect until it's believed. Hebrews 4:2 says, *"For unto us was the gospel preached, as well as unto them: but the word preached did not profit them, not being mixed with faith in them that heard it."* David believed God's Word and activated its power.

King Saul tried to give David his armor to wear, but he wouldn't take it (verses 38-39). That was just an attempt to change his focus from God to the flesh. David's trust was in the covenant and the God of the covenant, not Saul's armor. After all, Saul's armor wasn't doing him any good. He was hiding, along with the rest of the soldiers! David's faith rested in God alone.

God's covenant to us has promised us total victory in every situation. There's simply no reason for us to cower before our enemies. We have God's covenant promises. Activate them by faith, and watch your giants fall! (AW)

OCTOBER 24
PERSECUTION IS JEALOUSY
1 SAMUEL 17:28-30

"Eliab his eldest brother heard when he spake unto the men; and Eliab's anger was kindled against David, and he said, Why camest thou down hither? and with whom hast thou left those few sheep in the wilderness? I know thy pride, and the naughtiness of thine heart; for thou art come down that thou mightest see the battle" (1 Sam. 17:28).

There was more to Eliab's anger than just care for his father's sheep! Eliab was there when Samuel anointed David (1 Sam. 16:13). God had passed him over and chosen his younger brother to be king. Eliab was jealous of David.

"Only by pride cometh contention" (Prov. 13:10). Eliab's love for himself caused him to lash out at his younger brother. He was afraid, because if David was right—and Goliath was no match for a man in covenant with God—then Eliab was a coward. He had to condemn David's words, or they would condemn him!

This is the root of all persecution. If you throw a rock into a pack of dogs, the one that yelps the loudest is the one that got hit. So it is with persecution. Those who protest the loudest are the ones feeling the pressure of conviction.

Before you can defeat the giants in your life, you must withstand the critical remarks of others—especially your own family. If David hadn't overcome his older brother's criticism, he never would've overcome Goliath. Understanding that persecution is actually a defensive act of a person under conviction will help you keep your focus and fight the real battles. (AW)

OCTOBER 25
WHEN NO ONE'S LOOKING
1 SAMUEL 17:31-47

"Thy servant slew both the lion and the bear: and this uncircumcised Philistine shall be as one of them, seeing he hath defied the armies of the living God" (1 Sam. 17:36).

David had faith that God would enable him to kill Goliath and win the war. But no one else did. King Saul, the biggest and most powerful man in all of Israel, openly mocked David, saying that he wasn't up to the fight. That would've deterred most people, but David wasn't like most people.

Prior to this, David had kept his father's sheep. A lion and a bear had come after the sheep and he killed them both. This was on the backside of the desert. No one was around to see his valiant fight. It's likely that no one would have blamed him for running away!

But it was David's victory over the lion and the bear that gave him the assurance and faith that he'd be able to conquer Goliath as he had them. If David hadn't been faithful in the smaller things, he wouldn't have had the confidence to fight in this big thing.

Many people dream of slaying some giant of a problem or doing some great exploit, but they aren't faithful in life's everyday trials. They're waiting for the grandstands to be full before they give it all they have. But those who don't win the local trials never make it to the Olympics. David's faithfulness in the relatively small things was what enabled him to be ruler over much (Luke 16:10).

Be faithful in the trials you face today, and your faith will be strengthened for when the big tests come your way! (AW)

OCTOBER 26
MAKE SURE THEY'RE DEAD!
1 SAMUEL 17:48-58

"Therefore David ran, and stood upon the Philistine, and took his sword, and drew it out of the sheath thereof, and slew him, and cut off his head therewith. And when the Philistines saw their champion was dead, they fled" (1 Sam. 17:51).

We fight giants every day, but we often make the mistake of quitting before the battle is complete. Instead of destroying our enemies, we just chase them out of sight and leave them to return and fight another day. David declared, *"I have pursued mine enemies, and overtaken them: neither did I turn again till they were consumed"* (Ps. 18:37). Never was that illustrated in David's life more than when he fought Goliath.

David had a holy hatred for his enemy. He wasn't just trying to scare him off; he was out to kill him! David ran toward Goliath. He wasn't tentative; he was bold. He slung the stone and God made sure it hit its mark. Goliath, the giant of Gath, fell on his face before David.

But David wasn't through yet. The Scriptures don't say that Goliath was dead. He may have been, but he may not have. Certainly, the Philistines who were on the mountains watching couldn't tell for sure the fate of their champion. However, David left no doubt. He climbed up on top of the giant, drew Goliath's own sword, and cut off his head. Once David held the giant's head in his hand, there was no doubt in anyone who had won. Goliath would never fight again!

We don't know the exact reason why David chose five smooth stones from the brook (verse 40). We do know that there were four other giants in Gath (1 Chr. 20:4-8), one of which was Goliath's brother. Perhaps David was ready to take on them all.

If you have fought and obtained some relief, don't quit until the victory is complete. Chase the devil out of every corner of your life! (AW)

OCTOBER 27
SUBSTANCE ABUSE
PROVERBS 3:9

"Honour the LORD with thy substance, and with the firstfruits of all thine increase" (Prov. 3:9).

Many people in the church today have a problem with substance abuse. You can't hardly pick up a newspaper or watch television without hearing about some famous movie star or athlete who got into trouble because of it. Just as often you'll hear about folks checking into a substance abuse treatment center. There are many programs offering help, saying that we must follow a certain number of steps or do this routine to straighten out our lives. But that's not the kind of substance abuse I'm talking about. I'm referring to our abuse of money and possessions.

The word translated *substance* in Proverbs 3:9 is the Hebrew word *hown*, which means "wealth, riches, price, high value, enough, or sufficiency." While certainly it's a problem for a professing Christian to selfishly rack up money and possessions while neglecting everyone else, it's just as grave a sin to say a simple "no" when God tells you to give something small. I heard a woman minister talk about how the Lord dealt with her on obedience by telling her to give someone her favorite pair of earrings. Although she ultimately gave them, it was after much debate and arguing with God. That's an example of substance abuse. Spending money on things that a believer has no business buying is also an example. For a youth, using your tithe money to "just this once" buy the new CD you've been wanting is another example.

The Bible doesn't give us a five, ten, or twelve-step program to follow. God laid it out plain and simple, *"Honour the LORD with thy substance, and with the firstfruits of all thine increase."* *First-fruits* means "the first, beginning, best, chief or choicest part." Doctor Jesus is the answer to every malady we may have! Have you been guilty of substance abuse? Why not check in to the Lord's treatment program? In His presence, every problem can be wiped away—including substance abuse! (BN)

OCTOBER 28
LOOK UP!
MARK 6:35-44

"And when he had taken the five loaves and the two fishes, he looked up to heaven, and blessed, and brake the loaves, and gave them to his disciples to set before them; and the two fishes divided he among them all" (Mark 6:41).

Jesus faced an impossible task. There were 5,000 men who needed to be fed, not including women and children. All He had were five loaves of bread and two small fish. Although Jesus was God, He was also man. This situation was more than His sinless natural mind could comprehend. He had to look beyond the natural and tap into His Father's supernatural ability. That's why He looked up!

Jesus took His eyes off the natural realm and looked into the spiritual realm. The Greek word translated *looked up* means "to look up; by implication, to recover sight." This word—*anablepo*—was translated *receive* seven times and *received* seven times in reference to blind eyes being opened. When Jesus looked up, His spiritual eyes were opened to the power of God. That was more than enough to accomplish this miracle.

There's a spiritual answer to every physical problem we face. It's always there and is just as real as the natural impossibilities we see. God's supply is infinitely greater than our lack. In order to appropriate that supply, we need to "look up" and receive spiritual sight. Those who are blind spiritually have just as much difficulty in the spiritual realm as a physically blind person has in the natural realm. We need to see with our faith.

Can you see by faith? If you can see it on the inside, you can have it on the outside! (AW)

OCTOBER 29
WHAT DO YOU NEED?
JOHN 6:66-69

"Then said Jesus unto the twelve, Will ye also go away?" (John 6:67).

A friend of mine married a woman who had been verbally and physically abused in her first marriage. Therefore, she clung to this new godly husband as if her life depended on it. She became co-dependent and smothered him. If he would've left her, her whole world would have collapsed. That's not healthy!

A real breakthrough came one day when he told her how much he loved her and reassured her of his commitment to both her and the marriage. Then he said, "But I don't need you." He wasn't rejecting her. He was just trying to make her understand that he was complete in Christ—with or without her. He loved her and wanted her, but he could make it without her, because his foundation was Jesus. That's how it should be!

This was what Jesus was doing with His disciples. He loved them, wanted them to be with Him, and had chosen each one individually. But when the multitudes left, He asked His disciples if they wanted to leave too. Jesus wasn't encouraging them to go, but He wouldn't have fallen apart if they had. He didn't need them in the sense that He couldn't do without them. His total security was in His relationship with His Father.

Unknowingly, we've allowed ourselves to become dependent on many things other than the Lord for our stability and security. They may even be good things like mates and children. In fact, some would even argue that it's correct to be that way. However, Jesus Christ is the only foundation that will support the pressures of life.

What must you have to be satisfied? The only things that'll let you down are those you lean on. (AW)

OCTOBER 30
FIRST CONTACT
JOHN 4:1-26

"There cometh a woman of Samaria to draw water:
Jesus saith unto her, Give me to drink" (John 4:7).

This is reminiscent of the way Elijah ministered to the widow of Zarephath (1 Kin. 17:10). Although both Elijah and Jesus began their ministry to these women by asking them to give, there's much more to this story than meets the eye.

The Samaritans and the Jews were separated by the two strongest hatreds on earth: racial and religious prejudices. For Jesus to even speak to this woman, much less ask for an act of kindness, was radical. It got her complete attention. It also distanced Jesus from the hatred other Jews displayed. It showed He valued her. What a way to introduce yourself!

The worse the differences are between individuals or groups of people, the greater impact that even the simplest act of kindness can make. Before we can win people to the Lord, we first need to win them to ourselves. That is, we must show them that we love them and gain their trust. Failure to do this has turned many evangelistic efforts into big turnoffs for the lost. They can perceive that they aren't loved—just used and abused. That's not the way the Lord ministered to this woman.

Jesus honored her, thereby revealing His love. That immediately opened a door through which He entered, and began to share the great spiritual truths of who He was. The woman had to open the door first. Jesus didn't break it down.

Ask the Lord to give you opportunities to express love and value to others. The greater the disparity between their lifestyle and yours, the greater the impact your attempt to bridge the gap will make. Remember—love never fails! (AW)

OCTOBER 31
POWER EVANGELISM
JOHN 4:1-26

"The woman answered and said, I have no husband. Jesus said unto her,
Thou hast well said, I have no husband" (John 4:17).

Jesus told this woman what He was able to do. Then He demonstrated by telling her things He could only know through the power of the Holy Spirit. The New Testament example of evangelism was done with power—not just words. Some of the last words Jesus gave His disciples before leaving the earth were that supernatural signs would follow their ministries (Mark 16:17-18). *"And they went forth, and preached every where, the Lord working with them, and confirming the word with signs following. Amen"* (Mark 16:20).

Jesus operated in the word of knowledge (1 Cor. 12:8) to prove to this woman that His promises about giving her water that would quench her thirst forever were not just idle words. If Jesus used the power of God to demonstrate and validate His words, how can we expect to be successful with less? People need to experience God's power in the natural in order to convince them that He can work in the spiritual realm.

Just imagine what would happen to a person you are praying for if they experienced a supernatural healing or you "read their mail" through the gifts of the Holy Spirit. You can see the impact it had on this woman at the well. She instantly knew that Jesus wasn't an average guy. She knew God was working through Him, and that opened her up to what He had to say.

The gifts of the Holy Spirit weren't just for Jesus and the first-century apostles. They are for us today, to empower us to be more effective witnesses for the Lord (Acts 1:8). Let God flow through you in His supernatural power today! (AW)

NOVEMBER 1
DON'T CHANGE THE SUBJECT!
JOHN 4:1-26

"Our fathers worshipped in this mountain; and ye say, that in Jerusalem
is the place where men ought to worship" (John 4:20).

The Lord had touched a sensitive spot in this woman's heart. The conversation moved from the generic to her secret sins. Like so many people, when it got too personal, she changed the subject. She started asking questions about the proper place to worship. This wasn't sincere. Her lifestyle suggested that worshiping God wasn't a high priority for her, no matter where it was done; she didn't have a compelling desire to get her theological questions answered; she just wanted out of the spotlight.

Jesus masterfully got her back on track. He revealed that the form and place of worship is not the important thing. The Lord sought people to worship Him in their hearts. He turned her attention back to the condition of her heart and her personal relationship with Him.

Not much has changed. It's amazing how similar things are today. People would still rather debate theology than deal with their personal relationship with God. Individuals use these techniques to divert attention away from the real issue. The only thing that counts is your personal relationship with the Lord.

A person doesn't have to figure out all the mysteries of God to receive salvation. Don't let anyone divert you away from the real issue. Only one thing is critical for the person who isn't born again—what will they believe about Jesus? Stay on track. You may not have all the answers, but if you know the Lord, you have what the unsaved need. Share Him. (AW)

NOVEMBER 2
WHAT TO FORGET—WHAT TO REMEMBER
PHILIPPIANS 3:13

"Forgetting those things which are behind, and reaching
forth unto those things which are before" (Phil. 3:13).

God's Word tells us to remember many things. We are not to forget God's benefits of forgiveness, healing, strength, and mercy (Ps. 103:1-4). We are commanded to remember our former days and the fight of faith we endured (Heb. 10:32). God also commands us to remember His many other works.

So why then does Paul command us as believers to forget those things that are behind? He isn't only telling us to forget the sins, but also the blessings and triumphs of the past. How does this verse fit in with the many commandments to remember both the good times and the bad? What are we to forget and what are we to remember?

First, we are to forget anything that hinders us from advancing. In the Christian life, we're either advancing or retreating. We never stand still. God wants us to advance, and any hindrance should be removed, including our past.

Second, we are to forget yesterday when it's at the forefront of our minds. God promises to keep us in perfect peace as our minds are stayed on Him. When the past overshadows our ability to have our minds stayed on the Lord, we are to forget the past, assign it to oblivion, and advance in our spiritual growth.

Third, we are to forget the past when it's a stronghold. We are to cast down imaginations and high thoughts that exalt themselves against the knowledge of God. When the past exalts itself in our minds against the power of God's Word, we need to take authority over Satan's power in Jesus' name.

Ask yourself a question: Do you control your memories, or do they control you? If you can control them, they can be a blessing. Past successes can bring great anticipation of future blessings. Past sins can teach the strategies of Satan so you won't fall for them again. Yesterday is to be remembered when you're ready. (BY)

NOVEMBER 3
IT AIN'T OVER YET!
PSALM 73:1-28

"Until I went into the sanctuary of God; then understood I their end" (Ps. 73:17).

This Psalm was confusing to me until I spent some time studying and praying about it. Then I saw that it expresses the feelings that every true child of God has felt at one time or another.

In the first sixteen verses, Asaph was lamenting the prosperity of the wicked. He said that it looks like the wicked are getting away with sin. They seem to prosper and not have the worries that believers do. Sound familiar?

In our society today, the only people who can be discriminated against are Christians. Every value we hold dear is being assaulted, and if we speak out, we're called "bigots." Immorality isn't only practiced—it's flaunted! Television programs, movies, newspapers, magazines, and books are filled with trash. The people who influence us the most are, as a whole, the most immoral people in the nation. Yet, they receive infinitely more money and attention than the people who are godly. It's been said that character is no longer an issue in politics. At times, it appears that way.

This Psalm reveals that this situation is only temporary. The Lord, in His mercy, allows the ungodly to flourish for a while. But make no mistake, their end is certain. An axiom of Scripture is, **"Be sure your sin will find you out"** (Num. 32:23). Payday is coming. There is a reward for the godly and a punishment for the ungodly.

Take a lesson from Asaph today, and look at things through the eyes of Scripture. Your faith in Christ will be rewarded! (AW)

NOVEMBER 4
GLORIFY GOD
ROMANS 1:16-25

"Because that, when they knew God, they glorified him not as God, neither were thankful; but became vain in their imaginations, and their foolish heart was darkened" (Rom. 1:21).

In verses 18-20, Paul shows that each one of us has an intuitive knowledge of God within our hearts. This leaves us without an excuse for our rebellious behavior. We all know better in our hearts. In this verse, Paul admits that our foolish hearts can become darkened or hardened. When this happens, the foolishness of our imaginations drowns out the revelation the Lord placed in our hearts. This is a terrible condition! How can it be avoided?

In this verse, Paul gives the reason why this happens. There is a progression of actions that must take place to numb us to the voice of God within. First, we must quit glorifying God as God, and second, we must become unthankful. Unless these two things happen, our hearts can't become hardened to God and our internal compass will keep bringing us back to Him.

What does it mean to glorify God as God? Simply put, it means to exalt Him above everything and everyone else. If sickness has come against you, you need to put God higher. You need to exalt the promises of God that guarantee healing above the word of the doctor, which is a negative report. If you're hurting financially, you must remember that God is able to make all grace abound toward you and produce total prosperity in your life (2 Cor. 9:8). If your circumstances are causing you to worry or fear, then you aren't glorifying God.

We cannot lose the revelation God gave us unless we fail to glorify Him as greater than the things that come against that revelation, or become unthankful. Don't let that happen to you today—glorify God! (AW)

NOVEMBER 5
BE THANKFUL
ROMANS 1:16-25

"Because that, when they knew God, they glorified him not as God, neither were thankful; but became vain in their imaginations, and their foolish heart was darkened" (Rom. 1:21).

Once we know God in any area of our lives, we must exalt that revelation above anything that looks contrary, regardless of what we or others may think. We must also be thankful. Why is this important?

A thankful person acknowledges what someone else has done for them. They realize the contribution of another. Therefore, a thankful person is a humble person. Humility is a must in the kingdom of God. One of the strongest ploys of the Enemy is to try to get us to believe that we can make it on our own. Thankfulness constantly reminds us that God is our Source. We aren't self-made men and women; it's the Lord who gave us life, health, talents, and opportunities. We should be thankful!

People who aren't thankful become vain in their imaginations. They lose the perspective of God as their Source and begin to imagine that it's some virtue of their own that promoted them. They move off the foundation of faith in the Lord, and as they continue to build, they're destined to fall.

Thankful people think of and appreciate others and what they do for them. In relation to God, a thankful person knows that *"promotion cometh neither from the east, nor from the west, nor from the south. But God is the judge: he putteth down one, and setteth up another"* (Ps. 75:6-7).

Who is your source? Your thankfulness—or lack thereof—will tell. (AW)

NOVEMBER 6
DON'T DESPISE SMALL BEGINNINGS
ZECHARIAH 4:10

"For who hath despised the day of small things? for they shall rejoice, and shall see the plummet in the hand of Zerubbabel with those seven; they are the eyes of the LORD, which run to and fro through the whole earth" (Zech. 4:10).

My family and I are tremendously blessed, but we didn't start out where we are today. If you will take faithful steps, you'll see increase in every area of your life too. Don't despise the day of small beginnings. Sow what you have! It's amazing the ways the Enemy tries to deceive church people. Some have the concept that when they can sow $100 or $1,000, then they'll sow, but they won't turn loose of the nickel or the dime or the five or the ten that's in their pocket right now. Even if you consider it to be a baby step, sow seed somewhere in the ministry—your local church or somebody else's life.

There was a single woman in our church who was coming out of some bad past relationships that hurt her financially. She didn't make a whole lot of money, but after she gave her life to the Lord, she began to tithe and give offerings as she could. God was faithful to see that her rent and all of her bills were paid on time. She received her paycheck every other week. One Sunday, immediately after payday, a minister in the church was taking an offering for a special men's ministry event to provide scholarships to men who didn't have the money to attend. The Lord nudged her to give everything that was left in her checking account. It wasn't much—only ten dollars—but it was all she had left until the next payday. The Lord told her to tell the minister who was collecting the money, "This is for my husband." It was odd because she wasn't looking to get married. After she gave, she didn't give it another thought. There was also an announcement on the radio that the same event needed volunteers to work there. Three weeks later, at the conference, the woman sowed her time as well. It was there that she met the man who is now her husband. She had totally forgotten about the donation she made until a friend brought it to her remembrance. Guess how her husband—a missionary man—was able to come to the conference. That's right, on a scholarship. You go where you sow! The couple now lives in a beautiful house and are prospering spirit, soul, and body. As a matter of fact, she was able to leave her job to prepare their house for the family and ministry God has laid on their hearts.

This woman is an example of someone in the process of God's increase. She went from having ten dollars to last her for two weeks to having a wonderful marriage and home. Don't despise the day of small beginnings! Be faithful to sow what you do have, and God will provide the increase in every area of your life. (BN)

NOVEMBER 7
A PERFECT CHURCH?
ACTS 6:1

"And in those days, when the number of the disciples was multiplied, there arose a murmuring of the Grecians against the Hebrews" (Acts 6:1).

Many think that the early converts of Acts attended a perfect church. Some congregations are returning to the means and structure of the services recorded in this book, trying to find a church without problems. I'm sorry to shatter your dreams, but even the early church that began after the day of Pentecost had problems. This verse reveals that there was murmuring as the church grew. In addition to this, the previous chapter told of members lying to the Holy Spirit and to church leadership.

There is no perfect church! All churches have problems. The reason being is that all churches are run by people striving to hear from the Holy Spirit. Even if you could find a perfect church, why would they want you?

A lady informed me after service one Sunday that she was looking for a perfect church. I told her I'd shoot her and she would find it. The perfect church is in heaven. If you're looking for the perfect pastor, you'll meet Him when the trumpet sounds. His name is Jesus. In the meantime, you, like the saints in Acts, are asked to attend imperfect churches with imperfect pastors, imperfect music directors, and imperfect youth leaders.

You are to be committed to a church and not float around to many churches in a city or area. Many who "float" from one church to another think they are mature and "given" to more than one local church. Ephesians 4:14 tells us that babies are tossed to and fro, carried about by every wind of doctrine. It takes a mature believer to settle down in a church, call it home, and become committed.

Why would God call you to an imperfect church? So He can take your gifts and talents and offer them to the church. Walking in love together, we'll come a little more into spiritual maturity, striving to become the perfect church. (BY)

NOVEMBER 8
WHERE'S THE FRUIT?
NUMBERS 17:1-11

"And it came to pass, that on the morrow Moses went into the tabernacle of witness; and, behold, the rod of Aaron for the house of Levi was budded, and brought forth buds, and bloomed blossoms, and yielded almonds" (Num. 17:8).

Lack of respect for authority is one of the most common problems in our world today. We see it in the home, in the church, and in the attitudes people have toward government. Although it's everywhere, this isn't just a new problem of our modern times.

The people of Israel questioned Moses' and Aaron's authority to govern the nation. In Numbers 16, Korah slandered Moses' character and authority. He and all those associated with him were immediately swallowed up by the earth. Then another 14,000 Israelites who criticized Moses for the way he handled Korah died by a plague of the Lord. Moses' authority was under attack!

To resolve the issue, the Lord had Moses command the leaders of each tribe to take their rods, which symbolized authority, and write their names on them. Then all the rods were placed in the Holy Place overnight. When they came in the next morning, Aaron's rod had budded, blossomed, and produced almonds. The other rods were still just sticks. This forever settled the issue of whom God had chosen to rule the nation. The fruit made the difference!

There are many people who proclaim their own authority today and seek to exercise it over us in various ways. But we can always tell those who have God-given authority by the fruit they produce. Threats, boastings, and publicity don't prove authority. We can tell godly leaders by their fruit (Matt. 7:20). Those who are great in the kingdom of God are servants, not lords (Mark 10:44). (AW)

NOVEMBER 9
BIND OR LOOSE?
MARK 5:1-20

*"Because that he had been often bound with fetters and chains,
and the chains had been plucked asunder by him, and the fetters broken in pieces:
neither could any man tame him"* *(Mark 5:4).*

People attempted to bind this man. Isn't that typical? We usually seek to limit anyone or anything that threatens us. We think of how we can protect ourselves first. This leads to actions toward others that may be cruel and vicious, just as these people's treatment of this man. Then we justify our actions by reasoning that our own interests must come first.

Jesus was different. He loved this man that everyone else feared and hated. He didn't bind him. He loosed him. This is one of the great distinguishing characteristics between true Christianity and religion. The word translated *religion* in the New Testament means "to dock." This word paints a picture of binding a ship to a dock with ropes. The roots of this word always refer to some type of binding. Religion binds, but Jesus sets free.

In our day, religion has many people bound. Our performance-based doctrine binds people with rules and regulations instead of building a loving relationship. They're tormented and run from a "God" that binds. If people could see that Jesus loves them and wants them set free, they'd run and worship at His feet, just like this Gadarene demoniac.

You encounter people every day who are bound by religion or whom religion is trying to bind and put out of sight. Instead of following the world, follow the example of Jesus and loose them with the love of God. Without your intervention, they're doomed to a life of bondage among the dead. (AW)

NOVEMBER 10
GOD DOESN'T GIVE A HOLY HOOT!
ISAIAH 55:9

*"For as the heavens are higher than the earth, so are my ways higher
than your ways, and my thoughts than your thoughts"* *(Is. 55:9).*

God doesn't give a holy hoot about some of the things we get so uptight about here on earth. We need to let the main thing continue being the main thing! Now I enjoy nice things as much as anyone, but somehow those things just don't mean what they used to. Just let me reach more people for Jesus! Let me bless another missionary! Let me do something to see more souls come to the Lord!

When my wife and I visited the island of Grenada, we had quite an experience. We flew into San Juan and there was no electricity. They had more than eighteen inches of rain in one day and over a million people were without power, but we were able to check into our hotel. After searching around in the dark, we finally found the door to our room and went in. It was so pitch black that after my wife set her purse down, she couldn't find it again! When we woke up the next morning, we could finally see, because the sun was up. We laughed as I said, "You know honey, Americans are so spoiled. Thank God we have a decent bed to sleep in!" It's inconvenient when a woman can't locate her purse, but she finally found it. Some people just don't realize how blessed they are. In a third world nation, everything's delayed—if it happens at all!

After Grenada, we flew to Georgetown, Guiana. I'll never fuss about a rough road again! To me, the whole world looked like the old beat up Toyota we were in. There were even cows in the road—it was something else! Since it was nighttime, I was glad the taxi driver could see better than I could. I prayed, "God, give him x-ray vision!" And then there's some of the food I've seen in other countries. They were just thankful to eat!

God doesn't see things the same way we do. He doesn't accept someone based on the label of their clothes or the kind of car they drive. He looks at the heart. Are you concerned about the same things He's concerned about? Are you doing what you know to do with all that He's given you? You can count the seeds in an apple, but you can't count the apples that come out of a seed. God will cause you to prosper so that you can be a blessing. He'll prosper you so you can help provide for the end-time harvest. That's what it's all about! (BN)

NOVEMBER 11
GOD HAS A PLAN FOR YOU
JEREMIAH 1:4-10

"Before I formed thee in the belly I knew thee; and before thou camest forth out of the womb I sanctified thee, and I ordained thee a prophet unto the nations" (Jer. 1:5).

The Lord spoke to Jeremiah that he was called, sanctified, and ordained before he was born. But this wasn't unique to Jeremiah. John the Baptist (Luke 1:15-16), Jesus (Is. 49:1-5), and Paul were the same (Gal. 1:15)—and so are you!

Psalm 139:13-16 reveals how God possessed you in your mother's womb. He knew exactly what you'd look like before you were even born. Before you were formed, all your parts were written in His book. You didn't just happen! You didn't evolve! You were created by a God who has a specific purpose for your creation. He created you with special giftings to fulfill His purposes in your life. God has a plan for you!

Your greatest opportunity for happiness and success is in fulfilling God's purposes for your life. You may be able to use His talents to accomplish other things, but you won't experience God's anointing and blessing on those other efforts as you will if you devote those abilities to Him.

You may wonder, *How do I know what God wants me to do?* The answer comes in giving yourself completely to Him. When you make a total surrender to God, He begins working circumstances in a manner that lead you into His perfect plan for your life. Your part is to surrender. His part is to reveal. If you do your part, He'll do His. Then you'll experience a new fulfillment and joy that only those in the center of His will can know! (AW)

NOVEMBER 12
WHAT'S YOUR EXCUSE?
JEREMIAH 1:4-10

"Then said I, Ah, Lord GOD! behold, I cannot speak: for I am a child" (Jer. 1:6).

God had just revealed to Jeremiah that He had created him for a specific purpose. He had sanctified and ordained him to be a prophet to the nation of Israel. What wonderful news! How awesome to know that God had a special purpose when He created you. You aren't an accident. You were created on purpose to accomplish a specific purpose!

But Jeremiah wasn't blessed by this news—he was intimidated. He wanted out of God's plan for his life. Jeremiah thought it was greater than what he could do. If what you feel called to do isn't greater than what you think you can do, then it's probably not God. God is a big God and He calls us to big things. Man thinks small. God thinks big!

Jeremiah protested that he was only a child and couldn't speak. In truth, he was a grown man at this time. He was referring to his belief that he was inadequate for the task. Moses tried this same line on God (Ex. 4:10). We've all tried it. But the Lord commanded Jeremiah never again to say he was incompetent.

The truth is that none of us are capable of accomplishing God's will on our own. But it's also true that none of us are on our own when we submit to God's will. The Lord gives us special anointings and gifts to accomplish His will. All we have to do is yield. God does the rest.

Do you know what God's will is for your life? Are you lacking what it takes to get it done? You're in good company! Don't try to fulfill the task in your own strength and never again refer to your weakness. Go forward in His might instead! (AW)

NOVEMBER 13
YOU ARE THE CHRIST
MARK 8:27-30

"And he saith unto them, But whom say ye that I am?
And Peter answereth and saith unto him, Thou art the Christ" *(Mark 8:29).*

People often think how wonderful it would've been to be one of Jesus' disciples. They speculate that if they had seen the Lord with their own eyes performing all those miracles that it would have been easy to believe. Not so!

I once dreamed that I was one of Jesus' disciples. I witnessed the Lord raising Jairus' daughter from the dead. I saw blind eyes opened and deaf ears unstopped. I was walking down a road with all the disciples and we were talking about the incredible things we'd seen when Jesus walked right up to me and asked, "But who do you say I am?"

I was torn with emotion. Everything I'd witnessed and all my heart wanted to say, "You are the Christ," but how could I? As I looked at Jesus, He appeared like any other man. There was nothing special about His looks. There was no halo like you see in some pictures. All my sensory knowledge screamed that He was just a man. That's when I realized just how hard it was for Jesus' disciples to believe.

Finally, I gave Peter's reply. But to say, "You are the Christ" took all the faith I could muster. I had to look past His physical body and see who He was on the inside. Now I understand how it's actually easier for us who are removed from the scene to believe. We can read the Word about all the miraculous things He did and envision Him seated on the throne in heaven. The disciples were constantly battling the logic of how God could be in a human body.

You can believe in the Lord just as strongly as those who walked with Him during his physical ministry. Choose to believe today and reap the benefits! (AW)

NOVEMBER 14
IS YOUR HEART STILL BEATING?
HEBREWS 12:12-13

"Wherefore lift up the hands which hang down, and the feeble knees;
And make straight paths for your feet, lest that which is lame be
turned out of the way; but let it rather be healed" *(Heb. 12:12-13).*

This verse describes a person after they've been through the discipline of the Lord. Their hands are hanging down and their knees are weak because they're feeling sorry for themselves. Like a child after being disciplined, the pouting needs to end. It's time to live again!

Does this sound like you? Have you been disciplined by the Lord, but find it hard to forgive yourself? Have you asked yourself, "How could I have ever let myself become so foolish? How could I have disappointed the Lord so much?"

The good news is: There's restoration after forgiveness. Many Christians will try to tell you that God may forgive you, but you can never rise to a level of usefulness with the Lord again. They say, "You can be forgiven, but you can't be restored." A popular phrase is, "A bird with a broken wing can never fly as high." This may be true in nature, but it's not true in grace!

King David flew higher than he'd ever flown before. He became a greater king than ever. Although it took time and much healing, David wasn't only forgiven, but also restored by the power of God.

If you think you've failed so miserably that God can never forgive or use you again, take this test. Put you hand on your heart. Is it still beating? If so, then God isn't through with you. The only time He can't forgive or restore you is when you're dead. Until then, He has a plan for your life and you need to accept it.

Go ahead. Lift up your hands hanging down and your weak knees. Straighten out the path ahead and get back in the race. Heroes aren't people who never make mistakes. They are those who get up afterwards. (BY)

NOVEMBER 15
THANKFULNESS GLORIFIES GOD
LUKE 17:12-19

"There are not found that returned to give glory to God, save this stranger" (Luke 17:18).

Jesus healed ten lepers. He told them to go and show themselves to the priests as Moses commanded. As they went, they were healed. Yet, only one returned to give Jesus thanks. Verse 16 says that this man fell at Jesus' feet and gave Him thanks. Then in verse 18, the Lord said that this man glorified God. Therefore, giving thanks to God is glorifying Him.

Thanking and praising God means that you acknowledge Him as the fountain of your blessings. You are humbling yourself and proclaiming that it's the ability of God that has raised you up, not your own strength. Ungratefulness is like a child whose parents paid all the expenses to put them through college, but they just go out and brag on what they did without mentioning their parents' generosity. We'd think that young person was self-centered and spoiled, and we'd be right. Likewise, it's self-centered and arrogant to fail to thank God.

A very simple, yet profound, theology is, "There's only one God and you are not Him." We didn't make ourselves (Ps. 100:3). God is our Source and we must glorify Him accordingly. We do that by being thankful for all He has so graciously done for us. As the doxology, which many of us were raised with, says, "Praise God from whom all blessings flow."

A person who consistently gives thanks to God is someone who glorifies Him. They won't have a hardened heart. A person who doesn't consistently glorify God is someone who has dethroned Him and placed themselves on the throne. Let Jesus have His rightful place by thanking Him for all His goodness! (AW)

NOVEMBER 16
HEALED OR WHOLE?
LUKE 17:12-19

"And he said unto him, Arise, go thy way: thy faith hath made thee whole" (Luke 17:19).

Ten lepers cried out to Jesus for healing. He told them to act healed by showing themselves to the priests and to ask them to pronounce them cleansed. As they went, they were all healed. Yet, only one came back to the Lord to give Him thanks.

Jesus noticed that 90 percent of the lepers didn't return and that the one who did was a Samaritan. There is no indication that their lack of gratitude caused Jesus to withdraw the healing He had given. That's not the way God is. The Lord *"maketh his sun to rise on the evil and on the good, and sendeth rain on the just and on the unjust"* (Matt. 5:45). However, He did do something special for this one leper who offered thanks.

Leprosy causes parts of the body to decay and fall off. Lepers often were missing fingers or toes. All these men were healed, which meant that the leprosy was no longer in their bodies and no longer doing any damage. However, Jesus told the man who returned that he was made whole. This implied that not only did the leprosy depart, but any damage that the disease had done was repaired. It's possible that at that exact moment, his fingers and toes grew back. Praise the Lord!

Which would you rather have, healing or wholeness? Of course, everyone would rather be whole. Only the one who returned to give thanks was made whole. Why settle for less than God's best? Only those who learn to be thankful will see the greater miracles of God.

What has the Lord done for you? Thank Him! (AW)

NOVEMBER 17
BREAKING THE CURSE OF POVERTY
MATTHEW 6:25-33

"For your heavenly Father knoweth that ye have need of all these things" (Matt. 6:32).

The battle here is in the mind. God has already defeated poverty for us in Christ. We are blessed because we're in Him. To be able to partake in the blessing that is rightfully yours, you'll have to overcome some soul trouble. The soul is the life of the flesh. It's our mind, will, and emotions. John said, *"Beloved, I wish above all things that thou mayest prosper and be in health, even as thy soul prospereth."* (3 John 2). It seems that we need to get it in our mind—which is part of our soul—before we can get it into our wallets.

You're going to have to change the way you think about your money and stuff. First, you must give up ownership. Ownership is God's part of the relationship. Stewardship describes our part. According to Psalm 24:1-2, the earth, and everything in it, belongs to God. Second, tithing is a "must." The tithe isn't giving back to God His part, because we realize that it all belongs to Him. Third, when we get it right with what we already have—meaning we're good stewards—He'll allow us to steward over more. James 4:3 reveals, *"Ye ask, and receive not, because ye ask amiss, that ye may consume it upon your lusts."* The moment we lose sight of the ownership issue, we have become covetous and thereby cut off the blessing. God wants us to think right about money. *"No man can serve two masters: for either he will hate the one, and love the other; or else he will hold to the one, and despise the other. Ye cannot serve God and mammon"* (Matt. 6:24). If we fall in love with our money, we won't be able to do what He wants us to do with it.

"But godliness with contentment is great gain. For we brought nothing into this world, and it is certain we can carry nothing out. And having food and raiment let us be therewith content. But they that will be rich fall into temptation and a snare, and into many foolish and hurtful lusts, which drown men in destruction and perdition. For the love of money is the root of all evil: which while some coveted after, they have erred from the faith, and pierced themselves through with many sorrows" (1 Tim. 6:6-10). It doesn't say that money is the root of all evil; it says the love of money is. There are people who don't have a dime that are sinning all the time. Therefore, having money isn't the problem.

The next step in the process of getting free from poverty is to fill your soul (mind) with what God's Word says about prosperity and provision. You'll need to begin changing your mind with the Word of God. It's called renewing your mind. Prosperity begins on the inside and works its way out. Your soul begins to prosper the moment you believe and act on God's Word. Proverbs 22:9, Psalm 35:27, and Psalm 1:3 are great examples of scriptures you should be thinking about and speaking. Get a concordance, or search through your Bible, and find some scriptures on your own. If your thoughts were previously formed with lack, they can now be filled with God's abundance! By appropriating what Jesus already did for you, and acting on His Word, you'll break the curse of poverty in your life. (BN)

NOVEMBER 18
GOD'S WORD WILL MAKE YOU PROSPEROUS
JOSHUA 1:1-9

"This book of the law shall not depart out of thy mouth; but thou shalt meditate therein day and night, that thou mayest observe to do according to all that is written therein: for then thou shalt make thy way prosperous, and then thou shalt have good success" (Josh. 1:8).

Putting God's Word first in our attention and doing as it instructs will produce prosperity in every area of our lives. God's the one who made us. He knows what makes us tick and how He created this world to function. The Bible is like the owner's manual or the manufacturer's guide for humans. Success comes by following the instruction manual. Failure comes when we do it our way (Jer. 10:23).

Peter put it this way, *"His divine power hath given unto us all things that pertain unto life* and godliness, through the knowledge of him...Whereby are given unto us exceeding great and precious promises" (2 Pet. 1:3-4). Everything we need comes through the knowledge of God. That's what His Word is. It's His knowledge recorded for us in black and white. Verse 4 says that God's knowledge has given us great and precious promises. That's the Bible!

The world's system says, "The way to abundance is to hoard." God's Word says, "Give, and it shall be given unto you" (Luke 6:38). The world says, "The way to happiness is to put self first." Jesus said, "He that loseth his life for my sake shall find it" (Matt. 10:39). The world says, "Hurt me and you will die." Jesus said to turn the other cheek (Matt. 5:39).

God's Word is awesome! Put the Word first in your heart and actions, and watch prosperity come. (AW)

NOVEMBER 19
HOW FAR ARE YOU WILLING TO GO?
MARK 8:22-26

"And he took the blind man by the hand, and led him out of the town;
and when he had spit on his eyes, and put his hands upon him,
he asked him if he saw ought" (Mark 8:23).

We usually focus on the miracle this blind man received. But for a moment, think about the faith he exhibited.

Jesus took this man by the hand and led him out of town. Remember, this man was blind. He didn't know where he was going, and he was putting himself at risk. If Jesus decided to just leave him, what would he do? He couldn't find his way back on his own—he couldn't see! This man was committed. He was expecting to be healed. He made no other arrangements.

What if this man would've decided to stop following Jesus as soon as he discerned that he was getting out of the area familiar to him? After all, if he remained blind he'd be in trouble. It's probable that thoughts of unbelief like that would've stopped him from receiving his healing. He had to go all the way with Jesus. So do we.

There's no record that the Lord explained where He was taking this man or how far away it was. He just told him to hold onto His hand and follow Him. Isn't that enough? We often don't know exactly where the Lord is leading us or how things will go if we don't receive our miracles. But as long as we're holding Jesus' hand, we should feel safe.

How far are you willing to go with the Lord?

Jesus didn't fail this blind man and He won't fail you either. You can feel His hand as you fellowship with Him today. You don't need a "Plan B" or "Plan C" in case Jesus doesn't work. No backups are necessary. He's more than enough! (AW)

NOVEMBER 20
FREEDOM FROM ARROGANCE
PSALM 131:1

"Lord, my heart is not haughty, nor mine eyes lofty" *(Ps. 131:1).*

Unlike many leaders today, David wasn't afraid to share his secrets of success. He didn't fear someone taking his insights and becoming more successful than him. David was completely secure in himself and in the Lord. He wished others success and didn't hesitate to share what he'd learned in the process of becoming a successful king. One of four secrets described in Psalm 131 is David's freedom from arrogance.

Arrogance is exaggerated self-esteem. It's both the source of Lucifer's original sin (Is. 14:12-14 and Ezek. 28:16) and all of our personal sins. An arrogant person competes with everyone around them. This sin causes them to condescend to those they consider beneath them and to be jealous of those who seem better. They're too proud to admit their own weaknesses or recognize anyone else's strengths.

They can tell a woman how to be a better housewife, a businessman how to better manage his company, and a computer operator how to access the newest technology. The arrogant can teach others, but can't be taught themselves. How can you teach someone who thinks they know everything? Arrogance is the only disease that makes everyone sick, except the one who has it.

The enemy of the arrogant is the confident. The confident person relies on God's grace and not their own ability. David's security didn't come from his position as king but from his relationship with the Lord.

He could lose his kingdom and not lose his security. If you met with King David, you'd walk away saying, "He is still a shepherd. He's just wearing a crown!" (BY)

NOVEMBER 21
SUPERNATURAL BREAKTHROUGH
1 KINGS 18:33-35

"Fill four barrels with water, and pour it on the burnt sacrifice, and on the wood. And he said, Do it the second time. And they did it the second time. And he said, Do it the third time. And they did it the third time. And the water ran round about the altar; and he filled the trench also with water" *(1 Kin. 18:33-35).*

There comes a time when enough is enough. Israel had fallen deep into sin. They were worshiping Baal. God said, "We're going to take care of a lot of things at once here. We are going to see repentance and revival. It's time to have a showdown with this humanistic, demon-worshiping crowd. It's time!" There is again going to be a time when God says, "It's time. I've had enough!"

The prophets of Baal already had twelve hours worth of jumping around and cutting themselves trying to get their god to move on their behalf without success. Around noon, it was Elijah's turn. He mocked them saying, "Maybe your god's on vacation." Elijah sent them to pour out four barrels of water on the offering. He sent them three times. That's twelve barrels of water! Remember, they were at the end of three years of drought! Elijah was sowing what was most precious to him at the moment. Twelve barrels of water would go a long way when you've had three years of drought! Desperate times call for desperate measures. He sowed, believing God. Verse 41 says, **"And Elijah said unto Ahab, Get thee up, eat and drink; for there is a sound of abundance of rain."** He saw with the eye of faith what was ahead. **"And it came to pass in the mean while, that the heaven was black with clouds and wind, and there was a great rain"** (verse 45).

It's amazing how some people have a hard time understanding this. Somewhere along the line, there's always going to be supernatural sacrifice before there is supernatural receiving. Somebody sacrificed in prayer. Somebody sacrificed in giving. Somebody sacrificed in going out to minister. It doesn't always mean that it's a hard thing to do. When your heart's engaged and in love with Jesus, even a sacrifice isn't the challenge it used to be. Notice carefully, Elijah was willing to sow for his family, so to speak, and toward national revival. He was willing to sow what was most precious and most needed at the time, in order to see a breakthrough in every realm of his life. There was revival in Israel. Evil was put away and—hallelujah—there was rain. The outpouring of the Lord and the outpouring of what they naturally needed most—rain. Do you see the key? Only God could supply what they really needed, and He did. Elijah sowed water and they reaped rain in abundance. In <u>one day</u> there was national revival!

We have to get our faith out there. I believe entire cities will be won in a day! I believe it'll come down to testimonies like this. Maybe it'll be you in your workplace or your school—standing up and challenging the evolutionists, the humanists, the Satanists. Then God shows Himself strong on your behalf and pours out the flood of His blessing. Lord, do it again! Let it come in buckets, in waves. Let it overflow the troughs, in Jesus' mighty name! (BN)

NOVEMBER 22
MONEY IS THE LEAST AREA OF FAITHFULNESS
LUKE 16:1-13

"He that is faithful in that which is least is faithful also in much: and he that is unjust in the least is unjust also in much" *(Luke 16:10).*

This is an amazing statement from Jesus that has many applications. But in context, Jesus was speaking about money. The whole parable about the unjust steward is talking about his unfaithfulness with money. Jesus repeats this truth in the very next verse and substitutes the words "unrighteous mammon" for "that which is least." This leaves no doubt that money is the lowest level of stewardship.

This brings up some serious questions. If money is least, and yet we can't trust God with our finances, then how can we trust Him in greater things like our eternal destiny? How can a person say, "Oh yes, I know I'm going to heaven, but I can't trust God to tithe." If we don't have enough faith to trust God to give, then how can that faith get us to heaven?

Jesus used this same reasoning to minister to the rich young ruler (Mark 10). This man had an outward show of devotion, and he professed that he'd done everything right. But Jesus saw his heart. Therefore, He told him to sell everything he had and give it to the poor. Jesus would be able to tell by his response to this command about money how he really felt about God in his heart.

Our use of money says volumes about our faith in other areas. No one can profess true faithfulness to God who isn't faithful with their money. Money is the entry level of faithfulness. Financial stewardship is the very least state of faithfulness. It's like the bottom rung of a ladder. We can't go any higher if we don't take that first step. Be faithful with your giving and God will move you up the ladder to greater things. (AW)

NOVEMBER 23
DON'T FORGET
PSALM 106:1-48

"They forgat God their saviour, which had done great things in Egypt" (Ps. 106:21).

The reasoning that the Israelites used (or didn't use) was amazing. It was as if they forgot all that the Lord had done to bring them to the land of Canaan. God brought them out of Egypt, which was the most powerful nation on earth at the time. It wasn't done through their might. Supernatural plagues brought the Egyptians to their knees. Neither did the Israelites leave empty. A nation who had been enslaved for 400 years departed wealthy!

It should've been obvious that the Lord favored them and willed for them to succeed. He didn't bring the children of Israel out of Egypt so they could die in the wilderness. That would be inconsistent with everything He'd already done for them. He knew there were giants in the land when He made the promise to give it to them, but He planned for them to succeed—not fail.

In other words, the events that brought the Israelites to the land of Canaan were so miraculous that there could be no doubt that God had done it. Therefore, it should've been apparent to everyone that regardless of what challenges lay ahead, the Lord was with them to bring His promise to pass. However, they missed the obvious. How?

Three times in this chapter the Scriptures reveal that the Israelites forgot the great things God had done for them (verses 7, 13, and 21). Your memory is one of the most important factors in keeping your heart in tune with the Lord. Make a special effort this Thanksgiving season to remember the goodness of God. You'll find it builds your faith! (AW)

NOVEMBER 24
THE POWER OF MEMORY
2 PETER 1:10-13

"Yea, I think it meet, as long as I am in this tabernacle, to stir you up by putting you in remembrance" (2 Pet. 1:13).

Peter's time on earth was limited. This was possibly his last exhortation to the people he loved so much. Yet, instead of imparting one more piece of information, he reminded them of what they already knew. He used the power of their memories to stir them up.

Memory is a powerful thing. One sight, sound, or smell can trigger emotions and actions that we may not have experienced in years, all because it causes us to remember. Memory is a function of our minds. Peter said, *"I stir up your pure minds by way of remembrance"* (2 Pet. 3:1). We must think to remember. It takes effort, but it's worth it.

One of the ways that the Lord told us to remember is through setting aside special days to commemorate special events. This was one of the main purposes of the Sabbath (Deut. 5:15) and feast days of the Old Covenant (Deut. 16:3). They served as constant reminders of the Lord's blessings.

This is the purpose behind the American holiday Thanksgiving. It's specifically for reminding us of our meager beginnings and that without God's aid, the United States of America would not exist. Those who forget that God conceived this nation tend to think it can carry on without Him.

Regardless of your nationality, thanksgiving should be operative in your life. We need to *"forget not all his benefits"* (Ps. 103:2). The reason the Lord told us not to forget is because we will forget if we don't put forth some effort. Use this holiday to remember all the goodness of God toward you. (AW)

NOVEMBER 25
IT'S GOOD TO GIVE THANKS!
2 CORINTHIANS 9:8-11

"Being enriched in every thing to all bountifulness, which
causeth through us thanksgiving to God" (2 Cor. 9:11).

Our Thanksgiving holiday is rich in godly tradition. Of course, most people have heard of the original Thanksgiving, where the pilgrims gave thanks to God for helping them survive their first winter in the New World. Many presidents of the new United States had celebrations commemorating this original event. However, it was in the midst of the U.S. Civil war in 1863 that President Lincoln issued a proclamation making Thanksgiving an official holiday.

The original proclamation was actually written by William H. Seward, the Secretary of State. President Lincoln expressed similar sentiments when he called for a national day of prayer that same year. Here's an excerpt from that proclamation:

We have been the recipients of the choicest bounties of heaven; we have grown in numbers, wealth, and power as no other nation has ever grown. But we have forgotten God. We have forgotten the gracious Hand which preserved us in peace and multiplied and enriched and strengthened us, and we have vainly imagined, in the deceitfulness of our hearts, that all these blessings were produced by some superior wisdom and virtue of our own. Intoxicated with unbroken success, we have become too self-sufficient to feel the necessity of redeeming and preserving grace, too proud to pray to the God that made us.

These are profound words that are even truer today than when they were first written. Use this holiday season to humble yourself, and remember the God who's blessed you. (AW)

NOVEMBER 26
THE BIBLICAL PERSPECTIVE IS THE RIGHT PERSPECTIVE
ISAIAH 55:8-9

"For my thoughts are not your thoughts, neither are your ways my ways, saith the LORD" (Is. 55:8).

We need to understand some very important things from a biblical perspective. First of all, God wants you blessed. Second, Satan wants you poor. Third, Jesus bore the curse of poverty for all of us. And fourth, God is not the problem—He's the answer!

"Beloved, I wish above all things that thou mayest prosper and be in health, even as thy soul prospereth" (3 John 2). The word translated *wish* literally means "pray." Prosper comes from a compound word meaning "to be well off, fare well; and to lead by a direct and easy way, to have a successful, prosperous and expeditious journey." God's will is for us to prosper in every area of our lives, including financially.

"The thief cometh not, but for to steal, and to kill, and to destroy: I am come that they might have life, and that they might have it more abundantly" (John 10:10). Who's the thief? The devil. Satan is the one who wants to convince believers that they should be poor. But Jesus came to give us abundance—hallelujah! *Abundance* means "great plenty, an overflowing quantity, and ample sufficiency." He became poor so that we could be rich (2 Cor. 8:9). Not so that we could be greedy or selfish, but rich so that we can bless others from the overflow of the blessings He pours out on us!

One of the curses of the Law was poverty (Deut. 28). What good news to know that Jesus bore all those curses for us when He was crucified! *"Christ hath redeemed us from the curse of the law, being made a curse for us: for it is written, Cursed is every one that hangeth on a tree"* (Gal. 3:13).

Believing the Word of God is the balance and the key to receiving all that God has for us on this earth. I can sit down with you for hours and tell you that God wants you to prosper, but until you believe His Word for yourself, it won't be operative in your life. It all comes from God's Word. *"This book of the law shall not depart out of thy mouth; but thou shalt meditate therein day and night, that thou mayest observe to do according to all that is written therein: for then thou shalt make thy way prosperous, and then thou shalt have good success"* (Josh. 1:8).

Obedience to the Word will bring the blessing to you. What is obedience? It's doing what the Word says, not what you "come up with" in your own mind. If someone tells you something, or you have an opinion about something, and it disagrees with what the Bible says, you need to stick with the Word and throw the other stuff out! Judge all things from the biblical perspective. (BN)

NOVEMBER 27
WORRY IS ALWAYS FUTURE
EXODUS 17:3

"Wherefore is this that thou hast brought us up out of Egypt, to kill us and our children and our cattle with thirst?" (Ex. 17:3).

When we face a tragedy or a trial, we usually lose sight of all of God's blessings that brought us to this point. The children of Israel had only been in the wilderness a few days when they came to a place where there was no water to drink. They began complaining to Moses, calling the situation "his fault." They also felt like they had God's plan figured out. He brought them there to kill them!

Let's look at the stupidity of this argument. The Israelites had been in captivity for 400 years in Egypt. Even with the oppression, they continued to increase in population. When Moses arrived, God spared the Jewish people through ten plagues. While the Egyptians suffered and even died, the Israelites were protected by God. He then parted the Red Sea for them to travel safely across and drowned the Egyptian army behind them. Did God do all of this just to bring them to this one spot and kill them?

You've done the same thing! You've looked at your bills, your lack of food in the cupboard, and your overdue mortgage and cried, "I'm going to die right here!" Stop and think about what you just said. God saved you years ago, filled you with His Holy Spirit, healed your body, delivered you from demonic influence, performed miracles for you and your family many times, and supplied all of your needs again and again. Do you really think He's done all of these wonderful things just to bring you to this point and watch you die? No!

Worry is always future. God has taken care of you every moment of every day. This won't fail somehow tomorrow. God's grace isn't going to run out today. Worry is blasphemy against His promises. The God who has always taken care of you won't fail you tomorrow, next week, or next year. He'll continue to walk with you and provide until Jesus comes. *"I have been young, and now am old; yet have I not seen the righteous forsaken, nor his seed begging bread"* (Ps. 37:25). (BY)

NOVEMBER 28
YOU NEVER PUT GOD FIRST AND COME IN SECOND
1 KINGS 17:9-16

"And Elijah said unto her, Fear not; go and do as thou hast said: but make me thereof a little cake first, and bring it unto me, and after make for thee and for thy son" (1 Kin. 17:13).

Here was a desperate situation, but there was a man of faith and a woman of faith who were willing to do whatever it took for breakthrough. In many circles today, Elijah would've been criticized for saying "Go make me a little cake first." There was only enough meal and oil for this widow woman to make something for her son and herself. Then they thought they'd die. And here walks up a man of God saying, *"Fear not; go and do as thou hast said: but make me thereof a little cake first, and bring it unto me, and after make for thee and for thy son"* (1 Kin. 17:13). But Elijah, how could you take advantage of a poor widow like that? He wasn't taking advantage of her. He was giving her an opportunity to be blessed with a miracle! Elijah knew that God was a "sure thing." *"For thus saith the LORD God of Israel, The barrel of meal shall not waste, neither shall the cruse of oil fail, until the day that the LORD sendeth rain upon the earth"* (1 Kin. 17:14).

"And she went and did according to the saying of Elijah: and she, and he, and her house, did eat many days. And the barrel of meal wasted not, neither did the cruse of oil fail, according to the word of the LORD, which he spake by Elijah" (1 Kin. 17:15-16). By putting the man of God first, the widow woman was really putting God first. What happened as a result of that offering? A miracle. And what was that miracle? She and her family were sustained until the drought broke. This woman knew the principle: You will never go wrong by putting God first. And it paid off!

As believers, we aren't supposed to be worried about what we're going to wear or what we're going to eat. God promised to take care of all our needs. Jesus spelled it out very plainly, *"But seek ye first the kingdom of God, and his righteousness; and all these things shall be added unto you"* (Matt. 6:33). Paul wrote, *"Know ye not that they which run in a race run all, but one receiveth the prize? So run, that ye may obtain"* (1 Cor. 9:24). When we put God first, we'll never come in second! (BN)

NOVEMBER 29
FAITH TO RECEIVE
MARK 9:14-24

"Jesus said unto him, If thou canst believe, all things are possible to him that believeth. And straightway the father of the child cried out, and said with tears, Lord, I believe; help thou mine unbelief" (Mark 9:23-24).

Your faith is the key to receiving from God. It is faith in the love, mercy, and grace of God Almighty. It is faith in the atoning sacrifice and resurrection of the Lord Jesus Christ. It's your faith in His promises—that He will do what He said He would do. Actually, He's already done it. We just have to accept it as ours. You're never too young for a miracle, and you are never too old. The man in Mark 9 wanted desperately to believe. He realized that his faith played an important part in the miracle that was to come forth. He asked the Lord to help him, and He did.

Consider the following examples of receiving on the basis of faith. They apply to healing, but the same principle works for every need. In Matthew 9:22, it was the woman with the issue of blood; in Mark 10:51-52, it was a blind man; in Luke 17:17-19, it was the one leper that returned to give thanks. All these people had one thing in common—Jesus told them, *"__Thy faith hath made thee whole.__"* I believe He clarified the point in Mark 11:22-24 (emphasis mine), *"And Jesus answering saith unto them, __Have faith in God__. For verily I say unto you, That whosoever shall say unto this mountain, Be thou removed, and be thou cast into the sea; and shall not doubt in his heart, but shall believe that those things which he saith shall come to pass; he shall have whatsoever he saith. Therefore I say unto you, __What things soever ye desire, when ye pray, believe that ye receive them, and ye shall have them.__"*

If we believe, we receive the things we desire when we pray. When do we get the desire? When we pray. When do we believe? When we pray. When do we receive the things we desire? When we pray. Faith through prayer works for you both individually and corporately. Just as a body of believers has corporate goals, you should have individual goals. You should pray about those goals. Faith believes, confesses, works, praises, and rests! The question isn't, "Can God?" Yes, God can. The question is, "Will you believe?" I say, "Yes, God can, and yes, I will!" (BN)

NOVEMBER 30
THERE'S ALWAYS MORE!
EPHESIANS 3:20

"Now unto him that is able to do exceeding abundantly above all that we ask or think, according to the power that worketh in us" (Eph. 3:20).

If our shadows aren't healing people, there's more. There's always more with God! We serve a limitless God. There is nothing that is unobtainable in the spiritual realm. The only limit on God is the end of our faith—that is, where we stop using our faith. It's God's time to take the limits off! There's always a way with Him! *"Enlarge the place of thy tent, and let them stretch forth the curtains of thine habitations: spare not, lengthen thy cords, and strengthen thy stakes; For thou shalt break forth on the right hand and on the left" (Is. 54:2-3).*

"__For your shame ye shall have double__; and for confusion they shall rejoice in their portion: therefore in their land they shall possess the double: everlasting joy shall be unto them" (Is. 61:7, emphasis mine). God wants you to have at least twice as much—a better marriage, a better job, more profitable businesses, more revival, and more souls! *"Now he that ministereth seed to the sower both minister bread for your food, __and multiply your seed sown, and increase the fruits of your righteousness__" (2 Cor. 9:10, emphasis mine).* Enlarge! Expand! Raise the bar! Expand your vision!

Faith receives the promises of God. Faith always finds a way. We are not fear-people. We are faith-people. Trust God and believe His Word! The Word is constant. *"God is not a man, that he should lie; neither the son of man, that he should repent: hath he said, and shall he not do it? or hath he spoken, and shall he not make it good?"* (Num. 23:19). *"Heaven and earth shall pass away, but my words shall not pass away."* (Matt. 24:35).

Go beyond what is normal, usual, expected, or necessary. If you're going to receive like you've never received, you must sow like you've never sown. Wayne Myers said, "I've never received more by sowing less." With God, there's always more! (BN)

DECEMBER 1
SUPER-NATURAL
PSALMS 119:128

"Therefore I esteem all thy precepts concerning all things to be right; and I hate every false way"
(Ps. 119:128).

God works through the natural laws of the universe to bring prosperity to the people doing His will. *"For as the rain cometh down, and the snow from heaven, and returneth not thither, but watereth the earth, and maketh it bring forth and bud, that it may give seed to the sower, and bread to the eater"* (Is. 55:10). What rain does to bring forth fruit in the earth, the Word does to bring forth seed and bread. God uses the natural and blesses it. It's His "super" on our "natural." He blesses the work of our hands so we'll be a blessing to others. *"When thou cuttest down thine harvest in thy field, and hast forgot a sheaf in the field, thou shalt not go again to fetch it: it shall be for the stranger, for the fatherless, and for the widow: that the LORD thy God may bless thee in all the work of thine hands"* (Deut. 24:19).

Both faith and natural laws come from the same source—God. God used natural laws to bring increase to the children of Israel. *"And all these blessings shall come on thee, and overtake thee, if thou shalt hearken unto the voice of the LORD thy God"* (Deut. 28:2). Abraham's flocks grew by natural means, blessed by God. God didn't just make things appear out of nowhere; He blessed what Abraham had and increased it. Whoever owns something has the right to determine how it's used. Who owns everything? God. So everything you have should increase godliness in your life in some way. The person who uses what they have in a godly way will receive increase. Your greatest increase will come from how you use what you have, not from what you don't have.

God lays out His wisdom and His law for us. By knowing His ways, we'll know how to prosper. *"Treasures of wickedness profit nothing: but righteousness delivereth from death. The LORD will not suffer the soul of the righteous to famish: but he casteth away the substance of the wicked. He becometh poor that dealeth with a slack hand: but the hand of the diligent maketh rich. He that gathereth in summer is a wise son: but he that sleepeth in harvest is a son that causeth shame. Blessings are upon the head of the just: but violence covereth the mouth of the wicked"* (Prov. 10:2-6). The Word gives us the spiritual laws. The spiritual laws describe reality whether people admit it or not. For example, God doesn't want His children to be bogged down with debt. He shows the consequence of this in Proverbs 22:7. *"The rich ruleth over the poor, and the borrower is servant to the lender."* We must control our lives to live comfortably on what we make. Make use of what you have, and God will supply what you lack.

We must be willing to change to be able to receive more from God. Until we're willing to change more, we've received everything we can. God's way is the right way. When we do it His way, we win. (BN)

DECEMBER 2
TURNAROUND
LUKE 11:37-42

"But rather give alms of such things as ye have; and, behold, all things are clean unto you. But woe unto you, Pharisees! for ye tithe mint and rue and all manner of herbs, and pass over judgment and the love of God: these ought ye to have done, and not to leave the other undone"
(Luke 11:41-42).

The Pharisee in this scripture was concerned about ritual, but Jesus was concerned about the heart. If cleaning up the inward man was the topic, why do you think Jesus turned to the man's giving? It sounds very similar to what He told the young man in Mark 10:21-23: *"Then Jesus beholding him loved him, and said unto him, One thing thou lackest: go thy way, sell whatsoever thou hast, and give to the poor, and thou shalt have treasure in heaven: and come, take up the cross, and follow me. And he was sad at that saying, and went away grieved: for he had great possessions. And Jesus looked round about, and saith unto his disciples, How hardly shall they that have riches enter into the kingdom of God!"* People who are whole are givers, not hoarders. They look at an offering as what they can share, not just what they can spare. If your income belongs to God, your outcome will be established. Prosperous people determine where their money goes. Poor people have given that privilege up through debt.

The key to turnaround for me was tithing. The tithe forces you to face the issues of surrender and submission. There's liberty in that. It ends the struggle over who will rule: you, your money, or God? The non-tithing Christian is saying that they have the faith to trust God for eternal salvation, but not with ten percent of their money.

The stronghold lies in the thought life. It requires a faith response to activate the power of the Word. Your mind can't figure out God or His ways. We need to pay attention to 2 Corinthians 10:5, *"Casting down imaginations, and every high thing that exalteth itself against the knowledge of God, and bringing into captivity every thought to the obedience of Christ."* Your thought life is really where you live! It's not so much what happens to you, as what you *think* about what happens to you that affects you the most. Prosperity must be an internal reality first. The scorner is a scorner because their thoughts are full of scorn. Someone coined the phrase "Life is rough and then you die." That's not the confession of a believer! "Life is great and then we go to heaven!" Prosperous people have prosperous thought lives. Their souls prosper because they think on the Word.

Turnaround takes time. It takes twenty-one days to form a habit but an entire year to make it a part of your life. Sure, God can do it in a day. But change begins with a decision right now to do what the Word says regardless of the circumstances. Change takes place when the decision to do what's right, because it's right, has been acted on. Make up your mind to be a tither—not because of the blessing but because it's God's will. Then, the turnaround and blessing will come! (BN)

DECEMBER 3
SMALL SEEDS CAN MEET TALL NEEDS
LUKE 13:19

"It is like a grain of mustard seed, which a man took, and cast into his garden; and it grew, and waxed a great tree; and the fowls of the air lodged in the branches of it" (Luke 13:19).

The seed in your purse or pocketbook will never help the kingdom of God; it's the seed you take out and sow that'll grow! I remember hearing how they opened up some pyramids in the Middle East and found seeds thousands of years old. They were still there, but they hadn't helped anyone. Good intentions never grow a crop; seeds can only grow when you plant them!

No seed is too small. After a seed is sown, it becomes tall and great and blesses others. Small seeds can meet tall needs! A tiny little mustard seed could even fall out of your hand, but when you come back a few years later, it'll be a big tree. Big trees offer big shade. The Bible says that even the birds will fly and lodge in the limbs of that tree.

We've seen that in our lives. I've lost count of how many hotel bills we've paid over the years for ministers who were burned-out, tired, and discouraged. We told them, "If you can get here, we'll give you a hotel room for a few days." They'd come into our morning prayer services and regular services and be a part of what God was doing. Before long, they'd go home rekindled by the fire of God. They were able to go back out and help others. Our seeds may be small—a hotel room, a mis-sionary, a van, a lunch, even a smile—but they can meet tall needs when we plant them! (BN)

DECEMBER 4
THE BETTER DISH
LUKE 10:42

"Mary hath chosen that good part" *(Luke 10:42).*

Jesus made this statement to Martha, Mary's sister. The Greek word for *good part* means "the better dish." This must have been a hard statement for Martha to accept.

Martha had been working all day to prepare the meal for Jesus and His disciples. The opening of this story tells us she was "cumbered," or weighed down, by the preparation of the food, drinks, and table settings. She must have wanted each table setting to be perfect, each disciple to have enough of her prize-winning dishes, and each drinking glass to stay filled.

Martha was also angry at her sister. Instead of helping serve food, Mary was sitting at Jesus' feet listening to His every word. Finally, Martha shouted at the Lord, "Don't You care that Mary has left me all alone to serve? Tell her to help me." Jesus didn't tell Martha that laboring and serving were wrong, but she'd become too worried and overtaken by her work. Mary had chosen the better dish—sitting and learning at Jesus' feet.

We often get caught up serving the Lord and working in the church. If we're not careful, we can forget about the greatest dish of all—learning God's Word. It's through the Word that Jesus fellowships with us. True power for service comes through God's promises and fellowship with Him. This is where our hearts become truly committed to the Lord. We should serve Him out of a committed heart of love.

This is what Martha was missing. She thought that by working, she would find favor with the Lord. She worked hard to impress Him and His disciples. Mary found the true way to His heart. She put communion with Jesus first in her life. Her works would then count for the Lord. We are saved "unto good works," but we don't work to be saved! (BY)

DECEMBER 5
LOOK ON THE FIELDS!
JOHN 4:35-38

"Say not ye, There are yet four months, and then cometh harvest?
behold, I say unto you, Lift up your eyes, and look on the fields;
for they are white already to harvest" *(John 4:35).*

Part of sowing seed to reap our harvest is helping God reap His harvest. His harvest is souls. The Word of God says to look on the fields. It's amazing how many people come to church and never look on the fields. They hear the songs, they listen to the message, they do the things people do in church, but they leave and never look on the fields. God wants us to look out for the needs of others. When your stomach's full, don't forget that there are those who don't have sufficient food. When your home is comfortable, never forget that there is someone else who doesn't have a comfortable dwelling.

Can we do everything for everyone? No. But God wants us to look for opportunities to do what we can. Look for people who need Jesus. Look for those who will respond to the Gospel. Live alert and don't live selfishly. Live with your eyes open. This isn't to bring condemnation or pressure, but to challenge you to look for opportunities where you can make a difference. One church or one person can't respond to every need in the world today—even here in our own city. I realize that. I can't respond to every need presented to me. But if we'll look, we can respond to those needs we do see. Then we can happily do something about it!

Behold—look on the fields! Look at the people you work with. Study the needs of people's lives, and then do what you can. Tell them about Jesus. But don't lose your vision of the fields! A church that loses the vision of the fields, especially those fields immediately surrounding them, is a church in the process of dying. I want to live alert. Yes, I want to be blessed. But I want to be one that when God needs someone to do something on this earth, He can use me to be a blessing. By sowing into other's lives, God will multiply it back to your own! (BN)

DECEMBER 6
LIFT UP YOUR EYES
JOHN 4:35

"Lift up your eyes, and look on the fields; for they are white already to harvest" (John 4:35).

This phrase "lift up your eyes" was used many times in the ministry of Jesus. Before the feeding of the five thousand with five loaves and two fishes, Jesus "lifted up his eyes." Before raising Lazarus from the dead, He stood in front of an empty tomb and an unbelieving crowd and "lifted up his eyes." We are told that when Jesus taught or prayed before the multitudes, He "lifted up his eyes."

This means more than just looking toward heaven with your physical eyes. It's a redirecting of your attention from this natural world and its circumstances to the realm of the Holy Spirit. We sometimes think of God sitting on His throne in heaven, but He's actually much closer than that. He's an ever-present help in time of need! If we will acknowledge His presence and look to Him for help, we'll be delivered.

To receive divine healing, the Israelites were commanded to look at the brazen serpent. The serpent represented Jesus on the cross bearing our curse. The look by the natural did not heal, but seeing the image through the eyes of faith would bring divine deliverance. The look of faith for us will bring supernatural help, wisdom, and guidance from the Holy Spirit.

Christians often want to spend long periods of time in prayer before fighting a spiritual battle. They believe hours of intercession are needed before laying hands on the sick or counseling another believer. What did Jesus do as He went through His day? Needs came at Him so fast that He didn't have time to go into His prayer closet. He spoke at the synagogue, healed a man let down through the roof, cured Peter's mother-in-law, healed the woman with the issue of blood, and raised Jairus' daughter from the dead all in one day. Jesus knew the power of God was ever present. It was but one glance away. He "looked up."

Are you faced with a need? Get your attention off yourself. Help is a look away! (BY)

DECEMBER 7
TRAMPLED BY UNBELIEF
2 KINGS 7:1-20

"And that lord answered the man of God, and said, Now, behold, if the LORD should make windows in heaven, might such a thing be? And he said, Behold, thou shalt see it with thine eyes, but shalt not eat thereof" (2 Kin. 7:19).

Some people are their own worst enemy! Second Kings 6:25 tells us about a great famine in Samaria. Since the city was under siege by the king of Syria, food was scarce, prices were ridiculously high, and people were doing desperate things just to stay alive. Have you ever fallen upon desperate times? God can turn it around in a day! Elisha came in and announced that the Lord declared that by the very next day, prices for food would fall to practically nothing. That would set anyone to dancing and shouting—or would it? The officer assisting the king was a man full of doubt and unbelief. He declared, "That couldn't happen even if the Lord opened the very windows of heaven!" That unbelief cost him his life! Elisha answered, *"Behold, thou shalt see it with thine eyes, but shalt not eat thereof"* (2 Kin. 7:2).

In a miraculous move, God caused the Syrian army to hear the clatter of speeding chariots and galloping horses, as if a great army was approaching. They became so scared that they ran away and left everything behind. Four lepers discovered the riches that were there for the taking and reported it to the gatekeepers of Israel. News got back to the king and his scouts confirmed it. This ignited a mad dash of people plundering the deserted Syrian camp. The king's official, who said there was no way that God could turn it around in a day, had been assigned to guard the city gate. During the human stampede to plunder the Syrians, he was trampled to death by the rush of people.

The same God who miraculously provided for the Israelites is faithful to provide for us today. It's our job to be faithful to Him and believe that His Word is true. Let's never be guilty of being trampled by unbelief! (BN)

DECEMBER 8
WHO'S LISTENING?
ROMANS 8:31

"What shall we then say to these things? If God be for us, who can be against us?" (Rom. 8:31).

When Jesus instructed His disciples in faith, He told them to speak to the mountain (Mark 11:23). The occasion for this lesson was a dead fig tree Jesus had just spoken to the day before. In another teaching on faith, the Lord told His disciples to speak to a sycamine tree and command it to be plucked up (Luke 17:6). Are you beginning to understand? Faith works as we speak against problems.

When Joshua needed more daylight to finish his battle against five kings, he commanded the sun and moon to stand still (Josh. 10:12).

Paul joins with Joshua, Jesus, and others when he tells us to speak to the circumstances of life and say, "If God be for me, you can't be against me" (Rom. 8:31). Jesus didn't pray to God to heal; He spoke to sickness and demons and commanded them to go. I can't find a single place where Jesus prayed for sickness. But over and over again, I see that He spoke to sickness.

If we can speak to mountains, trees, sickness, and the circumstances of life, they must be able to hear! Jesus said the sycamine tree would obey. If good trees will one day clap their hands at the return of Jesus and oceans will roar at His coming, they must be able to respond to the voice of God's Word.

Why not speak to your checkbook as if it can hear? Why not speak to your cancer as if it has ears? Speak to them and say, "Checkbook, I command you to open up the provisions of God. You've been against me too long. Cancer, if God be for me, you cannot be against me. I rebuke you and command you to leave this body in the name of Jesus. Come out by the roots, and be cast into the sea!" Jesus said they will obey you! (BY)

DECEMBER 9
WHAT YOU MAKE HAPPEN FOR SOMEONE ELSE,
HE'LL MAKE HAPPEN FOR YOU!
PROVERBS 11:24

"There is that scattereth, and yet increaseth; and there is that withholdeth more than is meet, but it tendeth to poverty" (Prov. 11:24).

There is a popular radio minister in our church who was led of the Lord back in 1974 to give $900 to help another preacher pay off his ministry tent. Money was scarce at the time, and what he gave was originally going to go toward his own house. But he went ahead and sowed it in obedience. The years that followed brought great challenge and growth through difficult circumstances. After learning some things the hard way, they ended up in bankruptcy and had two homes foreclosed.

In 1992, the Lord started speaking to his wife and him to believe for another house. There was simply no way in the natural, but they believed God would honor the word He spoke to their hearts. They looked at houses and found a builder who would work with them. He told them, "You give us $2,000 and we'll start the house." At that time, they'd never received any more than $20 to $100 in special offerings!

Then in June 1993, they experienced revival in what's now their home church. They started to sow into the revival and soon had $20,000 extra toward their house. By that time, they'd been turned down by two or three mortgage companies. They kept pressing in and giving. They gave into a first fruits offering. You sow where you want to go. It was money they needed, but God said to help their daughter. She was believing for a house, so they sowed to help her as well.

One night in the fall of 1993, the Lord spoke to him in the radio studio and said, "Do you remember that $900 you gave Me? I'm getting ready to give that back to you with interest." He told him, "Figure it out with ten percent a year compounded." It came out to almost $50,000 for nineteen years! The minister gasped, "Oh, my!" Something was about to hit! They found a mortgage company that could help them and kept giving faithfully.

The mortgage broker took three contracts to the underwriters in April 1994. Two were spotless and the minister's had a bankruptcy and foreclosure on it. The broker said, "You won't believe this!" The minister answered, "I might." The broker explained that the other two were turned down, but his had been accepted! About a week before closing, all the money that they needed was in. Looking at their bank account, they noticed that the harvest started directly coming in during the revival when they began stepping out and aggressively sowing. That's when it really took off—the whole time they were obedient to tithe, sow, and believe the Word in faith.

Make a note of this: What you make happen for someone else, God will make happen for you. Do you have a need? Sow some seed! (BN)

DECEMBER 10
DON'T THROW MONEY—SOW IT!
HEBREWS 11:4

"By faith Abel offered unto God a more excellent sacrifice than Cain,
by which he obtained witness that he was righteous, God testifying of his gifts:
and by it he being dead yet speaketh" (Heb. 11:4).

God testified of Abel's gifts. Why? Because Abel offered his sacrifice by faith. He didn't give by faith in himself or faith in his gift, but by faith in God. This is a powerful principle I've learned. It's something that needs to be stressed for living in God's abundance. We are to be givers, but we must give in faith based on God's Word. We hear all kinds of appeals, but we should have His mind on where and how much we're to sow. Don't ever throw your money—sow it! Sow it on purpose—in faith—believing!

It's not just a minister's thing. The widow woman in 1 Kings 17 who gave the last little meal that she had was blessed. It wasn't just the prophet who got blessed! She too was blessed until the famine ended. Her obedience blessed the prophet, but it also brought blessing to her own house.

No, it's not just a preacher thing. I watch children who really catch the concept of giving. It's amazing what you see God do for a child. When you tell young children something, they believe it. They don't weigh the pros and cons or analyze the variables; they simply believe. They have faith. When the children of one of our church members were smaller years ago, they agreed for the Lord to give them a van for the family. That wasn't what their parents really had in mind. But in the process of looking for a car, the salesman said, "I don't believe I have the car you want, but I have a van here." Out of curiosity, they looked at it and decided they liked it. So instead of buying the car, they bought the van. As they drove down the road, the children were all rejoicing that God had answered their prayer.

Don't just throw your money; keep your faith active and operative every time you give! (BN)

DECEMBER 11
DON'T YOU BELIEVE WHAT YOU PREACH?
JOHN 6:29

"Jesus answered and said unto them, This is the work of God, that ye believe on him whom he hath sent" *(John 6:29).*

One time, in an emergency situation, a widow came forward and said that God told her to empty her savings. I was hesitant to receive that offering, but then she piped up and said, "What's the matter? Don't you believe what you preach?" Ouch! That was some of the hardest money to receive I've ever experienced. Yet in a matter of thirty days, she came right back up to the platform, shook her finger in my face, and declared, "Let me tell you what God did for me!"

Her deceased husband had worked for the railroad. One of his former co-workers came by and asked her if she'd heard about the new benefits. He further explained that the railroad wasn't telling people about these benefits unless they knew how to look for them. She told him that she hadn't heard about the benefits. The man checked into it and as a result, her benefit package increased by $400 a month as long as she lived, plus she received a $5,000 lump sum in cash. Her little meager savings that she'd emptied out was more than doubled in return. She knew that if she took care of God's house, He'd take care of hers. This woman took God at His Word!

There's a valuable lesson in this. God's Word works—every time! **"So shall my word be that goeth forth out of my mouth: it shall not return unto me void, but it shall accomplish that which I please, and it shall prosper in the thing whereto I sent it"** (Is. 55:11). God has done His part. The answer to the difficult is in the simple. He's given us His Word so we may prosper and be in health (3 John 2). Our part is simply to believe Him and act in faith on His Word! (BN)

DECEMBER 12
WHERE'S YOUR EBENEZER?
1 SAMUEL 7:3-13

"Then Samuel took a stone, and set it between Mizpeh and Shen, and called the name of it Ebenezer, saying, Hitherto hath the LORD helped us" *(1 Sam. 7:12).*

God had just won a great victory for the Israelites. As they assembled to pray and repent as a nation, the Philistines attacked them. The people cried out to God for help and the Lord was violently agitated and irritated with the Philistines. That's what the word *thundered* in verse 10 means. God routed the Philistines before the Israelites.

Samuel placed a large stone at the site of the battle and called it Ebenezer. The Hebrew word *Ebenezer* means "stone of the help." Samuel was placing a visual reminder for everyone present, and generations to come, that God was the one who had helped the people of Israel defeat their enemies.

The Lord commanded the observance of many feasts to remind His people of things He had done. He also commanded us to reverence the landmarks of others by not removing them (Deut. 19:14, 27:17; Prov. 22:28, 23:10). All of this stresses the importance of having markers that remind us of God's faithfulness.

Psalm 103:2 says, **"Forget not all his benefits."** The reason we're commanded not to forget is because we will if we don't make an effort to remember. That's what the stone Ebenezer was for.

Do you have Ebenezers in your life? Each one of us has many instances where God has been faithful, but whether or not you've marked that spot is a different matter. Let the Lord direct your memory back to His faithfulness and put a marker there in your mind. Then visit that place often! (AW)

DECEMBER 13
OFFENSES
MARK 4:17

"Afterward, when affliction or persecution ariseth for the word's sake,
immediately they are offended" (Mark 4:17).

As a pastor, I can tell you that offenses are the number one reason why people leave the Word of God, their walk with Jesus, and the church. Affliction and persecution come to every Christian, but some handle them better than others. Pressures are designed by Satan to steal the Word out of your heart. It's not you the devil hates—it's the Word in your heart. God's Word believed and spoken will overthrow Satan's hold on you and others.

An offense is just a molehill magnified into a mountain. Offenses are never major issues, only minor. They can be disagreements over carpet colors in the church, wall colors, or pews vs. chairs. Many become offended because the music is too loud or not loud enough, the room's too cold or too hot, or we stand too long for worship. I've even had people become offended because I didn't say "hi" to them in the hallway. Many times I simply didn't see them.

Eventually, offenses are like glasses. When you put them on, you see the whole world through the lens of your offenses. You judge the preaching, the music, and those in positions of leadership—all through your offenses. When you leave the church, Satan has you right where he wants you!

An offense is a side issue to take you away from the real issue—the Word of God. What does it matter if you have a chair or pew to sit on? Many around the world sit on the ground to hear the Word. The temperature and volume are nothing more than side issues. I've spoken in churches that had no sound system, heat, or air conditioning. The people attended only because they wanted to hear the Word.

This verse comes from the parable of the sower and the seed. All that's needed for spiritual growth and victory over Satan is a sower (minister), seed (the Word), and ground (the hearts of people). Anything else should be treated as a blessing, but not as an opportunity for offense! (BY)

DECEMBER 14
YOU GET WHAT YOU BELIEVE FOR!
HEBREWS 11:6

"But without faith it is impossible to please him:
for he that cometh to God must believe that he is, and that
he is a rewarder of them that diligently seek him" (Heb. 11:6).

Everything in the Word of God is based on faith, Not just faith in faith but faith in God. From Genesis to Revelation, it's all faith! *"By faith Abel…by faith Noah…by faith Abraham"* (Heb. 11:4, 7, 8) *"The just shall live by faith"* (Heb. 10:38). The Word clearly tells us that *"without faith it is impossible to please"* God.

We must mix faith with our giving! A farmer doesn't just go out and plant a bunch of miscellaneous seeds and expect to get a good crop of corn. He plants corn seeds. It's the same for us. We must target our sowing. At our church, every time we take an offering we speak, in faith believing, over our giving. We declare out loud that we are believing for jobs and better jobs, raises and bonuses, benefits, sales and commissions, settlements, estates and inheritances, interest and income, rebates and returns, checks in the mail, gifts and surprises, finding money, bills paid off, debts demolished, houses paid for, cars paid for, royalties received, multiplication, and new businesses. All of this is so we can finance God's end-time harvest and properly support the needs of our church, our families, and ourselves. As a result, we've been receiving many wonderful testimonies of these things happening in the lives of the people who are standing in faith for them.

We don't just throw our money—we sow it! What are you believing God for? Are you speaking His Word over that seed? Some people believe for nothing—and they're getting all that they believe for! (BN)

DECEMBER 15
CHRISTIANITY IS SUPERNATURAL!
LUKE 1:26-38

"To a virgin espoused to a man whose name was Joseph, of the house of David; and the virgin's name was Mary" (Luke 1:27).

The virgin birth is so incomprehensible that it has always been one of Christianity's main targets of criticism. Skeptics cite the impossibility of such a thing as proof that the Bible can't be true. Yet, the virgin birth of our Lord Jesus Christ is one of the cornerstones of the Christian faith.

Mankind produces offspring in his own likeness and image (Gen. 5:3). Therefore, if Jesus had just been the natural product of a man and woman, He would've had a sin nature (Rom. 5:12) and, therefore, could not have been our sinless sacrifice. Isaiah prophesied that the Messiah would be born of a virgin (Is. 7:14). This had to happen to give Jesus the pure life of God instead of the corrupted blood of man. There is no room for compromise on this issue!

Some true believers in the Lord and His Word try to find natural explanations to the miracles of the Bible to make it more palatable to unbelievers. They try to reconcile the Genesis account of creation with evolution, the children of Israel crossing the "Reed" Sea instead of the "Red" Sea, etc. However, there's simply no way to explain away the supernaturalness of the virgin birth. This couldn't have happened any other way but through a supernatural act of God.

Christianity is supernatural in every respect. God became a man, allowed Himself to be put to death as our sacrifice, then rose from the dead and now lives forever. Those who believe this and trust His sacrifice are "born again" and have the same nature and power as God. Christianity is supernatural! *All other attempts to explain God's relationship to man are superficial.* (AW)

DECEMBER 16
WHAT DO YOU EXPECT?
LUKE 1:26-38

"And when she saw him, she was troubled at his saying, and cast in her mind what manner of salutation this should be" (Luke 1:29)

Amazing! The angel Gabriel didn't say anything negative or derogatory to Mary. He said, "Hail," which is the Greek word *chairo* that was translated "glad, joy, rejoicing" fifty-nine times in the New Testament. Gabriel told Mary to rejoice because she was highly favored of God, the Lord was with her, and she was the most blessed woman who had ever lived. What was so disturbing about that?

The reality is that most of us aren't accustomed to praise. We're too acquainted with our faults. We may consider it rude for others to mention them, but we can relate when they do. Praise is uncomfortable. It causes us to blush. When it comes from God, it can be frightening. Why is that?

It's because we have a wrong image of God. We tend to see Him as a harsh, condemning, Almighty God instead of a loving heavenly Father. We expect judgment from Him, not mercy—and certainly not praise. God is Almighty and just, but above all things, He is love (1 John 4:8). That doesn't mean He overlooks sin. No! He deals with sin. Through Mary's faith, her sins had been forgiven and she was truly blessed of the Lord.

Amazingly, what we now have through Jesus is even better than what Mary had. If you are the least of all believers, you're greater than Mary (Matt. 11:11). Yet, like Mary, we don't tend to see ourselves as God sees us. If Gabriel had rebuked her, she probably wouldn't have been troubled. She would've said, "It must be God." Don't make the same mistake. Recognize that all believers are blessed and highly favored of the Lord. Rejoice! (AW)

DECEMBER 17
QUESTIONS AREN'T ALWAYS BAD
LUKE 1:26-38

"Then said Mary unto the angel, How shall this be, seeing I know not a man?" (Luke 1:34).

Contrast this encounter with the angel Gabriel to the one Zacharias had just six months earlier. Gabriel told Zacharias that he would have a son by a miraculous birth. Zacharias asked him how a thing like that could be, since both he and his wife were beyond childbearing ages. Zacharias's unbelief so angered Gabriel that he struck him with dumbness for nine months until the birth of his son (Luke 1:18-20).

Here, Mary asked a similar question, but the results were much kinder. Since God is not a respecter of persons (Rom. 2:11), it must be assumed that the heart motivations behind their questions were different. Zacharias asked his question in unbelief, a statement of scorn rather than a true inquiry. Mary asked her question for information, a very different motivation and a wise move.

If Abraham had questioned the Lord about who his promised seed would come through, he would've avoided the birth of Ishmael and the whole Arab-Israeli conflict we have today. Questions in themselves aren't wrong. It just depends on the attitude or reason for asking them. Without this question and Gabriel's answer, Mary might have assumed that this child would come through the natural union between Joseph and her.

All of us have trouble understanding the ways of the Lord. He told us, *"My thoughts are not your thoughts, neither are your ways my ways, saith the LORD. For as the heavens are higher than the earth, so are my ways higher than your ways, and my thoughts than your thoughts"* (Is. 55:8-9). We need wisdom that only God can give. He doesn't mind us asking questions, as long as our hearts are right. (AW)

DECEMBER 18
ALL THINGS ARE POSSIBLE!
LUKE 1:26-38

"For with God nothing shall be impossible" (Luke 1:37).

The virgin birth is inexplicable except as a miracle. There's no possible way for a virgin to have a baby. With God, all things are possible.

However, the Bible reveals that there are some things that are impossible. Hebrews 6:18 says that it's impossible for God to lie. It was impossible for Satan to keep Jesus in the grave (Acts 2:24). It's impossible for anyone who was once enlightened and now fallen away to be "born again" again (Heb. 6:4). It certainly is impossible to please God without faith (Heb. 11:6).

The *Amplified Bible* translates this verse as, *"No word from God shall be without power or impossible of fulfillment."* In other words, anything that God has promised in His Word is possible.

God's Word not only proclaims what He's willing and able to do, but it also carries the power of God to accomplish whatever He promises. God's Word becomes a self-fulfilling prophecy when mixed with faith. The one word "come" from the lips of Jesus had enough power in it to enable Peter to walk on water (Matt. 14:29). The word of the Lord that Gabriel brought to Mary had the power to produce the virgin birth, if she received it.

What has God spoken to you? It doesn't matter how impossible it may look. The only question is, "Lord, is this really from You?" If so, then the power it takes to accomplish the task is contained in the Word itself. Mix it with faith, and nothing that God has promised you is impossible! (AW)

DECEMBER 19
THE WORD BECAME FLESH
LUKE 1:26-38

"And Mary said, Behold the handmaid of the Lord; be it unto me according to thy word.
And the angel departed from her" *(Luke 1:38)*.

The virgin birth of Jesus was an absolute miracle. Everything about it was natural except one thing: A man didn't provide the seed. The Holy Spirit of God placed the seed in Mary's womb. First Peter 1:23 calls God's Word the "incorruptible seed." The Greek word translated *seed* is *spora*. This comes from the same root from which we get the word "sperm." God's Word is His seed or sperm (Mark 4:14).

Gabriel took the Word of God that had been spoken through prophecy about the Messiah and brought it to Mary. Then the Holy Spirit moved upon her as He did over the waters of the earth in Genesis 1:2. He took God's seed and impregnated Mary with it. Therefore, John's description of this is very accurate. **"And the Word was made flesh"** (John 1:14).

A similar process is involved in every miracle we experience. In a very real sense, we must become pregnant with God's Word. The Word must be received into our hearts and nurtured over a period of time before there is actual manifestation of the miracle. A woman goes through stages of pregnancy. Likewise, when God's Word first takes root in our hearts, it's not always obvious—even to us. Eventually, it begins to show that His Word is working in us. Finally, there's the birth of what we have believed.

No one but Mary has ever had a virgin birth, but even that birth took a seed to make it happen. You must conceive to give birth. Put God's Word in your heart today, and get ready to receive your miracle! (AW)

DECEMBER 20
THINK ABOUT THIS
LUKE 1:39-45

"And it came to pass, that, when Elisabeth heard the salutation of Mary,
the babe leaped in her womb; and Elisabeth was filled with the Holy Ghost" *(Luke 1:41)*.

This story has become so familiar to us that it's easy to miss the miracles!

Mary and Elisabeth were cousins (Luke 1:36). They knew each other. Surely Elisabeth was aware that Mary was engaged but not yet married. She was just a teenager. Yet, Elisabeth prophesied about Mary being pregnant—not just pregnant, but carrying the Messiah. That was awesome! This certainly didn't come out of Elisabeth's mind. She never would have said those things. They were illogical.

Notice also that Elisabeth referred to Jesus as her Lord (verse 43). He had just been conceived! Jesus would've been called a "fetus" today, yet He was Elisabeth's Lord. The angels also proclaimed Him Lord at His birth (Luke 2:11). Jesus grew physically, but He was Lord from the moment of conception!

It's also interesting to note that John the Baptist, who was just a six-month-old "fetus" at the time, leapt for joy in his mother's womb. This means that a six-month-old "fetus" has emotions. It's also when John the Baptist was filled with the Holy Spirit. Before he was visible outside of the womb, God considered him a person and filled him with the Holy Spirit!

Elisabeth spoke these words without reservation. She placed a blessing on Mary for believing what the Lord had told her and then reassured her that it would surely come to pass (verse 45). What an encouragement and confirmation this must have been to Mary! **"Think on these things"** (Phil. 4:8). (AW)

DECEMBER 21
MAKE GOD BIGGER
LUKE 1:46-56

"And Mary said, My soul doth magnify the Lord" *(Luke 1:46).*

Magnify means "to make greater in size, extent, or effect." How could Mary make God any greater in any of these ways?

God is who He is regardless of what we think about Him. Our unbelief doesn't diminish who God is, but it can diminish how much of the Lord and His provision we receive. In that sense, we can limit God (Ps. 78:41), or decrease Him and His ability in our lives. Every time we think *Can God?* we make Him smaller in our own minds. How can we change that?

"I...will magnify him with thanksgiving" (Ps. 69:30). That's what Mary was doing here. Thanksgiving magnifies God in our lives. Through thanksgiving, we exercise the power of our memory, which stirs us up (2 Pet. 1:13). Thinking about God's goodness and faithfulness in our lives builds faith (Col. 2:7).

Whatever our minds focus on is what gets magnified. Too often, we focus our minds on the negatives of the past or future. Sometimes Satan puts no more than a toothpick in our path, but by the time we get through meditating on all the different ways that it could hurt us, it's increased to the size of a baseball bat, which the devil then uses to beat our brains out. We need to magnify the Lord by reminding ourselves of all His faithfulness.

Mary magnified the Lord and brought the greatest miracle into the world that's ever been. You can see your miracle come to pass too. Start magnifying the Lord, and watch your perception of God's greatness increase! (AW)

DECEMBER 22
SOUL & SPIRIT
LUKE 1:46-56

**"And Mary said, My soul doth magnify the Lord,
And my spirit hath rejoiced in God my Saviour"** *(Luke 1:46-47).*

Gabriel told Mary that her cousin Elisabeth was in the sixth month of a miraculous pregnancy too. No doubt, Mary went to see her because she hoped Elisabeth might understand that she was pregnant without a physical relationship. Mary was bound to be apprehensive. How could she expect anyone to believe that she was pregnant without a sexual relationship? These verses reflect the absolute joy Mary felt when her cousin confirmed all that had happened before she told her anything.

Mary had already rejoiced in her spirit. She believed Gabriel and experienced the Holy Spirit overshadowing her and conceiving Jesus. Now she rejoiced with her soul too. This is very important!

Sometimes you'll hear people criticize others for their outward display of emotion toward the Lord saying, "They aren't in the Spirit." The truth is that rejoicing in the spirit and rejoicing in the soul are two different things. Our born-again spirits always have the fruit of joy in them, but our souls only rejoice at times, as we choose. The Holy Spirit has released joy into our spirits and the rejoicing of our souls is our choice.

The whole concept of being under the control of the Holy Spirit when we dance, lift our hands, or speak in tongues has kept many people from doing these things. Actually, our spirits are always rejoicing, and we can praise the Lord with our souls and bodies when and as we will.

Follow the lead of your spirit today, and rejoice with your soul too! (AW)

DECEMBER 23
JOSEPH: MAN OF GREAT FAITH
MATTHEW 1:18-25

"Then Joseph being raised from sleep did as the angel of the Lord had bidden him, and took unto him his wife" (Matt. 1:24).

Many amazing things happened at the birth of our Lord Jesus Christ. However, the faith of Joseph is often overlooked. Think of how much faith he had to have operated in!

After the angel Gabriel appeared to Mary, there's no mention in Scripture of her telling Joseph anything. In fact, Mary went to see Elisabeth with haste (Luke 1:39). It's possible that in her excitement, she forgot to tell Joseph she was even leaving. When she returned three months later, *"She was found with child"* (Matt. 1:18, emphasis added). This implies that Mary didn't tell Joseph what had happened, but he observed that she was pregnant.

How would you react if your fiancée turned up pregnant and told you it was a virgin birth? I'm sure Joseph had those same thoughts. His mercy toward her showed that he loved her, but he also planned to divorce her, which means he didn't believe her. Then the angel of the Lord appeared to Joseph in a dream and explained the situation to him. Even at that, it took a strong faith to believe what he was told!

This had never happened before and would never happen again. No one would believe him. To everyone else, it would appear that Joseph was marrying someone who had already been unfaithful. In the eyes of the world, this marriage would always be tainted. Yet, it's to his credit and a testimony to his great faith that Joseph obeyed the Lord by going ahead and marrying Mary.

If Joseph and Mary could believe God for the virgin birth of Jesus, surely we are able to believe what He has spoken to us! (AW)

DECEMBER 24
GOD CAN USE ANYONE OR ANYTHING
LUKE 2:1-5

"And Joseph also went up from Galilee, out of the city of Nazareth, into Judaea, unto the city of David, which is called Bethlehem; (because he was of the house and lineage of David)" (Luke 2:4).

The prophet Micah prophesied that the Messiah would be born in Bethlehem. Yet Joseph and Mary lived in the Galilean town of Nazareth. This was a problem. How would God work this out? In this case, He actually used Caesar Augustus to move Joseph and Mary into the proper place. This reveals some very important things to us.

First, we mistakenly think that the Lord only uses those who are totally devoted to Him. That certainly wasn't the case here! Augustus was one of the most corrupt Caesars of them all. He proclaimed himself to be "God." Yet, he was the one God used to move the parents of our Lord to the proper place. Totally unknown to him, Caesar was used of God.

Also, it doesn't appear that Joseph and Mary were aware of Micah's prophecy. If they were, you'd think they would've headed to Bethlehem on their own, in obedience to that word. Yet, God used circumstances to get them to the exact spot that Micah had prophesied the Messiah would come. This says that we don't have to bring God's will to pass on our own; He's able to divinely structure our circumstances to direct our paths in His ways. All we must do is seek Him and He'll direct our paths (Prov. 3:6).

Have you been worrying about how the Lord is going to work things out? Be encouraged! God can use the most unlikely people and circumstances to direct your path. Just trust in Him! (AW)

DECEMBER 25
NO FRILLS FAITH
LUKE 2:6-7

"And she brought forth her firstborn son, and wrapped him in swaddling clothes, and laid him in a manger; because there was no room for them in the inn" (Luke 2:7).

This is absolutely amazing! The King of kings and Lord of lords was born in a barn because no one would give His parents a room in the inn. If we were God, we would've saved Herod the trouble of killing all the newborn baby boys in Bethlehem by retaliating and doing it ourselves. Jesus was the Creator and His creation had no room for Him. That could really bother a lesser God!

Yet, I believe the Father delighted in the setting in which Jesus was born. After all, a room in the greatest palace on earth would still have been a shambles compared to the splendors of heaven that Jesus had left. Nothing could compare, so why try? Besides, love and humility motivated this awesome act of God becoming man (Phil. 2:8). Jesus said Himself that He was meek and lowly of heart (Matt. 11:29). He's a humble God.

The Lord could have come in some spectacular way. He could've been born in the greatest palace. He could have forced everyone to believe on Him, but that's not His way. Likewise, He could manifest Himself to you in such awesome ways that it would take no faith on your part, but that's not His way. He loves faith. He loves you too, but you can't please Him without faith (Heb. 11:6).

Are you missing God's subtle miracles all around you just because you're looking for something spectacular? If you had found Jesus lying in a stall in a barn, would you have had the faith to believe? The Lord delights in revealing Himself in subtle ways. Don't miss Him like they did in Bethlehem! (AW)

DECEMBER 26
THE WAR IS OVER
LUKE 2:8-20

"Glory to God in the highest, and on earth peace, good will toward men" (Luke 2:14).

A couple of Japanese soldiers were found on one of the South Pacific islands years after the end of WWII. Due to temporary deafness from bomb explosions, they had missed the announcement via airplane and were unaware of the war's end. Many years later, they were still hiding in the jungle fighting the war. How sad. However, many Christians still think that the war is on between God and man. That's even sadder!

These angels weren't proclaiming that there would be peace among men. That certainly hasn't happened since Christ came, and it's not what we see happening now. Jesus even declared that He wasn't sent to bring peace among men (Matt. 10:34-36). These angels were praising God that the war between God and man was over.

Prior to Christ coming to the earth, God dealt with mankind through the Law. The Law was a system of rules and regulations with appropriate punishments for disobedience. The only thing wrong with that system was that we all broke the Law. Therefore, we all came under the curse instead of the blessing. There was no peace, because of our sins. Jesus ushered in a new way for God to deal with mankind. We can now be totally clean and free of all sin, not because of our performance, but because of our faith in Jesus.

The war is over. The peace treaty has been signed in the blood of the Lamb. Are you enjoying that peace, or are you still suffering the hardships of war because you missed the announcement? There is peace and goodwill toward you from your loving, heavenly Father today. (AW)

DECEMBER 27
REVELATION KNOWLEDGE
LUKE 2:21-40

***"And it was revealed unto him by the Holy Ghost, that he should not see death,
before he had seen the Lord's Christ"*** *(Luke 2:26).*

A pastor friend of mine told me that before he received the baptism of the Holy Spirit, the thing that upset him the most about charismatics was what we called "revelation knowledge." He had two doctorate degrees and had been through seminary, yet he'd hear ministers like me on the radio (whom he could tell had no formal training) expound the Scriptures in ways he had never heard before. He said he had studied those same scriptures hundreds of times and had missed the simple, obvious truths that we brought out. It upset him and at the same time made him desire what we had.

This was how Simeon operated. ***"It was revealed unto him by the Holy Ghost."*** This wasn't something he was taught by man. It was revelation knowledge: knowledge that didn't come from observation or instruction, but was intuitive. This revelation knowledge is available to all born-again believers who will receive this ministry of the Holy Spirit.

Simeon had no natural way of knowing which of the thousands of babies he saw would be the Christ. He simply kept his heart in tune with the Holy Spirit, and that knowledge was supernaturally imparted to him at the appropriate time.

This shouldn't be hard to believe. In nature, we see birds, fish, and animals migrate to the exact spots their parents came from without ever being there before. They didn't learn that in school. If God can speak to His animal creation, doesn't it make sense that He can also speak to us supernaturally? Listen for the voice of God on the inside of you today. (AW)

DECEMBER 28
DANIEL'S INFLUENCE
MATTHEW 2:1-11

***"Saying, Where is he that is born King of the Jews?
for we have seen his star in the east, and are come to worship him"*** *(Matt. 2:2).*

It is remarkable that these men from the East would interpret the appearance of any star, regardless of how unusual it might be, as a sign of the birth of the Jewish Messiah. What did they know about Jewish prophecy?

Matthew 2:1 calls these men ***"wise men."*** The actual word used in the Greek text was *magos,* which was of foreign origin, denoting a Magian (hence Magi) or an Oriental scientist or magician. It's commonly believed that they came from Persia. This is significant because Babylon was where Daniel had been taken as a captive and elevated to the head of all the magicians. When the Persians captured Babylon, he continued in this position.

Daniel was the prophet to whom God gave the interpretation of Jeremiah's seventy weeks prophecy, which pinpointed the coming of the Messiah (Dan. 9:2, 24; Jer. 25:11). As head of the magicians (or scientists) in Persia, it's certain that Daniel made this knowledge known to his colleagues. No doubt, they had been studying his prophecy and were anticipating the event. Therefore, it's very understandable that the appearance of a new star moving in a different fashion would be taken as a special sign of the Jewish Messiah's birth.

The Jewish scholars were taken by surprise, but the Persian magicians were not. They had been studying God's Word through Daniel. The Word makes us wise unto salvation (2 Tim. 3:15). You can be a wise person too, if you'll let God's Word instruct you! (AW)

DECEMBER 29
GIVING BUILDS A MEMORIAL BEFORE GOD
ACTS 10:4

"And when he looked on him, he was afraid, and said, What is it, Lord?
And he said unto him, Thy prayers and thine alms are come up for a
memorial before God" (Acts 10:4).

Cornelius was *"a devout man, and one that feared God with all his house, which gave much alms to the people, and prayed to God alway"* (Acts 10:2). Here was a Gentile who was "doing the stuff." He was a man who loved God, was a big giver, and was always praying. Cornelius wasn't doing any of these things to try to "buy" God, but was simply planting seeds the whole time. It's obvious he wasn't giving to selfishly get, because he was surprised when the angel appeared to him. His prayers and generosity were building a memorial before a loving, all-sustaining God. *"He that hath pity upon the poor lendeth unto the LORD; and that which he hath given will he pay him again"* (Prov. 19:17). If you put your money in a bank, it'll gain only a small amount of interest. When you're generous to help those in need, God will repay you far more than any bank could!

Because he put God first with his heart, life, and substance, the Lord sent him a divine connection—a divine appointment. This man, Cornelius, went on to be part of the first New Testament Gentile revival! He and the others with him heard the glorious Gospel, were saved, and filled with the Holy Ghost. Hallelujah!

Every time you are generous to give, every time you humble yourself, every time you honor the Lord with everything you have, you are sowing seed for revival in your life and in the lives of everyone around you. You are raising up a memorial to Almighty God. Like Cornelius, when you honor the Lord with a right heart, He'll prosper you! (BN)

DECEMBER 30
JUBILEE
LUKE 4:18-19

"The Spirit of the Lord is upon me, because he hath anointed me to preach the gospel to the poor; he hath sent me to heal the brokenhearted, to preach deliverance to the captives, and recovering of sight to the blind, to set at liberty them that are bruised, To preach the acceptable year of the Lord" (Luke 4:18-19).

Jesus returned from the Jordan River after being given power by the Holy Spirit. He came into His hometown and spoke in the synagogue as He had done many times before. However, the sermon was different this time, because Jesus was different. He spoke about the anointing of the Lord to heal the sick and deliver the afflicted. He also declared that He had come *"to preach the acceptable year of the Lord."*

This was the year of Jubilee (Lev. 25). During this event, which occurred once every fifty years, every possession went back to its original owner and all slaves were released. It was a legal holiday. The only way someone could miss repossessing lost articles was to be ignorant of the Law.

Why did Jesus compare His public ministry to this Old Testament event? He was anointed to bring back to us what had been taken by Satan! This was why He called healing from blindness *"recovering of sight to the blind."* During Jubilee, slaves were also freed. Through Jesus, we have *"deliverance to the captives."* The Gospel is also preached to the poor. The riches taken by Satan have been given back to the redeemed!

Jesus told us that He wouldn't just give us the blessing, but He'd also remove the curse. Sight replaces blindness, liberty is for the bruised, and healing is for the brokenhearted. Jesus removes blindness and gives sight. Why is this important? Christ gives us what is rightfully ours and removes what's rightfully someone else's. Everything, good and bad, goes back to its original owner. Therefore, Jesus took the blessing away from Satan and gave it to its original owner—us. He also took the curse from us and gave it back to its original owner—Satan. This new creation jubilee doesn't just last one year—it's eternal! (BY)

DECEMBER 31
TO RESOLVE OR NOT TO RESOLVE?
PROVERBS 4:20-27

"Ponder the path of thy feet, and let all thy ways be established" (Prov. 4:26).

The end of the old year and the beginning of a new one is a great time to take inventory of what has happened in your life and plan for what's ahead. Some people don't think it's good to look back, and they certainly don't think it's good to make New Year's resolutions. But this passage of Scripture tells us to *"ponder the path of thy feet."*

Ponder means "to weigh mentally." You can't weigh something unless you have something to weigh it against. If you don't have any goals, there's no way to evaluate whether or not you're making progress. We all need something to shoot at. Otherwise, we'll shoot at nothing and hit it every time!

There are dangers associated with setting goals and making resolutions. If we stretch ourselves too far, we are destined to fail. This just adds to our sense of guilt and frustration. The Bible advocates vision and goal setting, but we need to exercise wisdom. We shouldn't set goals arbitrarily, independent of God. Establishing goals contrary to His will just absorbs all our time and keeps us from Him.

It's beneficial to look back and remember the good and learn from the bad. In order to plow a straight row, we must fix our eyes on a point far out in front of us. Use this time to see if your life is going in the direction the Lord wants it to. If it's not, then there needs to be some changes. It's foolish to keep doing the same things expecting different results. Ponder the path of your feet today, and take the appropriate steps! (AW)

OTHER CONTRIBUTING WRITERS

Bob Nichols

Bob has an interesting and colorful background, spanning 50 years in full-time ministry In 1964 God called him to start a church where ALL FAITHS CAN GROW FAITH. In July of 2003, their new facility was finished, which houses Calvary Academy state-of-the-art school and gymnasium. Bob Nichols is used by God in teaching evangelism with a unique ability to minister to pastors; he shares that gifting in seminars around the world. He believes that in this hour, we must unite to finish the job of evangelizing the world.

Bob Yandian

Bob Yandian is a gifted teacher, pastor and author. He attended Trinity Bible College. Bob is an international teacher and founder of School of the Local Church, a nine month ministerial training Bible school. Described by many as a "pastor's pastor" Bob is renowned for his detailed expository teaching of God's Word as well as his diverse topical instruction Bob's background includes several years with Kenneth Hagin Ministries and Rhema Bible Training Center, where he served as an instructor and held the position of Dean of Instructors.

OTHER BOOKS BY ANDREW ARE NOW AVAILABLE!

SPIRIT, SOUL & BODY   *Item Code: 318*

Have you ever asked yourself what changed when you were "born again"? You look in the mirror and see the same reflection—your body hasn't changed. You find yourself acting the same and yielding to those same old temptations—that didn't seem to change either. So you wonder, *Has anything really changed?*

The correct answer to that question is foundational to receiving from God. If you lack this basic understanding, you'll forever ask yourself doubt-filled questions like: "How could God love somebody like me?" and "How can I possibly expect to receive anything from the Lord? I don't deserve it. I'm not good enough!"

Spirit, Soul & Body will help you to eliminate those and other doubt-filled questions that destroy your faith. If you have trouble receiving from God, this is a must-read!

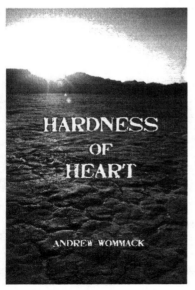

HARDNESS OF HEART   *Item Code: 303*

You might be surprised to find that every Christian has a varying degree of hardness in their heart. Listen as Andrew establishes from Scripture what causes this and then how to cure it. This understanding is vital to great faith and success in your Christian life.

THE NEW YOU & THE HOLY SPIRIT

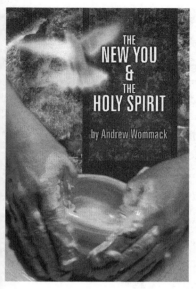

Item Code: 323

The New You

It's very important to understand what happened when you received Jesus as your Savior. It's the key to keeping the Word that was sown in your heart from being stolen by Satan. Andrew's teaching gives a solid scriptural foundation that will help you understand.

You'll learn through Scripture that true salvation includes, but is not limited to, the forgiveness of your sins. It's the forgiveness of sins that makes intimate fellowship with the Lord possible, but much more was provided, more than you may have ever imagined.

The Word is very clear about past, present, and future sins. You may be surprised when you read about that. Andrew will explain how salvation comes by grace through faith and will contrast the difference between Christianity and other religions of the world.

The Holy Spirit

Learn why the baptism of the Holy Spirit is an absolute necessity! Living the abundant life that Jesus provided is impossible without it. Before Jesus' disciples received the Holy Spirit, they were weak and fearful men. But, when they were filled with the Holy Spirit on the day of Pentecost, each one became a powerhouse of God's miraculous power. In Acts 1:8 Jesus tells us that same power is available to us.

If you believe the Bible is truly the Word of God, then you must also believe the baptism in the Holy Spirit is God's will for everyone. Many teach that the baptism of the Holy Spirit is received at salvation and the accompanying miracles of old are not for today, but that's just not true.

Many also ask, "Do we have to speak in tongues when baptized in the Holy Spirit?" No, you get to. It's like a pair of tennis shoes—they all come with tongues. In this book, Andrew establishes the validity of speaking in tongues, talks about the many gifts that accompany it, shares other little-known benefits, and explains how to begin speaking in tongues.

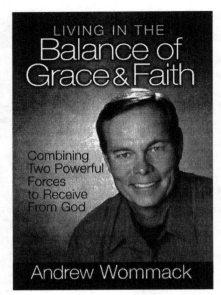

LIVING IN THE BALANCE OF GRACE AND FAITH *Item Code: 228*

This is the first book we published, and it explains one of the biggest controversies in the church today. Is it grace or faith that releases the power of God? Neither—it has to be a combination of both. Just as sodium and chloride are poisonous by themselves, grace or faith taken without a proper understanding of how they relate will kill you. However, when sodium and chloride are mixed together they make salt, which is impossible to live without. So it is when faith is mixed with God's grace that the results are miraculous.

THE EFFECTS OF PRAISE *Item Code: 309*

Every Christian wants a stronger walk with the Lord. But how do you get there? Many don't know the true power of praise. It's essential. Listen as Andrew teaches biblical truths that will not only spark understanding but will help promote spiritual growth so you will experience victory.

HARNESSING YOUR EMOTIONS

Item Code: 313

We all have emotions, but do they rule us, or do we rule them? Psychologists and Christians alike agree that actions are the result of inner thoughts and feelings, emotions. But that is where the agreement ends. The Word says that sin is conceived in our emotions. If that is true, then the Word must also give us a way to harness our emotions. Andrew's teaching will present you with a new perspective on emotions

THE TRUE NATURE OF GOD

Item Code: 308

What is the real nature of God? Is He harsh, as viewed through many Old Testament instances, or is He meek and gentle of heart, as Jesus portrayed? This book will trace God's dealings with man all the way from the Garden of Eden to the present and show one consistent nature of God through it all. This teaching will answer many questions and leave you with a much greater faith in the goodness of God.

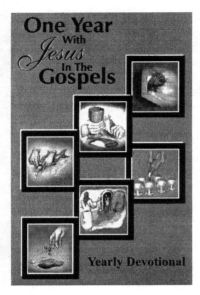

ONE YEAR WITH JESUS IN THE GOSPELS *Item Code: 311*

This is a one-page-per-day devotional book that highlights teachings and actions of Jesus from the Gospels. You will receive fresh revelation and a new love for the Lord as you follow Jesus through the Gospels day by day. Each devotion has a practical application of Jesus' teaching that will help you to put these great truths into practice each day of the year.